Contributions of Selected Rhetorical Devices to a Biblical Theology of the Song of Songs

Contributions of Selected Rhetorical Devices to a Biblical Theology of the Song of Songs

Mark McGinniss

WIPF & STOCK · Eugene, Oregon

CONTRIBUTIONS OF SELECTED RHETORICAL DEVICES TO A BIBLICAL THEOLOGY OF THE SONG OF SONGS

Copyright © 2011 Mark McGinniss. All rights reserved. Except for brief quotations in critical publications or reviews, no part of this book may be reproduced in any manner without prior written permission from the publisher. Write: Permissions, Wipf and Stock Publishers, 199 W. 8th Ave., Suite 3, Eugene, OR 97401.

Scripture quotations taken from the New American Standard Bible®,
Copyright © 1960, 1962, 1963, 1968, 1971, 1972, 1973,
1975, 1977, 1995 by The Lockman Foundation
Used by permission. (www.Lockman.org)

Wipf & Stock
An Imprint of Wipf and Stock Publishers
199 W. 8th Ave., Suite 3
Eugene, OR 97401

www.wipfandstock.com

ISBN 13: 978-1-60899-634-6

Manufactured in the U.S.A.

To my wife,

שֶׁאָהֲבָה נַפְשִׁי

Who deserves so much more than a simple dedication

Who has been a constant source of encouragement

Who has allowed me not only to study the Song

but to experience its message

To you, Joy, this book is gratefully and lovingly dedicated

זֶה דוֹדִי וְזֶה רֵעִי

Contents

Acknowledgments / ix

Abbreviations / x

1. Introduction / 1
2. The Use of the First Person / 14
3. Rhetorical Questions / 78
4. Poetic Characters / 139
5. Conclusion / 224

   Appendix 1—A Chart of the Occurrences of the Hebrew First Person in the Song of Songs / 227

   Appendix 2—A Suggested Thematic Outline / 234

Bibliography / 235

Acknowledgments

THE WRITING OF A dissertation (the process by which this book was borne) is a solitary endeavor, but the completing of it takes a special community. I would like to express my appreciation to the library staff at Baptist Bible College & Seminary for all their assistance in securing the necessary sources for this project. Special thanks to Janet McClain and Sharon Gardoski, who, as good detectives, tracked down all needed resources.

I am especially grateful to the administration of BBC&S, President Jim Jeffrey, Provost Jim Lytle, and Deans Howard Bixby and Mike Stallard, who structured my responsibilities at the seminary to allow time to study, write, and pray this work into existence. My heartfelt thanks to my colleagues at Baptist Bible Seminary, who were free with their libraries, and freer with their encouragements and prayers. I appreciate their friendship more than they know. A special measure of my gratitude goes to Dr. Richard Engle, who painstakingly read this manuscript multiple times as a dissertation and book. My thanks to Drs. Alan Ingalls and Mike Stallard for their keen insights, helpful suggestions, and guidance in this project. A special thanks to Christian Amondson of Wipf and Stock for seeing this project through to publication and to my copyeditor, Mark Dubis, who caught a "number of foxes" that could have spoiled this project.

No words are adequate to acknowledge the contribution and the sacrifice that my family has made to this project. To my wife, Joy, who carried more than she should and to my children, Jeremy and Kara, Drew and Temisa, Ian, Kasey and Kyle, who hopefully will have better memories of Dad other than him sitting in front of a computer. Thank you with all my love. Above all, I am grateful to my God who has extended mercy and grace beyond measure to one such as me.

Abbreviations

A&C	*Affirmation & Critique*
AAS	*Asian and African Studies*
AJSL	*American Journal of Semitic Languages*
ARTS	*The Arts in Religious and Theological Studies*
AThR	*Anglican Theological Review*
AUSS	*Andrews University Seminary Studies*
BDAG	*A Greek Lexicon of the New Testament and Other Early Christian Literature*, 3rd ed.
BDB	*Hebrew and English Lexicon of the Old Testament*
BH	Biblical Hebrew
BHS	*Biblia Hebraica Stuttgartensia*
BibInt	*Biblical Interpretation*
BibSac	*Bibliotheca sacra*
BN	*Biblische Notizen*
BRev	*Bible Review*
BT	*The Bible Translator*
BTB	*Biblical Theology Bulletin*
CBQ	*Catholic Biblical Quarterly*
CH	*Church History*
ChrCent	*Christian Century*
CR	*Currents in Research*
DBSJ	*Detroit Baptist Theological Seminary Journal*
ERT	*Evangelical Review of Theology*
IEJ	*Israel Exploration Journal*
GKC	*Gesenius' Hebrew Grammar*
GTJ	*Grace Theological Journal*

HER	*Harvard Educational Review*
IBHS	*An Introduction to Biblical Hebrew Syntax*
Int	*Interpretation*
IRM	*International Review of Missions*
JAAR	*Journal of the American Academy of Religion*
JAOS	*Journal of American Oriental Society*
JATS	*Journal of the Adventist Theological Society*
JBL	*Journal of Biblical Literature*
JETS	*Journal of the Evangelical Theological Society*
JHS	*Journal of Hebrew Scriptures*
JOTT	*Journal of Translation and Textlinguistics*
JMAT	*Journal of Ministry and Theology*
JNES	*Journal of Near Eastern Studies*
JRF	*Journal of Religion and Film*
JSOT	*Journal for the Study of the Old Testament*
OTTH	Old Testament Theology
POV	Point of View
RelSRev	*Religious Studies Review*
RQ	Rhetorical Question
RTR	*Reformed Theological Review*
SEÅ	*Svensk Exegetisk Årsbok*
SJOT	*Scandinavian Journal of the Old Testament*
Song	Song of Songs, Song of Solomon, Canticles
SofS	Song of Songs, Song of Solomon, Canticles
SoS	Song of Songs, Song of Solomon, Canticles
SR	*Studies in Religion*
STJ	*Stulos Theological Journal*
T&S	*Theology and Sexuality*
VT	*Vetus Testamentum*
WTJ	*Westminster Theological Journal*

1

Introduction

THIS WORK INVESTIGATES THREE literary devices used in the Song of Songs (SoS): the author's use of first person personal pronouns, rhetorical questions, and the various characters that inhabit its pages. Each of these literary tools is identified within their individual context within the Song. Once these tools are identified, this study offers suggestions concerning how the biblical author uses them rhetorically to communicate his theological message. This process will enable the reader to appreciate the biblical theology of this ancient love song.

NEED FOR STUDY

The rationalization for the present effort is sevenfold: (1) it seeks to refute the claim that the Song has no theology in and of itself; (2) by demonstrating some of its biblical theology through these literary devices, it will implicitly refute the allegorical interpretation of the ancient love poem by presenting a sound, literal, grammatical interpretation; (3) it will add to the church's understanding and her use of the SoS; (4) by following Schultz's admonition for a complete exegesis, it will complete the exegetical process of scholars who have previously done fine work on the Song but have fallen short of articulating its theological thrust; (5) although much has been written on the Song, some perplexing questions still remain, especially Solomon's role in the Song itself;[1]

---

1. One of the perplexing questions in research of the Song concerns the overall structure. While Roberts ("Let Me See Your Form," 757) has argued well for the unity of the Song (against an anthology view), he is unable to define an overall structure, but recognizes unity on a micro level. To demonstrate the lack of consensus concerning the overall structural organization of the Song, Exum (*Song of Songs*, 38–39) lists a number of scholars and their respective positions. Another question without consensus is the number of characters or voices in the Song. For example, Exum hears only three voices. Stoop-van Paridon (*Song of Songs*, 471), who observes the most voices, hears

(6) it will further the study of this piece of biblical poetry by demonstrating that a rhetorical methodology may be employed with profit in ancient Hebrew poetry; and (7) it plows new ground by demonstrating the importance of both a literary and a theological exegesis in the biblical theological enterprise; thus far, no project has attempted both from a literal-grammatical hermeneutical perspective.

First Rationalization

This study demonstrates the presence of a legitimate biblical theology in the Song and its usefulness for the church today. Martens recognizes the need for biblical theology today as a resource for the church: "Biblical theology is to the health of the church what the Centers for Disease Control in the USA is to a nations' health."[2] He further believes biblical theology serves the body of Christ:

> Biblical theology serves as a resource whereby the church can do a reality check to ensure that the faith community is not aberrant or one-sided in its belief. Norms for belief and behavior are important for the church in whose service the discipline of biblical theology is placed.[3]

This aspect of the Song has been overlooked.[4] While one can appreciate the work of a scholar such as House, he is incorrect when he states,

---

seven. Solomon's role is another perplexing problem. Is this well-known king of Israel the author, main character, or something else in the Song? While Dell ("Song of Songs," 24) does not articulate specifically how Solomon "pervades" the Song, she does suggest, "The character of Solomon seems to pervade the Song in a more profound way than is often assumed."

2. Martens, "Old Testament Theology Since Walter C. Kaiser, Jr.," 681. To reiterate, Martens states, "Apart from setting out the belief parameters, a biblical theology should deal with the praxis of the church, including matters of life-style" (ibid.). The Song deals with the area of physical intimacy, which is part of every believer's lifestyle, single or married.

3. Ibid.

4. Brueggemann (*Theology of the Old Testament*, 342) gives but a passing comment to the Song and that half page is simply illustrative. To see no significant theological contribution from the SoS in a book on Old Testament theology (OTTH) is an oversight that needs to be addressed, if not directly at least tangentially. Ten years later the situation has not changed appreciably. Waltke (*Old Testament Theology*, 163–64) in his hefty Old Testament theology (1040 pages) provides a scant page and a half. In his theology of the OT, Merrill (*Everlasting Dominion*, 638–40) allots the same amount of space. Gerstenberger has one reference to the Song (*Theologies of the Old Testament*,

"Song of Songs is artistically and thematically lovely but not particularly theologically enriching."[5] This biblical love song through its author's use of various rhetorical devices has a theological message for its original audience and its readers today. This challenges scholars such as Malul and Grossberg. Malul writes, "It is known that the OT was never intended for the modern audience, to begin with, but for its contemporaries. . . . Furthermore, and to make matters more difficult, it was written by, and perhaps intended for, only part of its contemporaries, a certain elite."[6] Grossberg contends, "There are no ostensible theological, religious or moralistic intentions in this strangely secular work."[7]

A chasm has developed between theology and the exegetical work of scholars on the Song. This project seeks to span that gulf and contribute to Stoop-van Paridon's goal of further work on the aspect of human love. She is worth quoting at length as she summarizes her research and suggests a need for further study:

> In the love between the young man and the young woman in the SofS, all the layers of their human personalities are emphatically involved, including their erotic-sexual potential. This love is

---

36). Eichrodt lists six (*Theology of the Old Testament*, 562). The OT theologian Gerhard von Rad has but one reference in his two-volume theology (*Old Testament Theology*, 479). Preuss has but five, which describe the physical attributes of the female form (*Old Testament Theology*, 428).

The theology of the Song has also been overlooked in various systematic theologies as well. This is evidenced in a perusal of their scripture indices. Erickson in his massive systematic tome has no listing for the Song of Songs at all (*Christian Theology*, 1249–70). John F. Walvoord lists none either in his two-volume abridged theology of Lewis Sperry Chafer (*Systematic Theology*, 1:417–32; 2:519–38). While Grudem has an entire chapter on man as male and female (22), there are no references to the Song in this chapter nor in his partial scriptural index (*Systematic Theology*, 454–71; 1267–70.). The same is true for Lewis and Demarest's *Integrative Theology* (542–62). Charles Hodge had the foresight to include the topics of marriage, celibacy, and monogamy in his nineteenth-century systematic theology. However, he never references the Song to prove his position (*Systematic Theology*, 3:368–87). There are also no references to the Song in his very limited *Index to Systematic Theology* as well (80–81).

5. Paul House, *Old Testament Theology*, 469. While it may be true that the Song does not contain the same level of theological import as does Genesis or Deuteronomy, for example, it is nonetheless worthy of theological reflection. Schultz ("Integrating Old Testament Theology and Exegesis," 196) notes very well that although some biblical books may "contain fewer theological 'calories' per pericope, they are still legitimate objects of theological analysis."

6. Malul, *Knowledge, Control and Sex*, 10.

7. Grossberg, *Centripetal and Centrifugal Structures*, 56.

unique and faithful, and this is the subject dealt with in the SofS. If one sees in this love primarily an image of the love of God for mankind, then the message of the SofS has not been appreciated. Then one step has been omitted, a step which is essential and which implies that this human love is holy, including its erotic-sexual dimension. This acknowledgement has been made a number of times in the past, but often it has not, because scholars recoiled from it. A further coordinated, multidisciplinary study of this human love may lead to illuminating and liberating results.[8]

From other theological quarters there are concerns that take the theology of the Song deeper than the author intended. Walton and Stuart recognize such a trend: "An increasingly common theological assumption is made that our human sexual activities are merely symbolic representations of a deeper sacred reality."[9]

Second Rationalization

In a recent commentary on the Song of Songs (2005), systematic theologian Robert Jensen proposes "to discover how this evocative poetry solicits a theological reading."[10] While noting the theological importance of its genre and its poetic devices, his conclusion is that the Song is "about the love of Israel and the Lord."[11] Unfortunately, the theological reading that he proposes is a "theological allegory" dressed in the cloth of what he calls "canonical plain sense."[12] The theological import of certain literary devices need not lead a reader to such an incorrect allegorical reading. A correct understanding of the rhetorical strategy of the author leads to a plain-sense interpretation without the aid of an analogous relationship between Israel and her God (or between God and his church).

---

8. Stoop-van Paridon, *Song of Songs*, 497.

9. Walton and Stuart, "Editorial," *T& S*, 120. For instance, Bell's new book, *Sex God*, is an attempt to explore the connection between sexuality and spirituality. Bell (42) states, "Our sexuality is all of the ways we strive to reconnect with our world, with each other and with God."

10. Jensen, *Song of Songs*, inside jacket cover.

11. Ibid., 8.

12. Ibid.

Third Rationalization

This work follows a method suggested by Schultz in seeking to do exegesis by identifying the use of certain literary devices and suggesting theological observations communicated by them. Watson recognizes the value of the first part of this endeavor as part of his analysis of Hebrew poetry: "Having extracted as much data as possible from the chosen text, it remains to determine how the various poetic devices interact within the poem. Look for a dominant poetic device within each strophe or for the whole poem, and determine its function."[13] The author's use of the first person, rhetorical questions, and his characterizations are dominant poetic devices within their individual contexts that express certain theology. According to Schultz, such a method "that is consciously theological will also result in greater clarity regarding the contemporary implications and application of a given text."[14] This will increase the church's understanding and her use of the SoS for the present generation.[15]

Fourth Rationalization

Many contemporary scholars have undertaken fine work on the Song but have fallen short in completing the exegetical process by failing to articulate its theological thrust. While Munro provides an exceptional study in *Spikenard and Saffron: A Study in the Poetic Language of the Song of Songs*, which pioneers the use of various metaphors in the Song, she does not articulate the theology that flows from these metaphors nor does her work address the three literary devices this study focuses on.[16] Falk takes a literary approach to the study of the Song in her *Love Lyrics*

---

13. Watson, *Classical Hebrew Poetry*, 20. Watson continues his thought by noting that, after analysis, "the next essential step, then, is to find out why this poetic device has been used here" (31).

14. Schultz, "Integrating Old Testament Theology and Exegesis," 195.

15. Hart et al. (*Secrets of Eve*, 259) recognize the church's need to understand sexuality: "Hopefully, our study has raised enough issues to warrant an overhaul of how we help people develop a truly Christian understanding of sexuality, an understanding not distorted by toxic beliefs and attitudes." This project anchors a Christian's sexual understanding (and practice) in the word of God itself.

While it is the intention of this study to aid the church in her understanding of the Song and its view of sexuality, it may serve those outside the church as well. Yancey ("Holy Sex") remarks, "Unfortunately, few people look to the church for perspective on the true meaning of human sexuality, since they view the church as an implacable enemy of sex."

16. Munro, *Spikenard and Saffron*.

from the Bible, noting its contexts, themes, *wasfs*, and motifs.[17] However, her study did not pursue the relationship between these topics and theology, nor does she interact with the literary devices that are the focus of this study.

From the standpoint of OT theology, there is no question that the biblical theology of the Song of Songs has been researched, discussed, and debated. For example, Roy Zuck in *A Biblical Theology of the Old Testament* has contributed fifty pages on the biblical theology of the Song and wisdom books.[18] Paul House has a mere eight pages of the Song's theology in his *Old Testament Theology*.[19] Brevard Childs' *Introduction to the Old Testament* includes eleven pages on its canonical shape and theological implications.[20] The theological observations of these authors have been insightful. However, these works have not shown *how* these scholars came to their theological conclusions.[21] They simply make biblical-theological statements. This work seeks to demonstrate how the biblical author uses certain literary devices to build and communicate his theological message.

Fifth Rationalization

Although much has been written on the Song, perplexing questions remain. One of those questions concerns the characters in the Song, especially Solomon's role. At present there is no scholarly consensus concerning the voices in the Song. Exum states that they are simple "literary personae, literary constructs."[22] Bergant notes the characters are simply unnamed.[23] Phillips believes a historical but unnamed shepherd and the Shulammite are the male and female leads while Solomon, the king of Israel, is the interloper of their relationship in the Song.[24] A

---

17. Falk, *Love Lyrics*.
18. Zuck, *Biblical Theology of the Old Testament*.
19. House, *Old Testament Theology*.
20. Childs, *Old Testament as Scripture*.
21. In her excellent work on the study of the poetic language of the Song, Munro, *Spikenard and Saffron*, sought to identify the different groups of metaphors in the Song. Munro did not delineate how the metaphors aided the biblical author in communicating his theology.
22. Exum, "Ten Things Every Feminist Should Know," 27.
23. Bergant, *Song of Songs*.
24. Phillips, *Exploring the Song of Solomon*.

close study of the characters in the Song suggests the rhetorical part they play in the purpose of the biblical author and the theology that flows from their use.

Sixth Rationalization

It is the purpose of this thesis to further the study of the Song by demonstrating that a rhetorical method may be applied and used with profit in biblical Hebrew poetry. There is a rhetorical reason the author uses the three literary devices under investigation. For instance, concerning the characters, Sternberg remarks that the author has a rhetorical repertoire "through which the Bible shapes our response to characters."[25] Following a rhetorical approach will cast light on some of the questions concerning the biblical author's use of his characters in the Song.[26]

Seventh Rationalization

This treatise plows new ground by joining a literary and a theological study. By combining these, Schultz's suggested exegetical process is completed. In addition, there is a need in OT poetical studies to discover the various rhetorical devices the human author used to craft his divinely inspired message. Adele Berlin captures this need: "I would argue that we need to attend more to biblical poetry *qua* poetry—to give more attention to the *meaning* of a poem and to how a poem achieves its meaning."[27] Recently, Estes echoes Berlin by suggesting that future scholars of this ancient poetic text "must read biblical poetry as poetry, feel poetry as poetry, and hear biblical poetry as poetry."[28] He feels a close reading of the text is accomplished by "integrating the traditional attention to philological, historical, and theological issues with sensitivity to the poetic

---

25. Sternberg, *Poetics of Biblical Narrative*, 475.

26. Crenshaw recognized the need for such study as early as 1981. In his preface to *Old Testament Wisdom: An Introduction*, he states his intention to undertake "a study of the art of persuasion in Israelite wisdom (7). There is no published evidence that his project came to fruition. The rhetorical aspect of this study may anticipate such an endeavor.

27. Berlin, "On Reading Biblical Poetry," 26.

28. Estes, "Entering the Garden of Intimacy," 1. Petersen and Richards (*Interpreting Hebrew Poetry*) recognize the need for readers of Hebrew poetry to give attention to its literary devices. There is a need to "alert readers of Hebrew poetry to its literary features, many of which often have gone unnoticed" (7). This project helps fill the need recognized by these authors.

distinctiveness of the text."[29] He illustrates this close reading of the text by studying the sound play, literary structure, and imagery in a brief section of the SoS (4:8—5:1). This work follows suit by investigating other literary devices: rhetorical questions, characterization, and the author's use of the first person. This work expands and complements Estes' brief vision for the future study of biblical poetry. It also demonstrates that Estes' vision for the future study of poetical texts is sound and provides the integration that Estes envisions between historical and theological criticisms for future studies of biblical poetry.

SONG RESEARCH

Old Testament scholars suggest there is room for what this project proposes to accomplish. Berlin notes that the literary approach to the Bible has enjoyed popularity in recent years. However, the study of biblical poetry has not.[30] Estes concurs with Berlin when he writes, "Because poetry is aesthetically charged it is often neglected. This is particularly true in the case of biblical poetry."[31] While Berlin calls for work on metaphor in Hebrew poetry, this project seeks to investigate different but just as important rhetorical devices.

There is room for this project in current SoS research as well. For instance in a recent work, George Schwab seeks to enlighten the dark side of love in the Song through his *The Song of Song's Cautionary Message Concerning Human Love*. His 1999 work stands as a correction to those who recognize no dangerous side to love in the Song. P. W. T. Stoop-van Paridon wrote her 2003 work, *The Song of Songs: A Philological Analysis of the Hebrew Book*, to discern for herself the philological qualities of the Song. In her sometimes unique (and minority) interpretation, she studies the individual words of the SoS and not the theology. Steven Horine offers an integrative literary approach in his 1999 work, *An Integrative Literary Approach to the Song of Songs*. In this thesis he studies the nuptial imagery, which provides an interpretive framework for understanding the Song. In his tome of over eight hundred pages, *Let Me See Your Form: Seeking Poetic Structure in the Song of Songs* (2001), D. Phillip Roberts analyzes the structure of the Song from the bottom

---

29. Ibid.
30. Berlin, "On Reading Biblical Poetry," 25.
31. Estes, "Hermeneutics of Biblical Lyrical Poetry," *BibSac* 152 (1995) 416.

up. He concludes the Song is a unified work, but he was unable to establish an overall structure for the Song. In her 2006 MTh thesis for Oak Hill College, London, entitled "Song of Songs: A Biblical Theology," Ros Clarke attempts a biblical theology of the Song through the lens of two important themes: marriage and land. Based on the current published research on the SoS, there is a niche for a study that weds literary and theological exegesis and researches three distinct rhetorical devices and their contribution to the theology of the Song.

GOALS

The goal of this work is threefold: (1) to catalogue the use of the three literary devices; (2) to provide an explanation for the rhetorical function of these literary features; and (3) to suggest the biblical theology that naturally flows from the author's use of these three elements. In the context of a biblical ministry, the overall goal is to help the church better understand this most sublime song, apply it, and widen the wealth of scholarship concerning this ancient love poem.[32] Martens observes,

> A major goal of biblical theology is the shaping of a community, such that it will be clearly aligned with the biblical teaching. One aspect of biblical theology, to be sure, is of an academic nature in which scholars set forth proposals and engage in critique. But another function, and the more important, I propose, is targeted to the faith community.[33]

---

32. Wyrtzen (*Love Without Shame*, 119) believes the church's lack of appreciation for the SoS today is another factor in the epidemic of immorality: "We must learn how to artistically appreciate the beauty of the human body and to relish its delight in the marital relationship. The lack of appreciation and expression in evangelical circles is another factor in the epidemic of immorality." While Wyrtzen may be overstating the case, he does articulate the need for the church to understand (and apply) the theology of this erotic poem.

33. Martens, "Old Testament Theology," 688–89. Martens is worth quoting again regarding the practical value and desperate need of biblical theology: "Moreover, in the West, though not only there, biblical illiteracy is widespread. Christians individually and collectively as a church are in need of a biblical worldview, one which biblical theology helps provide" (ibid., 689). While Martens is advocating a whole-Bible theology, such a theology begins at the level of the individual book.

OUTLINE

This study consists of five chapters. This chapter deals with introductory issues. Chapters two through four focus attention on the three literary devices of the SoS: the biblical author's use of the first person pronouns, rhetorical questions, and the use of the individual characters in the SoS. These chapters identify the specific literary feature in context and suggest its rhetorical use by the biblical author. Each chapter concludes with theological observations that naturally flow from the author's use of each specific literary characteristic. Chapter five provides a conclusion and offers suggestions for future research. An appendix and bibliography completes the project.

METHODOLOGY

The methodology for this work is multifaceted. It is exegetical. Since the purpose is to seek to understand the theology of the biblical author through his use of certain literary devices, the method must be exegetical. However, it is important that a complete exegesis be undertaken. Richard Schultz explains the need for a complete exegesis to understand the theology of the biblical author:

> Exegesis is incomplete if it does not lay bare the theological thrust of a text, seeking to identify words, phrases, motifs, images and even structural elements that reveal aspects of God's will and work in the world as it places demands on or otherwise affects Israel, the nations and/or all humankind. These elements should be analyzed in terms of their function within the given text and synthesized in terms of their participation in and contribution to the theological emphasis of the book as a whole, whether structural or thematic in nature.[34]

In the same vein Bright calls for an exegetical process that is "not content merely to bring out the precise verbal meaning of the text but that goes on to lay bare the theology that informs the text."[35] Because there is theology in every biblical text, Bright strongly encourages interpreters to discover the theological concern of the biblical author: "It is incumbent

---

34. Schultz, "Integrating Old Testament Theology and Exegesis," 195.
35. Bright, *Authority of the Old Testament*, 170.

upon the interpreter to seek to discover what that theological concern is."[36] This work will navigate the course set by Schultz and Bright.

The approach will be canonical or, stated another way, it focuses on the final form of the text. The biblical text is the primary focus. For as Lim writes, "The texts become the centre of concern with the character, structure, composition, content and theological status coming to the forefront."[37] While Lim is concerned with the final form of narratives, the same approach may be followed in poetic texts as well. For as Lim rightly remarks, "The interpreter should then seek to attempt to understand the particular shape and function of individual books in the Hebrew canon."[38] Since the SoS is in the Hebrew canon, this proposed method is a valid one.

It is also rhetorical. While rhetorical studies have concerned themselves mainly with studies of biblical narrative, this method may be profitable in its application to poetry.[39] The reason for its profitability is based on the classic understanding of rhetoric. Patrick and Scult suggest that rhetoric is "the means by which a text establishes and manages its relationship to its audience in order to achieve a particular effect."[40] Because the Song is the product of an author (or, as some suggest, an artistic compiler), it is meant to somehow influence its audience. While it is not Hebrew poetry or narrative, Brent Strawn recognizes this exact dynamic in Deuteronomy as he studies repetition and exhortation. In Deuteronomy Strawn suggests rightly that this literary device was employed to produce a rhetorical effect and "in turn, an *ethical and theological result*."[41] It is vitally important to the exposition of the theology of the text to be able to ascertain the intended effect that the text is thought to have on its original audience. Patrick and Scult observe this dynamic:

> Any author must necessarily shape his or her language in one way rather than another, and insofar as we may assume artful

36. Ibid.
37. Lim, "Towards a Final Form Approach to Biblical Interpretation," 7.
38. Ibid., 5.
39. See Alter, *Art of Biblical Narrative*; Sternberg, *Poetics of Biblical Narrative*. Muilenburg ("Form Criticism and Beyond," 17) foresaw the importance of a rhetorical study even of repeated terms when he stated: "The repeated words or lines do not appear haphazardly or fortuitously, but rather in rhetorically significant collocations."
40. Patrick and Scult, *Rhetoric and Biblical Interpretation*, 12.
41. Strawn, "Keep/Observe/Do," 217.

deliberateness on the author's part, the shape and form of the discourse is an indication of how he or she means for us to take the message. It is thus through a text's rhetoric that a modern interpreter can recapture the possibilities for encounter the particular text holds.[42]

Noegel observes that Bergant's commentary on the Song (2001) falls short in this manner since she only catalogues the various poetic devices "without attention to their function in the poem."[43]

It is a biblical-theological approach. While a systematic theology approach is a valid pursuit after the biblical theology of an individual pericope has been assessed, this thesis will not seek to collaborate its findings with other canonical texts.[44] The goal is to discern the biblical theological meaning of the SoS. Lim states, "Biblical texts were shaped purposefully and purposely in order to function as a permanent theological witness."[45] By studying the literary devices of the Song, the theological witness will be evident. By following this multifaceted approach, this work aims to accomplish its purpose and aid the church in her understanding of this most sublime song.

ORIENTATION

Since this work studies three individual literary features of the SoS, it is purposefully narrow in its focus. Since the limit of this work is so narrowly defined, it is important to orient the reader to the overall structure of the entire poem. By understanding and recognizing these limits, the proverbial forest is not lost while one studies the bark of an individual tree.

While scholarly consensus may be moving away from an anthology interpretation to a unified work in recent years, there is no consensus concerning the overall structural division of the book.[46] Following

---

42. Ibid., 13.

43. Noegel, review of *Song of Songs*, by Dianne Bergant.

44. For a recent work that researches the topic of sexuality throughout the OT, consult Davidson's *Flame of Yahweh*.

45. Lim, "Towards a Final Form Approach," 10.

46. Exum (*Song of Songs*, 39) demonstrates this lack of scholarly accord by citing twelve different scholars and their structures since 1963. While there may be similarities, none agrees with one another. Exum herself parts company with all. Based on the dialogue of the two main protagonists, Exum suggests that the Song is simply composed of two long cycles of speeches (ibid., 38–40).

Dumbrell, the book may be divided according to seven cycles or major units: 1:1—2:7; 2:8–17; 3:1–5; 3:6—5:1; 5:2—7:10; 7:11—8:4; 8:5–14.[47] He observes that each of these units or cycles is composed of the following sequence: lover separated, expression of desire, and lovers united.[48] He believes this sequence is evident in every cycle except the last. In addition to Dumbrell's sequence, there may be an obstacle or problem that must be overcome by the couple in each of the cycles except the fourth.[49]

---

47. Dumbrell, *Faith of Israel*, 278–81. The term *cycle* is preferable since there is a reoccurrence of the themes of separation, expression of desire, obstacle, and union that are generally present in each of Dumbrell's units. Even though Exum (*Song of Songs*, 38) recognizes a different number of major units or structural divisions, she still recognizes that there are cycles evident in the Song.

48. Ibid., 279. Although Elliott (*Literary Unity of the Canticle*, 40) does not follow Dumbrell's outline of the book, she does recognize the theme of separation. She also believes the separation of the couple begins each of the six parts in her outline of the book.

49. For instance, the female lover's self-perception may be a problem in the first cycle (1:6; 2:1). In the second cycle, "little foxes" are a concern (2:15). The lost lover is a problem in the third cycle (3:3). There is no problem in the fourth cycle where the focus is on sexual intercourse. The problem in the fifth cycle is the reluctance of the female lover to be accessible to her lover's nocturnal advance (5:2–3). In the sixth cycle the problem may be the inability to enjoy public displays of affection because of social constraints (8:1). The problem in the seventh cycle may be a Solomonic mindset that believes love can be bought or enjoyed in the multitude of lovers (8:7, 11–12).

2

The Use of the First Person

THE PURPOSE OF THIS chapter is to discover the theological import of the author's use of the first person as a rhetorical device.[1] Therefore, it is important to start with an identification of the author's use of the first person throughout the Song. Schultz believes the accurate identification of words is the foundation for determining the theology that flows from those words, and he calls for a return to assessing their theological contribution. He states,

> Having discussed the macro components of textual exegesis—the structure of books, the genre categories that group together books, or individual texts, and themes that weave their way through entire books, encompassing numerous words and related phrases and descriptions—we must return to the micro components—those fundamental building blocks of the text: the words ... the accurate identification, understanding, and comparison of theologically significant words within a text can make a substantial contribution to the theological assessment of a text.[2]

This chapter will seek first to identify the uses of the first person personal pronouns throughout the entire Song in their various forms

---

1. This chapter is an expansion of my ThM thesis: "'Let Him Kiss Me': An Exploration of the Use of the First Person in the Song of Songs and Its Impact on the Theology of the Song."

2. Schultz, "Integrating Old Testament Theology and Exegesis, 192. The specific instances of the first person may be found in appendix 1. The scripture references listed in the body of this work are examples of the usage and are not necessarily exhaustive.

In his rhetorical analysis of Amos 2:6–16, Meynet (*Rhetorical Analysis*, 271) notes the importance pronouns play in this biblical passage and how the first person "frame(s) the center" of the passage. Meynet does not seek to complete the exegetical process by suggesting the theology that flows from such use of the first person. However, he does suggest that the rhetorical analysis does aid the interpretive process (327).

and from the mouths of various speakers.³ Following the recognition process, the function of the author's use of the first person personal pronouns throughout the various cycles of the Song will be suggested. In connection with the author's use of the first person, this chapter will seek to recognize the significant shifts in the use of the first person to either second or third person. Following the identification of such shifts, the functions of these shifts will be proposed. Then a number of theological observations that naturally flow from the biblical writer's use of the first person will be put forward.⁴ A summary of the significance of the first person as a rhetorical device will conclude the section.⁵

IDENTIFICATION OF USES OF THE FIRST PERSON

The use of the first person as it concerns the female lover evidences itself in three ways.⁶ There is the female "I" which is found as an independent

---

3. Although the first person pronoun is not marked for gender in BH, the context of the Song does give the reader enough information to determine the gender of the first person in most cases. It is in this manner that the concept of first person masculine or first person feminine is used.

4. This effort will help fill in the oversight of historical exegetes who believe, according to Knierim ("Criticism of Literary Features, Form, Tradition and Redaction," 3–4), that "the inclusion of the theology of a text into its exegesis was considered unscientific speculation." Knierim believes that OT exegesis must seek "to recover all data and all levels of meaning present in the text."

These observations will be concerned with the biblical theology of the SoS since this project limits itself to this example of ancient songs. Since the study is limited to one book, the observations will not be in the nature of a systematic theology.

5. According to Merrill ("Isaiah 40–50 As a Anti-Babylonian Polemic," 11), the use of the first person is a rhetorical device in Sumerian and Akkadian literature "especially in the hymns of self-praise and royal inscriptions." He also notes its rhetorical usage in Isaiah 40–55. He compares this section to Sumerian and Akkadian literature. This rhetorical device in Isaiah is used as a polemic to exalt Yahweh and debase the gods of Babylon. Sefati (*Love Songs in Sumerian Literature*) observes the use of the first person pronoun in the love songs of Sumer. While the examples of verbal repetition are varied, he does observe that verbal repetition is a major type of repetition used by ancient authors. He (69) gives this translated example for verbal repetition, where the repetition of the first person personal pronouns is readily apparent:

"My 'dear,' my 'dear,' my 'dear,'
My 'darling,' my 'darling,' my honey of the mother who bore her."

6. See the charts in appendix 1 (columns 1, 2, 3) for specific instances of these uses. While it is true that the first person is not marked for gender in BH, the context of the Song gives sufficient evidence to determine the gender of the first person in most cases.

personal pronoun אֲנִי, such as "I am black" שְׁחוֹרָה אֲנִי (1:5); and the "I" conjugated with the perfect or imperfect verbs, such as "I have kept" נָטַרְתִּי (1:6) or "I should become" אֶהְיֶה (1:7). The independent pronoun may also be found with the prefixed relative pronoun, -שֶׁ as in שֶׁאֲנִי (1:6). The pronoun "I" אֲנִי, independent or affixed to the relative pronoun, is present twelve times in the Song. According to Stoop-van Paridon this form is only found in the mouth of the female lover.[7] When it is conjugated with a verb (imperfect or perfect), it appears forty times. The second manner in which the first person is used of the female lover is "me" -נִי. The suffixed personal pronoun "me" -נִי is either attached to the verb (for example, "kiss me" יִשָּׁקֵנִי, 1:2) or appears suffixed to a preposition such as "to me" לִי 1:7).[8] There are some cases where the personal pronoun "me" is translated by the English "mine" to show possession or ownership, as in 2:16, "my beloved is mine," דּוֹדִי לִי. The pronoun "me" -נִי suffixed to either verb or preposition is used thirty-three times. The third example of the first person referencing the female lover is the suffixed possessive pronoun "my" -ִי with various nouns such as "my vineyard," כַּרְמִי; (1:6). From the mouth of the female lover this form occurs fifty-nine times throughout the Song.

The use of the first person as it reflects the male lover of the Song is used in two ways.[9] Unlike the female lover, the male lover never has the independent pronoun, "I," אֲנִי placed on his lips by the author. LaCocque notes that the female lover "is always the one who says . . . me, my soul . . . or even my heart."[10] The male "I" is always found with a verb, as an afformative with a perfect such as "I liken you," דִּמִּיתִיךְ (1:9) or preformative with an imperfect "I will go" אֵלֶךְ (4:6). This masculine "I" appears eleven times.

The second manner in which the first person masculine occurs is as the pronominal suffix "me." This pronoun is either suffixed to a verb (e.g., "let me see" הַרְאִינִי, 2:14) or to a preposition (e.g., "from me" מִנֶּגְדִּי, 6:5). Whether attached to a verb, preposition, or direct object marker (4:8), this form appears only eight times. The third way in which the first person is used of the male lover is the pronominal suffix "my" -ִי with

---

7. Stoop-van Paridon, *The Song of Songs*, 52.

8. LaCocque (*Romance She Wrote*, 43) states that the female lover "is always the one who says *'anî* (me) . . . or even *libbî* (my heart, me)."

9. See appendix 1, columns 6, 7, and 8, for specific instances of these uses.

10. LaCocque, *Romance She Wrote*, 43.

various nouns such as "my darling" רַעְיָתִי (1:9). This form in the mouth of the male beloved occurs thirty times. The total number of the combined uses of the personal pronoun "my" in regard to the male and female lover is eighty-nine, making it the most common form in the entire poem.

The use of the first person plural pronoun as it concerns the couple evidences itself in two ways.[11] First, the plural personal pronoun נו- from the mouth of the female is suffixed to prepositions, such as "catch for us" אֶחֱזוּ־לָנוּ, and to nouns, such as "our vineyards" כְּרָמֵינוּ (2:15),[12] "and over our doors," וְעַל־פְּתָחֵינוּ (7:14), and "our wall" כָּתְלֵנוּ (2:9). This form appears seven times from the mouth of the female lover.[13] The same form is on the lips of the male only once, in the phrase "in our land," בְּאַרְצֵנוּ (2:12). The second occurrence of the first person plural prefix, as it relates to the couple, is the use of "we" -נ, which is always part of the conjugation of an imperfect verb such as "let us run" נָרוּצָה (1:4) or "let us go" נֵצֵא (7:12). It is used five times. Each of these is from the perspective of the female lover. The only example of this form from the mouth of the male may be "that we may gaze at you" וְנֶחֱזֶה־בָּךְ (7:1).[14] The first person plural pronoun is also found in the mouths of the daughters of Jerusalem and occurs five times. For example, the daughters of Jerusalem state, "We will rejoice" נָגִילָה (1:4). The plural personal pronoun is also heard in 8:8, "what shall we do" מַה־נַּעֲשֶׂה. This form appears twice, but only in this verse. The personal pronoun, "us," נו- is used two times (8:8).

---

11. See appendix 1, columns 4 and 5, for specific instances of these uses.

12. There is some disagreement concerning the identity of the speaker of this verse. I have followed the translation of the NASB, which places the words of this verse in the mouth of the woman. Since the first person plural is used, it is either the woman or the man. The exact identity does not alter the observation.

13. According to Westenholz ("Love Lyrics," 2477), the use of first person plural forms by a female speaker appears frequently in Akkadian love lyrics between Inanna and Dumuzi.

14. Scholars are uncertain of the identity of the speaker in this verse. Some conclude that it is the male while others argue that this verse comes from the "daughters of Jerusalem." Based on the NASB and the verses which follow, I have chosen to place it in the mouth of the male beloved. Uncertainty concerning the speaker's identity does not greatly impact the theology of the Song. Longman (*Song of Songs*, 91) remarks that the speaker is ambiguous. Murphy (*Song of Songs*, 138) puts the verse in the mouth of the woman. Hess (*Song of Songs*, 38) believes it is best to see the statement coming from the lips of both male and female. Keel (*Song of Songs*, 108) suggests the daughters of Jerusalem speak here as a group.

OBSERVATIONS OF THE AUTHOR'S USE OF FIRST PERSON

As it has been observed, there are a significant number of grammatical instances of the first person personal pronouns occurring in the Song. This is not unusual. For as Linafelt points out,

> To speak of erotic love is, to be sure, often a matter of speaking in the first and second person singular: an "I" addresses a "you." . . . And even where the demand to become one proves impossible or elusive, there remain the distinct satisfactions of the first person plural, the possibilities of "we."[15]

The author's repetitive use of the first person personal pronouns combines to create the first person point of view (POV).[16] The majority of the Song is written from this perspective.[17] It is important to recognize the point of view of the biblical text. Writing about biblical narrative, Berlin shows the importance of recognizing the biblical author's various points of view: "Recognizing the multiple points of view is the first step in discovering the point of view of the implied author; and this is the first step in discovering the meaning and the purpose of the story."[18] This is an important step to discovering the theology of the biblical author. Berlin lays out a legitimate track to follow. Although Joy Thompson is writing about the first person POV in modern English literature, her observations shed light on the Song: "With first person point of view, the reader sees inside the viewpoint character's mind, gaining full access to her thoughts and feelings."[19] This is evident in the opening verse of the Song. The audience overhears the woman's intimate desire to be kissed (1:2). Her erotic feelings are further revealed in her phrase "I am lovesick" כִּי־חוֹלַת אַהֲבָה אָנִי (2:5). The first person

---

15. Linafelt, "Arithmetic of Eros," 247.

16. Berlin (*Poetics and Interpretation*, 55) believes that to determine the point of view of the biblical author one must "attempt to isolate specific words, phrasing, and syntactic arrangements." The isolation (identification) and analysis of the first person in this chapter is such an endeavor.

17. Contra Kravitz and Olitzky (*Shir Hashirim*, 2), who recognize the change of style in 1:2 and state, "Since 1:3 is written in the second person, we have chosen to translate the first clause of 1:2 that way as well. We believe that this is the overwhelming viewpoint taken in the entire text."

18. Ibid., 82.

19. Thompson, "Talking Heads."

POV is uniquely suited to communicate the inner feelings of love for the main characters of the Song.

Thompson further notes that the first person POV establishes a more intimate relationship between the reader and the viewpoint character than with any other character.[20] In this song the first person POV is mainly that of the woman. It is from her lips that the majority of the poem is expressed, and it is she with whom the audience is most acquainted. Thompson believes that "one disadvantage with first person POV is that your viewpoint character must be present for all key scenes. She is the one telling the story, after all, and anything that the viewpoint character does not know or hasn't seen or been told, cannot appear in the story."[21] Although this first person perspective may have its limitations, this is the POV of the biblical author. The female lover is, in the terminology of Thompson, "the viewpoint character." Although the woman is not always speaking, she is always present in the mind of the audience through the speech of her beloved or other characters such as the daughters of Jerusalem or the brothers (e.g., 4:1–6; 6:4–9; 8:8). She is also present in the evaluation of her actions by the Song's author or his narrator's voice (5:1).

The first person POV is a rhetorical device that allows the author to include the audience in the action. Sharon Sorenson comments,

> The first-person point of view uses "I," "me," "my," and "our." It permits the author to tell the story from the point of view of a narrator or of one of the characters in the story, major or minor. Only those feelings, observations, and reactions which that narrator or character experiences can appear in the story. The advantage of first-person point of view, of course, is that it puts readers close to the action.[22]

Thompson remarks that the "use of first person POV also affects the pace of the story, providing a sense of reality and immediacy as reader and viewpoint character experience it hand-in-hand."[23] Although Jacobson writes concerning direct discourse in Ps 30, his observations convey the rhetorical purpose of direct discourse (which creates the first person POV) as it is used in Hebrew poetry:

20. Ibid.
21. Ibid.
22. Sorenson, "Points of View."
23. Thompson, "Talking Heads."

> Psalm 30 is a song of thanksgiving in which the psalmist praises God for delivering him from danger. But the psalmist does more than simply describe his past fall into sin and deliverance from trouble. *The psalmist transports the audience back in time to the moment of sin—or rather, the psalmist transports the past moment of sin forward in time to the audience by reenacting the moment through quotation.*[24]

The female lover of the SoS (since she is the major voice) transports the audience into her garden celebration of the physical relationship through the narrator's use of the direct discourse in first person. Jacobson captures the emotional connection between the author and his audience by the use of the first person POV: "This technique has the advantage of a sharp and precise focus. Moreover, you feel part of the story because the narrator's 'I' echoes the 'I' already in your own mind."[25] Because of this perspective, the individual female reader is able to become the female lover of the Song, and the individual male reader is able to become her beloved. Tremper Longman remarks, "These poems invite later readers to place themselves in the position of the woman and the man. In this way, the Song is similar to the book of Psalms, where the reader is implicitly encouraged to put him- or herself in the place of the first person speaker."[26] In the same manner the modern couple is encouraged to enjoy the same celebration of love in their own married lives as the couple of the Song.[27]

---

24. Jacobson, "*Many Are Saying*," 77. Emphasis is original.

25. "Elements of Literature," http://web.cocc.edu/lisal/literaryterms/elements_of_literature.htm#Points.

26. Longman, *Song of Songs*, 91. The use of the first person POV in the lament psalms especially has endeared those prayers to every generation of believers precisely because they are in first person. The reader does not simply read an ancient prayer, but through the "I" and the "me," the modern reader becomes the psalmist crying anew for God to look favorably on his plight and deliver him. For an excellent discussion of this dynamic in the Psalms, see Jacobson who investigates the rhetorical aspect of the direct discourse in the Psalter. For example, writing about the rhetorical function of the direct discourse in the Psalms in the community of faith, he states, "A third rhetorical function is that they provide a voice for modern readers who approach the psalms. Readers . . . seek to find themselves in texts" ("*Many are Saying*," 144).

Hosea also uses the first person POV rhetorically to persuade Israel to return to God by placing his entire audience at Bethel (Hosea 12:4). This is unique since Jacob was the one to wrestle with the angel alone (Gen 32:24, 25) and he alone spoke with God a thousand years earlier than Hosea's audience (Gen 31:13).

27. The same emotional connection is established in the Song by the author's use of the second person POV.

The Use of the First Person

The first person POV allows the author to communicate deep emotions and develop an intimate connection with the reader. Writing about the Song, Ryken observes, "It is almost continuously an outpouring of feelings.... The basic structure is what in modern literature we call stream of consciousness; meaning that it follows the shifting flow of actual thought and feelings."[28] The audience does not read about her desire to be kissed. Such a sentiment would be rewritten as "let her be kissed by him," which would constitute a third person POV of 1:2. The third person POV places the reader in the role of outside observer who would *hear* the desire to be kissed but would not *feel* her desire to be kissed. The reader is connected with the woman in a special way by the use of the first person POV. The reader not only shares the knowledge of the woman's desire for physical intimacy found in kisses but the reader experiences the desire to be kissed (and not just once but many times) as well.

The first person POV allows the reader to experience vicariously the celebration of love by overhearing the intimate dialogue of these two lovers. Jacobson asserts that direct discourse does not simply describe old circumstances but it "recreates such circumstances."[29] If the Song was written in the third person without direct (or indirect) discourse, the audience would make judgments about the characters being presented. By the use of the first person POV, the reader is invited into this celebration of love to become the characters of the song. The audience does not merely hear about love, which would be true of the third person POV, but it experiences love vicariously through the first person POV. Mairs notes that through this POV the audience is thrown into "confrontation, even contact" with the characters, "drawn into a relationship of implicit intimacy."[30] Gledhill, writing on the Song, concurs: "The couple are representative types of Everyman and Everywoman. They articulate our own most private and intimate longings, and as we read, we are drawn into their passions and tensions."[31] Jacobson comments, "People who

---

28. Ryken, *Words of Delight*, 272.

29. Jacobson, "*Many are Saying*," 78.

30. Mairs, *Voice Lessons*, 11. Although Mairs is describing the use of the first person POV in modern literature, her observation is nonetheless true when applied to this ancient love song. She could have been speaking about the intimacy found in the Song. Speaking of reading her students' literary work from the first person POV, she writes, "I was drawn into a relationship of implicit intimacy that my Yankee grandmother would certainly have condemned as inappropriate if not downright impertinent."

31. Gledhill, *Song of Songs*, 94.

read literature will read it as being literature, in part, about themselves. . . . Poetry does create *voices*. These voices do evoke responses in readers and readers will tend to resonate more strongly to the voices that are like them."[32] Through the use of the first person POV in the Song, the reader is moved to desire the same intensity of passion and intimacy in his or her own marriage or, if unmarried, to look for it at the proper time within the confines of marriage (2:7; 3:5; 5:8).

The highly repetitive use of the first person throughout the SoS in its various functions and forms and its use to create the first person POV may also give evidence of a unified composition. While Longman and others have seen the SoS as a collection of individual love songs, the biblical author's use of the first person argues for a single song. Such a study that focuses on the rhetorical aspect of the first person may, as Murphy observes, enable "us to discern a remarkable coherence of literary style and language throughout the Song."[33]

THE FUNCTION OF THE FIRST PERSON IN THE SONG

In this section the function of the first person by gender and case will be surveyed.[34] It will observe the first person feminine in the nominative, accusative, and genitive cases. Next, the first person masculine in the nominative, accusative, and genitive cases will be considered.[35] The first person common plural personal pronoun in all three cases will conclude

---

32. Jacobson, "*Many are Saying*," 144. Emphasis is original.

33. Murphy, *Song of Songs*, 67. For instance, the male lover's term of endearment for his lover is "my friend" רַעְיָתִי. As Murphy (ibid., 81) observes, "The nine attestations of this epithet are fairly spread evenly throughout the poetic units of 1:2–6:3, but none appear after the occurrence in 6:4." This absence may not argue against a unified composition since the male speaks less in those subsequent sections and he uses other terms of endearment to address his love.

34. BH is not marked for gender in the first person. These instances reflect the author's understanding of the gender of the person speaking.

Sternberg illustrates the rhetorical import of the biblical author's use of first person in the Saul-Agag story (1 Sam 15:20ff.). The use of the first person singular in Saul's case demonstrates that he "monopolized the credit but suppressed the blame" (*Poetics of Biblical Narrative*, 510). This rhetorical device moves the reader to increase his doubtfulness as to Saul's fitness for continued kingship. The first person carries rhetorical import in the SoS as well.

35. Following *IBHS* (126): "Biblical Hebrew is a language without a case system, though it is often helpful to look at various aspects of its nominal use in a case framework. . . . Nevertheless, from a historical, comparative, and syntactic viewpoint we can differentiate three distinct 'cases,' that is, syntactic functions, of the noun: nominative, genitive, and accusative."

this section. The charts in the appendix seem to give evidence of an intentional grouping, if not a pattern, of the use of the first person personal pronoun. This chapter will work through the function of the author's use of these personal pronouns by following seven cycles that seem to be the major sections or units of the Song.[36]

First Cycle (1:1—2:7)

In the first cycle of the Song there are nine uses of the first person feminine in the nominative case. Four instances function as the independent pronoun (1:5, 6; 2:1, 5). All the independent pronouns function as subjects. Five are affixed to both imperfect and perfect verbs (1:6, 7; 2:3 [2x], 7) and function as subjects as well. The first person pronouns and affixed verbs (as well as the use of the other cases in these verses in first person POV) provide numerous repetition of the /i/, י sound as in "unique" (1:5–6). This repetition of sound provides structural unity in these cola as well as rhyme or rhythm. Grossberg remarks that "repetition in its various forms is the most frequent cohesive device."[37] Roberts notes that the repetition of אֲנִי provides cohesion between the strophes (1:5. 6).[38] Glickman observes that אֲנִי functions as a poetic boundary marker for the subsection of 2:1–5. This subsection begins with אֲנִי and 2:5 ends with the independent personal pronoun as well.[39] Besides providing structural cohesion, Stoop-van Paridon observes that "the selective use of אֲנִי in relation to the female protagonist becomes her characteristic, a literary aid for identifying her as the speaker."[40]

The use of the independent personal pronouns in this cycle also demonstrates a self-awareness of the female lover.[41] She describes herself

---

36. While I realize that there is no consensus on the structural division of the book, generally speaking the grouping of the usage of the first person falls within these seven units or cycles. I prefer the term "cycles" because of the reoccurring themes of separation and the expression of desire, obstacle, and union that are generally present in each major section. Following Dumbrell (*Faith of Israel*, 278–81), these are the seven cycles or major units of the Song: 1:1—2:7; 2:8–17; 3:1–5; 3:6—5:1; 5:2—7:10; 7:11—8:4; 8:5–14.

37. Grossberg, *Centripetal and Centrifugal Structures*, 9.

38. Roberts, *Let Me See Your Form*, 116.

39. Glickman, *Solomon's Song of Love*, 201.

40. Stoop-van Paridon, *Song of Songs*, 52.

41. Concerning the male lover, there are no instances of the use of the independent first person pronoun. The first person pronoun is always affixed to a verb when it concerns the male. There is no self-awareness by the male beloved evidenced by the use of

in the first person: "I am black" אֲנִי שְׁחוֹרָה, "I am swarthy" שֶׁאֲנִי שְׁחַרְחֹרֶת, "I am the rose of Sharon" אֲנִי חֲבַצֶּלֶת הַשָּׁרוֹן, and "For I am lovesick" כִּי־חוֹלַת אַהֲבָה אָנִי (1:5, 6; 2:1, 5). The first three instances are self-deprecating. She thinks less of herself because of her physical appearance. This deprecating self-awareness provides her lover an opportunity to compliment her: "like a lily among the thorns, so is my darling among the maidens." He flatters her with almost her same words by repeating the word "lily" שׁוּשַׁן, which she has just spoken. This self-description also moves the reader to feel empathy for the woman. The audience is aware there is a problem (though a self-perceived one) in the relationship: her sunburnt skin. The use of the independent pronoun "I" אֲנִי in 2:1 is the first instance of a metaphor employed by the woman of herself: "I am the rose of Sharon אֲנִי חֲבַצֶּלֶת הַשָּׁרוֹן.[42] Her final self-description reveals how deeply she is "infected" with her lover: "Sustain me with raisin cakes, refresh me with apples, because I am lovesick" (2:5).[43]

The use of the first person personal pronoun in the phrase "for why should I be like" שַׁלָּמָה אֶהְיֶה כְּעֹטְיָה sets up a tease through the use of a rhetorical question that anticipates a negative answer (1:7). In the next instance the first person personal pronoun functions as a subject. Its individual use with two verbs (and *waw* conjunctive) may function to slow the action: "I took great delight and I sat down"[44] חִמַּדְתִּי וְיָשַׁבְתִּי (2:3). The verb יָשַׁב "sit, remain, dwell," may demonstrate the woman's desire to linger long over her lover. Not only does she desire his kisses (1:2), she desires to taste him as well (2:3). The last instance of the nominative case

---

the independent personal pronoun. This fits the POV of the Song since it is sung from the perspective of the female and not that of the male. The female voice is the typical voice that is heard the majority of the time in Ancient Near Eastern love poetry. By Brenner's accounting (*Israelite Woman*, 47) "the eight chapters of the song contain 117 verses. Out of these, sixty-one and a half are delivered by the woman speaker." Women's voices are also mentioned in Exod 15:21; Judg 5:1; 1 Sam 18:7; 2 Sam 1:20, 24; Eccl 12:4; Jer 9:17, 20; Ezek 32:16.

42. Munro (*Spikenard and Saffron*) has written well concerning the importance of the various metaphors in the Song, so there is no need to duplicate her efforts. It should be noted that the metaphors in the Song begin with a reference to one of the lovers. Many times they are referenced by the author's use of pronouns, for example, "I am," "you are," and "he is." Pronouns seem to be the building block of metaphors in the Song.

43. Roberts (*Let Me See Your Form*, 176) suggests the אָנִי may function as a mark of closure since it occurs at the end of the cola.

44. Translation is the author's. NASB omits the second independent pronoun.

is the refrain of 2:7. It is the voice of the woman who concludes this cycle with a warning to the young women of Jerusalem. Since she is the one expressing and initiating such intense love in this cycle, it is only proper that she be the one to warn others to take care not to awaken or arouse this powerful emotion until the proper time.

The use of the first person feminine in both the accusative and genitive cases translated by the English "me" demonstrates that the woman is the object of desire. She is the one who desires to be kissed ("may he kiss me" יִשָּׁקֵנִי, 1:2), to be drawn after her lover ("draw me" מָשְׁכֵנִי, 1:4; 2:4), to gain information about her lover's presence ("tell me" הַגִּידָה לִּי, 1:7). She is the one who needs to be sustained, refreshed and embraced (2:4–6). Her lover is identified as "a pouch of myrrh" צְרוֹר הַמֹּר (1:13) or a "cluster of henna blossoms" אֶשְׁכֹּל הַכֹּפֶר, (1:14). Through the use of metaphor, he becomes those items. He is those pleasant smells that surround her. Even though she is the object of his desire, it is clear from the use of the first person pronouns that he is her desire as well.[45]

But being the object is not always positive. In 1:6 she was the object of her brother's anger. This hostility caused her to neglect her own vineyard: "My brothers have been angry with me; they charged me with the care of the vineyards" בְּנֵי אִמִּי נִחֲרוּ־בִי שָׂמֻנִי נֹטֵרָה אֶת־הַכְּרָמִים. The ten uses of the feminine first person personal pronoun (in all three case functions) in 1:6 combine to produce a repetition of the same end sound. The same observation may be suggested for 1:13, 14; 2:4, 5.

In the first cycle the use of the first person feminine in the genitive case, which is translated by the English "my," demonstrates possession, exclusivity, and totality. It is "my breasts" שָׁדַי, "my beloved" דּוֹדִי, and "whom my soul loves" שֶׁאָהֲבָה נַפְשִׁי. This pronoun also demonstrates desire. It is "my head" לְרֹאשִׁי that wants to be held and "my taste" לְחִכִּי that wants to enjoy his fruit (2:3, 6).

In the first cycle the use of the first person masculine pronoun in all three case functions is limited to five instances. The only nominative case usage is "I liken you" דִּמִּיתִיךְ (1:9). This instance serves to introduce the first time the male beloved speaks. He begins with a culturally conditioned simile. In the same verse the genitive case appears two times: לְסֻסָתִי and רַעְיָתִי. These two phrases open and close the colon. This provides a repetition of ending sounds and provides an inclusion of theme:

---

45. That she is his desire is stated explicitly in 7:11. This Hebrew word for desire, תְּשׁוּקָה, is used three times in the entire OT canon: Gen 3:16; 4:7; Song 7:11.

she is "my mare" לְסֻסָתִי and "my friend" רַעְיָתִי.⁴⁶ These terms demonstrate a possessiveness, a desirability, and an intimacy on the male lover's part. His remarks show that their love is mutual. This is not a one-sided relationship. He desires and appreciates her as much as she desires and appreciates him. The phrase "my darling" רַעְיָתִי is repeated in this cycle in 1:15 and 2:2 as well. This is the beloved's favorite term of endearment for his female lover.

The first person plural pronoun occurs eight times in the first cycle. It appears in the nominative case five times and the genitive three (1:16, 17). It is used in the nominative case concerning the lovers once (1:4) and four times in connection with the daughters of Jerusalem (1:4, 11). The lovers' use of the first person plural is an accumulation of movement from the third person "he" (1:2) to the second person "your" and "you" (1:3) to the first person "me" (1:4a). Once the two lovers are together, they become a couple, "us." This reveals her desire to be with the one she loves as well as to be known as a couple and to get away as a couple: "draw me after you *and* let us run" רַעְיָתִי (1:4).⁴⁷ The employment of the plural genitive case shows a dissolving now of each lover as an individual into a couple (1:16, 17). It is not "his couch" or "her house." It is "our couch" עַרְשֵׂנוּ, "our houses" בָּתֵּינוּ, and "our rafters" רַהִיטֵנוּ. While Stoop-van Paridon is incorrect in her identification concerning the number of male characters or voices in the Song, her insight concerning the first person plural is helpful in highlighting its significance at this juncture. She notes that the "personal pronoun *our* occurs three times in 1.16 and 1.17. That focuses all the attention on the content: an accentuation of the contrast between the circumstances of the female protagonist now and her living conditions previously, with her beloved shepherd."⁴⁸ This use

---

46. The NIV does not account for the function of the genitive in its translation of 1:9. Instead of "my mare," the NIV simply translates it as "a mare." Gledhill (*Song of Songs*, 112) follows the NIV. Bloch and Bloch (*Song of Songs*, 144) recognize the genitive and translate it "my mare."

47. See Gen 2:24: "The two shall become one."

48. Stoop-van Paridon, *Song of Songs*, 96. While one may not agree with a number of her conclusions, Stoop-van Paridon's philological work on the Song is a valuable resource for understanding how the individual words function in this poem. This is evidenced in her keen observation concerning the personal pronoun *our* in this passage. Her observation highlights the importance of studying the individual words of the Song. Unfortunately, however, she misses the opportunity to shed light on the uses of other first person personal pronouns in the Song. For instance, this is the only significant discussion concerning the first person in chapter 1 of the Song.

of the first person plural pronoun here emphasizes for the audience that the two lovers are together. Between 1:16–17 there is a repetition of the /nu/ נוּ, /m/ מ, and /nah/ נָה sounds, which may function to tie the verses together and provide a rhythm if not a rhyme.

The use of the first person plural nominative case pronoun from the daughters of Jerusalem allows the audience to know that the feelings of the woman towards her lover are not unique to her: "We will extol your love more than wine" נַזְכִּירָה דֹדֶיךָ מִיָּיִן (1:4).[49] Her beloved is not only desirable to her but to every female. This heightens the desirability of the man. Fox states, "The girl moves back and forth between the first person plural, where she includes the other girls in her appreciation of her lover's beauties, and the third person plural, where she dances verbally out of the group to add a certain objectivity to her statement about the public estimation of his love worthiness."[50] Conversely, the same use of the first person plural nominative case pronoun from the daughters of Jerusalem allows the audience to sense that the feelings of the man towards his darling are not unique. The daughters of Jerusalem desire to adorn her beauty as well. "We will make for you ornaments of gold with beads of silver," תּוֹרֵי זָהָב נַעֲשֶׂה־לָּךְ עִם נְקֻדּוֹת הַכָּסֶף (1:11).[51] Her beauty is not only praised by her beloved but by all who see her. The use of this female choir allows the audience to identify and agree with their evaluation of the lovers individually, and it moves the reader emotionally deeper into the Song.[52]

Second Cycle (2:8–17)

In the second cycle of the Song there is one instance of the nominative case as an independent pronoun and it concerns the female lover (2:16). There are seven instances of the first person personal pronoun in the genitive case (2:8, 9, 10, 16, 17) in the same gender. When affixed to a preposition, the English translation is "me" (2:10, 16). When affixed to a noun, the translation is "my" (2:8, 9, 10, 16, 17). The use of the inde-

---

49. Murphy, *Song of Songs*, 127. He proposes that the woman may be part of the "we" in 1:4.

50. Fox, "Scholia to Canticles," 200.

51. Murphy, *Song of Songs*, 134. He suggests the man may be part of the "we" in 1:11.

52. The exact manner by which the audience identifies with the daughters of Jerusalem will be developed in chapter 4.

pendent pronoun in 2:16 "my beloved is mine and I am his" דּוֹדִי לִי וַאֲנִי לוֹ emphasizes mutuality, affection, "ownership,"[53] "mutual belonging,"[54] and exclusivity of the relationship between the couple. This may be the fundamental theme in the entire Song and it is communicated by the author's use of the first person.[55] Stoop-van Paridon concurs with this thematic use of the personal pronouns. She writes, "The relationship of the female protagonist and her beloved are the central theme which is emphasized by the personal pronoun in 2.3 and 2.4. She implicitly gives herself away by this: a loving relationship like this exists only between myself and my beloved shepherd."[56] Similar wording is also found in 6:3 and 7:11. Without the use of the first person personal pronouns, the same intimate effect could not be attained. Roberts remarks that there is a "phonological intensity with the succession of the three final י sounds."[57] The biblical author may have used the intensity of the sounds to communicate the intensity of the sentiment. This intensity of belonging draws the reader into desiring the identical mutuality, affection, and exclusivity in his or her marriage. This fundamental theme instructs the modern audience not by precept but by example. The Song instructs not only by an appeal to cognitive knowledge but by an appeal to the emotions.

The five instances of the genitive case (2:8, 9, 10, 16, 17) in the same gender make up the same phrase, "my beloved" דּוֹדִי. This is the favorite term of the female lover for her man. The use of the personal pronoun coupled with the term of endearment דוד captures the intimate relationship she has with her lover. This beloved is not just any beloved; he is "my beloved" דּוֹדִי. While other women may appreciate her beloved, he is hers and not theirs (1:4). Although Longman (following Murphy)[58] recognizes that this cycle opens and closes in chiastic fashion with the mention of gazelles, stags, and mountains (2:8, 17) and that these literary devices unify this cycle, they fail to note that "my beloved" דּוֹדִי should also be included in the list of literary devices. The repetition of this term of endearment, "my beloved" דּוֹדִי may prove to be more of a structural

---

53. Longman, *Song of Songs*, 125.
54. Gledhill, *Song of Songs*, 140.
55. Pope, *Song of Songs*, 405.
56. Stoop-van Paridon, *Song of Songs*, 105.
57. Roberts, *Let Me See Your Form*, 228.
58. Longman, *Song of Songs*, 117.

device than the chiastic theme of animals and mountains that unite not only the ending cola but the middle ones as well.⁵⁹

The final two instances of the genitive case in this cycle are affixed to prepositions. The English translation is "me" (2:10, 16). In 2:10 the conventional formula introducing speech in a narrative is presented: "my beloved answered me and said to me," עָנָה דוֹדִי וְאָמַר לִי. This shows that she is both the object of his speech and his desire. The sixfold repetition of the /i/ יִ sounds and the use of the imperatives may serve to move this colon along more quickly. It creates the sense of desire and immediacy the young man is feeling.

In the second cycle of the Song (2:8–17), there are no uses of nominative case pronouns as it concerns the male lover. There are five instances of the genitive case in regard to the male (2:10, 13, 14). Two times the term "my darling" רַעְיָתִי, is used (2:10, 13). As stated previously, this is the beloved's favorite term for his lover. Not only is she "my darling" רַעְיָתִי, she is also "my beautiful one" יָפָתִי. In the second half of this verse the two terms of endearment are sandwiched in the middle of the colon. The syntactical pattern of the first half of the cola is

>   imperative + prepositional + term of endearment
>   קוּמִי לָךְ רַעְיָתִי "arise with you my darling"
>   The second half pattern is
>   term of endearment + imperative
>   יָפָתִי וּלְכִי־לָךְ "my beautiful one, and come"

These terms of endearment run on top of each other (ending one colon and beginning the other). This device allows the audience to experience how the beloved feels about his darling. He is emphatic in his feelings about her. With the use of the affixed pronominal suffix, "my" ("my darling," "my beautiful one"), the theme of exclusivity on the man's part is demonstrated. Not only is she his darling, his beautiful one, but she is also "my dove" יוֹנָתִי (2:14). Here the author applies a metaphor to explain some characteristic or characteristics about his love. The function of this metaphor may relate to "the dove's ability to hide and nest in hidden, out-of-the-way places."⁶⁰ Since he would also like to hear her voice as

---

59. דוֹדִי "my beloved" occurs in 2:8, 9, 10, 16, 17. Gazelles, stags, and mountains only appear in 2:8, 9, 17. The gazelle and stag are only used as similes in relationship to the male beloved.

60. "Dove," *Dictionary of Biblical Imagery*, 217. This concept may find support in Ps 55. Here the psalmist wishes to "fly" away to a solitary place like a dove where he could

well as see her, the dove metaphor may relate to the soft cooing of a dove. This fits since the man's desire is to be able to see her and listen to her voice. The implication is he wants to be alone with her and enjoy her completely.

In 2:14 there are two instances of first person pronouns with regard to the male lover in the accusative case. These two pronouns are affixed to two hiphil verbs: "let me hear" הַשְׁמִיעִינִי and "let me see" הַרְאִינִי. The beloved's request both to see and hear his lover may communicate the total desirability of his darling. The reason for the request is because "your appearance is beautiful" מַרְאֵיךְ נָאוֶה and "your voice is sweet" קוֹלֵךְ עָרֵב. He desires her for her beauty and her words.

In 2:12 the first person plural personal pronoun in the genitive case is employed. In this stanza spring has begun to blossom. The evidence of spring explodes over verses 11, 12 and 13. But the blooming of spring is not simply in "the" land or "my" land or even "your" land. Spring has broken out in "our land" בְּאַרְצֵנוּ. This use of the first person plural functions to show that this couple does not hold anything as their own. There is no selfishness in their relationship. Whatever is his is hers, and whatever is hers is his. This theme is summarized at the end of this stanza when the female lover declares she herself belongs to him and he belongs to her: "my beloved is mine and I am his" דּוֹדִי לִי וַאֲנִי לוֹ. In 2:15 the first person plural genitive construction "our vineyard" כְּרָמֵינוּ. is heard from the mouth of the female and denotes the same theme of mutuality as 2:12.[61] While the exact identity of the speaker in 2:15 is in doubt, it may be one of the lovers since it is their relationship (see "for us" לָנוּ) which is in jeopardy because of the "little foxes." The genitives function to show the mutuality of the relationship.[62]

---

be safe and secure. If the place is truly solitary, then Gledhill (*Song of Songs*, 137–38) may be correct in viewing the man's wish to see her in some state of nudity.

61. There is discussion concerning the identity of the speaker of 2:15. Because the woman has been the one to discuss vineyards up to this point (1:6), and because she surely utters 2:16, she is the likely speaker of 2:15.

62. Stoop-van Paridon, *Song of Songs*, 121. Stoop-van Paridon says of the personal pronoun "our" that it "can also be understood in a more general sense and not with a strictly possessive meaning; cf. 'our district,' 'our rivers,' 'our country.'" Her examples still include the aspect of possessiveness.

Third Cycle (3:1–5)

In the third cycle there are no uses of the first person masculine or first person common plural pronoun in any case. The cycle opens with the use of the first person feminine genitive case pronoun "upon my bed" עַל־מִשְׁכָּבִי (3:1). This may seem to contradict the mutuality that was mentioned previously (2:15). However, it is precisely because the lovers are not together that the first person singular pronoun is used instead of the plural. In this report of her dream she views herself as alone in bed.[63] They are not together. Since they are apart, this suggests a new cycle (as evidenced by the author's use of the first person singular by the female and her desire to search for him). This first phase of the new cycle, separation, is communicated by the use of the *singular* first person pronoun in contrast to the previous use of the first person *plural* pronouns when the couple is together (2:15). The other five instances of the first person feminine genitive case pronouns appear in 3:1, 2, 3, and 4. The phrase "whom my soul loves" שֶׁאָהֲבָה נַפְשִׁי is repeated four times within the first four verses. This repeated phrase serves to remind the audience of the object of her frantic search and of her desire for him. The phrase may also mean that she loves him with her whole person as evidenced by the use of "my soul" נַפְשִׁי.[64] In 3:1 the use of this phrase supplies an additional internal /i/ יִ sound which may add to the panicky feeling of not being able to find her love. The יִ sound appears five times within only seven words (3:1). Its sound is heard twenty times throughout this cycle. The fifth instance of the first person feminine genitive case pronoun is "to the house of my mother" אֶל־בֵּית אִמִּי (3:4). The use of this pronoun, "my," may serve to carry the /i/ יִ sound throughout this cycle, and thus it provides cohesion in this cycle. It appears as an end sound ten times and as an internal sound twelve times. It could be that it functions to close the cycle before the adjuration refrain.[65] The interpretation of the phrase is still debated.[66]

---

63. Since this is a dream, it is difficult to tell if she is truly alone in bed or if she is only dreaming that she is alone.

64. Longman, *Song of Songs*, 129. See Gen 2:7 where God formed Adam from the dust of the ground and man became a "living being" לְנֶפֶשׁ חַיָּה.

65. Roberts, *Let Me See Your Form*, 269.

66. Longman, *Song of Songs*, 131. He summarizes the choices of אֶל־בֵּית אִמִּי וְאֶל־חֶדֶר הוֹרָתִי, as a place of security, of generations of lovemaking, the womb (i.e., the act of sex), or the place where marriage was arranged.

The accusative case first person pronoun in regard to the female lover appears only once: "the watchmen who make the rounds of the city found me" מְצָאוּנִי הַשֹּׁמְרִים הַסֹּבְבִים בָּעִיר (3:3). This instance may function as a contrast in this lost-and-found cycle. The beloved is lost but the watchmen find the woman. The Hebrew word מְצָאוּנִי "found me," which opens verse 3, may serve to foreshadow the fact that since the watchmen found her, she would find her lost beloved. This discovery takes place before the end of the next cola.

The most prolific use of the first person in this cycle is in the nominative case. It appears fourteen times in only five verses. Its possible function is at least the repetition of the /ti/ sound תִי as well as to build the sense of anxiety in the woman as she frantically searches for her lover.[67] Could it be that the first person nominative case pronouns are an example of rhetorical parallelism?[68] There are seven uses of the first person nominative case pronouns in verses 1 and 2 of the "lost" section of this cycle. There are none in verse 3. But there are six in verse 4 in the "found" section. Do multiple instances in the "lost" section parallel the multiple instances in the "found" section?[69] If nothing else, the repetition of the first person nominative case pronouns provides strong cohesion for the cycle.[70] Alter notices "the prominence of verbatim repetition" in this section (3:1–4) which is created by "a thread of verbal recurrences."[71] He suggests the selection "would sound like this: I sought the one I so love, I sought him, did not find him, let me seek the one I so love, I sought him, did not find him, the one I so love, I found the one I so love."[72] While Alter's observation that there is verbal repetition is true, one cannot discount that the repetition of the first person also aids the "verbatim repetition" the biblical author is employing in order to create the sense of anxiety in the female lover. The use of the first person nomi-

---

67. "I sought him," "I must arise," "I must go about," "I must seek," "I sought but," etc.

68. Kaiser (*Toward an Exegetical Theology*, 219) states, "rhetorical parallelism designates features which are intended to produce a certain literary effect." This is parallelism of literary features versus parallelism of meaning or thought (semantic) or grammatical parallelism.

69. Also present is the direct object marker אֶת in 3:1, 2, 3, 4, 5. This may give more evidence of parallelism. This may be evidence of vertical parallelism mentioned by Watson (*Classical Hebrew Poetry*, 158), who observes vertical parallelism built around the *waw* ו of 2 Sam 1–3.

70. Roberts, *Let Me See Your Form*, 263.

71. Alter, *Art of Biblical Poetry*, 188.

72. Ibid.

native case ends with the adjuration refrain (3:5; cf. 2:7). This address to the daughters of Jerusalem breaks the passion and intensity of the previous verses. This break provides the audience with an opportunity to catch its breath and to contemplate the consequences of arousing love. In the third cycle there are no instances of any masculine case first person pronouns.

Fourth Cycle (3:6—5:1)

In the fourth cycle there are only two instances of any pronouns that refer to the female lover. The rest of the first person pronouns (twenty-two instances) are employed in regard to the masculine gender. In this cycle the POV is predominantly second person spoken from the man to the woman. Even though the woman is not speaking, the reader feels she is present through his vivid description of her (4:1–5), his passionate desire for her (4:7–15), and his complete enrapture with her love (5:1). The object of the man's desire is not simply any female but "my darling" רַעְיָתִי (4:1). She is his intimate. In the same way "my beloved" דּוֹדִי, shows her desire and intimacy with him, רַעְיָתִי. The same term is used in 4:7. This term, "my darling" רַעְיָתִי, is "centered" between two identical expressions of her beauty. This placement may serve to center the reader's attention not only on the object of the following physical description, or *wasf*, but on their close friendship as well.

This cycle also introduces another term of endearment, "my sister bride" אֲחֹתִי כַלָּה, which is used two times (4:9, 12). Again, the possessive demonstrates the lover's intimacy and closeness that is further deepened by the familial term "sister."[73]

The multiple uses of the genitive case first person pronoun in 4:1, 7, 9 are incremental steps in the increase of passion that will climax in 5:1.[74] Because she is willing to open herself to him (as demonstrated by the "my"), the male lover is able to possess her and enjoy her completely

---

73. Murphy (*Song of Songs*, 156) remarks, "The use of the term 'sister' has nothing to do with brother-sister marriage. The words 'brother' and 'sister' occur frequently in Egyptian love poems as terms of endearment."

74. Each noun coupled with the possessive "my" is repeated twice: "my darling" (4:1, 7), "my sister bride" (4:9, 12) and "my heart" (4:9 twice). This may be a literary device that allows the reader to experience the passionate build up of the couple to the climax in 5:1.

(5:1). If she is not his, he would never have been able to enter the "locked garden" גַּן נָעוּל (4:12).

The first person is suffixed to a preposition three times: "to me" לִי and "with me" אִתִּי (4:6, 4:8 twice).[75] The first cola of 4:8 presents disrupted word order beginning with the preposition suffixed with the first person and the verb ending the cola. The repetition of the phrase "with me" אִתִּי and its placement may emphasize his intense desire to be together with his lover. The phrase "to me" לִי which opens the second cola of 4:6, might show sole possession. The way in which the beloved is described, "I will go my way" אֵלֶךְ לִי (more fully, "I will go my way to the mountain of myrrh and to the hill of frankincense.") Since the geographical reference is to some part of the female's body, the male may infer that the route he is taking over her body is "my own way" and no one else's.[76] The nominative case use of the first person pronoun is evident in this verse as well: "I will go," אֵלֶךְ. The accusative case appears in the clause, "you have ravished my heart" לִבַּבְתִּנִי, which is used two times (4:9). Longman remarks that the emphasis of this verb is one that intensifies or causes a state of being. "According to its use in the Hebrew Bible *leb* refers to one's inner life. . . . Here, the focus is on the emotions, and the word refers to the man's excited emotional state as he thinks of the woman."[77] Although it is clear in this cycle that the man is sexually aroused by his lover, this clause shows that his excitement is not simply genital. His whole being is moved by the ravishing beauty that is before him. She is exclusive in her sexuality. It is reserved for one man only. This is one of the few places in the Song where the audience experiences what effect the woman has on the man. Although she is the main speaker throughout the Song and it is mostly her desire and arousal the audience hears, the male lover is not unmoved by his lover.

75. Although the BHS apparatus suggests גני as emendation for 4:12, there is no manuscript evidence for such a reading. Therefore, it is excluded from this study. Structurally, the noun without the possessive better fits the context since according to Bascom ("Hebrew Poetry," 102), "garden" functions as a key word in the chiastic structure of the poetic discourse 4:12—5:1. Also, since the male lover is the speaker (as evidenced by the direct address, "my sister bride") the garden cannot be the male "my" garden until she offers it to him in her invitation in 4:16.

76. Garrett ("Song of Songs," 192) believes the reference to "mountain" and "hill" is not to a literal geographic location in Israel but is an allusion to the woman's breasts: "They are a straightforward metaphor for breasts . . . He intends to get himself to these mountains."

77. Longman, *Song of Songs*, 151. Also see *IBHS*, 400.

The remaining uses of the first person pronouns in this cycle cluster together in 5:1. There are four perfect verbs conjugated with the first person pronoun. There are eight genitive case pronouns. This strophe is unique in that every word except the last word in the first cola ends with a first person marker. The parallelism is also distinctive in this verse because lines a, b, and c all begin with a perfect first person verb followed by a first person genitive case pronoun suffixed to a noun. Each concludes with a prepositional phrase and a first person genitive case pronoun suffixed to a noun. The preponderance of the /i/ י sound cannot be missed in this strophe. These first person characteristics provide "intense semantic and thematic cohesion."[78] Stoop-van Paridon observes the "four suffix (perfect) conjugations are each followed by substantives with possessives. This extravagant use of language indicates how positively and enthusiastically the speaker reacts to the preceding words of verse 4.16."[79]

Another function of the first person in this cycle is the interplay between the female "my garden" גַּנִּי (4:16) and the male "my garden" גַּנִּי (5:1). By her invitation and through the mysterious union of the physical relationship between a man and a woman, her "my garden" in 4:16 becomes the male's "my garden" in 5:1.[80] Klein, Blomberg, and Hubbard suggest this morphing of her garden into his garden is actually the center of a chiasm that encompasses the entire book and "provides a starting point for further interpretation."[81] According to these authors, the center of the chiasm is the main focus of the SoS. While this point is interesting, there is no consensus concerning the overall structure of the Song by scholars as of yet. Whether this is the center point or not, the list of the genitive case pronoun ("my") used by the male lover does demonstrate his complete possession and enjoyment of "her garden."[82]

---

78. Roberts, *Let Me See Your Form*, 367.
79. Stoop-van Paridon, *Song of Songs*, 241.
80. Bekkenkamp ("Into Another Scene of Choices," 80) is surely reading too much into the text at this juncture when she states that "*her* garden is *his* garden only as long as she loves him." From the female lover's point of view, not loving him is never a viable option as evidenced in the rest of the Song.
81. Klein, Blomberg, and Hubbard, *Introduction to Biblical Interpretation*, 301–2.
82. Stoop-van Paridon, *Song of Songs*, 221. She correctly notes the frequency of the "personal pronoun with the verb and the substantives" in this section of the Song (4:9–15); however, she fails to elucidate its significance.

Fifth Cycle (5:2—7:10)

The fifth cycle is the second dream cycle that begins with the woman dreaming or retelling her dream (first dream is 3:1–5). The first eight verses of this cycle are filled with thirty-nine instances of the use of the first person pronouns in various case functions.[83] The man speaks six instances and the rest are from the woman. What is evident in this section of the fifth cycle (5:2–8) is that the use of the first person determines the structure of the cycle.[84] The cycle begins with the first person independent pronoun, "I" אֲנִי (5:2), and the last word of the "lost" section is again the first person independent pronoun, "I" אָנִי (5:8). The first person pronoun functions as an envelope figure for this section. Its function is delimitation, distinguishing the beginning and the ending of the section.[85] This envelope figure sandwiches four first person verbs (5:3), then two first person verbs each with the addition of the emphatic first person independent pronoun (5:5, 6). The cycle concludes with four first person verbs (5:6, 8) before the final first person independent pronoun. The repetition of the first person also provides a phonological structure in this section as well. There is a continual reoccurrence of the /i/ ִי sound which may serve to tie the section together by sound as well as structure. The use of the first person also aids the theme and the transition of this section. This is evidenced by the use of the accusative and genitive cases. Although she is in bed alone, she is the object of her lover's desire (5:2).[86] He desires her to "open to me" פִּתְחִי־לִי. Her reluctance to grant access to her lover changes in 5:5. The reason for the sudden change in her demeanor towards her lover is unknown. However, the change is evident by the use of the independent first person pronoun used in conjunction with the first person finite verb: "I, even I, arose to open to my beloved" קַמְתִּי אֲנִי לִפְתֹּחַ לְדוֹדִי (5:5). This combination of independent pronoun and finite first person verb provides emphasis to her actions. Following *IBHS*, this syntax reflects a *psychological focus*, and the first person is

---

83. Not all instances of the first person will be noted in this cycle since they have already been mentioned in other cycles. There are seven uses of the first person from the mouth of the male lover. Six of those are composed of affectionate terms such as "my sister," "my darling," and "my dove," which have been already referenced (26, 29).

84. The chart that covers this cycle in appendix 1 shows in visual form the structural connection and parallelism of the first person.

85. Watson, *Classical Hebrew Poetry*, 284.

86. The male lover's use of four affectionate terms consecutively gives further evidence of his desire (5:2).

used to emphasize her self-assertion, which at this time is a change of action.⁸⁷ In this instance Stoop-van Paridon recognizes the rhetorical importance of the independent pronoun in connection with the verb קַ֫מְתִּי. *IBHS* labels it as pleonasm.⁸⁸ Stoop-van Paridon further quotes Christianson who captures the rhetorical effect that this may have had on the Hebrew readers: "In support of this, אֲנִי must have had a unique rhetorical effect on Hebrew readers when read aloud, stylistically marking instances of importance."⁸⁹ Muraoka suggests the rhetorical effect of this construction is meant to move the "listener or reader to share his concern, interest, or consciousness."⁹⁰ Stoop-van Paridon believes Muraoka has noted well the significance of this feature. He regards the pronoun as a "means to give expression to the agitated, excited self of the maiden now ready to welcome her man."⁹¹ Thus, the author desires the audience to experience the woman's anxiety in not being able to find her lover. In 5:6 she is still the object because she desires her lover to "answer me" עֲנֵ֫נִי. Exum recognizes the importance of the personal pronoun "I" in this section as structural. She believes the personal pronoun marks the division of this nocturnal scene into three parts: "I was sleeping" (5:2), "I arose" (5:5), and "I opened" (5:6).⁹² While the section has definite erotic overtones, Exum may go too far to suggest that these first person pronouns imply sexual intercourse at this point. The immediate discipline by the watchmen (and the absence of her lover) mitigates against such a sexual high point.

This use of the accusative case continues the theme of the female as the object: the watchmen "found me" מְצָאֻ֫נִי. The first person accusative case closes 5:6 and opens 5:7. She continues as the object of the discipline of the watchmen throughout the verse: "they struck me" הִכּ֫וּנִי "they wounded me" פְצָע֫וּנִי, and "they took my shawl from me" נָשְׂא֤וּ אֶת־רְדִידִי.

---

87. *IBHS*, 296. To further make the point, Muraoka (*Emphatic Words*, 58) states that this syntax alludes to "strong emotional heightening" and "focused attention or deep self-consciousness." Murphy (*Song of Songs*, 165) remarks that "the opening words of v 5 (קַ֫מְתִּי אֲנִי) and v 6 (פָּתַ֫חְתִּי אֲנִי) are emphatic." He further notes the "pleonastic use of אֲנִי in Ecclesiastes."

88. *IBHS*, 692. Pleonasm is defined as redundancy.

89. Stoop-van Paridon, *Song of Songs*, 272.

90. Muraoka, *Emphatic Words*, 48.

91. Ibid.

92. Exum, *Song of Songs*, 192.

The use of the first person demonstrates that the woman is the object of her lover's and of the watchmen's discipline. Her own desire is evidenced by "my soul went out" נַפְשִׁי יָצְאָה and by her emphatic use of "to my beloved but my beloved" לְדוֹדִי וְדוֹדִי.⁹³ However, her desire goes unfilled because of her initial reluctance to meet her lover.

The placement of elements of this section, her adjuration, the daughters' question, and the *wasf* (5:8—6:1) allow the tension to build as to whether or not she will once again be united with her beloved.⁹⁴ Her conversation with the daughters allows the woman to sing her man's praise, thus rekindling the passion that was lost in her midnight refusal of her lover's advances.⁹⁵ She concludes her praise with "this is my beloved and this is my friend" זֶה דוֹדִי וְזֶה רֵעִי (5:16). Although the praise of 5:16 is with her lover absent (as evidenced by the lack of the first person POV), he materializes in 6:3 during her praise of him in the first person POV: "I am my beloved's and my beloved is mine" אֲנִי לְדוֹדִי וְדוֹדִי לִי. Once the man is present to the audience through the authors' use of the first person POV, he begins to praise his lover's beauty and her awesomeness (6:4–9). His praise contains his common terms of affection for her. All are affixed with the first person pronoun: "my darling" רַעְיָתִי (6:4), "my dove" יוֹנָתִי, and "my perfect one" תַמָּתִי אַחַת (6:9). He not only finds her beautiful but her eyes have such an effect that he requests her to "turn your eyes from me, for they torment me" הָסֵבִּי עֵינַיִךְ מִנֶּגְדִּי שֶׁהֵם הִרְהִיבֻנִי (6:5).⁹⁶ Here the use of the first person may be phonological since the /i/ יִ sound is repeated three times. His praise of his darling has the ef-

---

93. Murphy, *Song of Songs*, 165.

94. *Wasf* is an Arabic term which means description. It has been applied by scholars to describe the lengthy physical depiction of each of the lovers by the other (Longman, *Song of Songs*, 140–41).

95. Instead of maintaining the same formula of telling him how wonderful he is when he is present, the author uses the daughters as an audience to change the formula so the audience would not tire of the description and would be kept wondering what happens next. Watson (*Classical Hebrew Poetry*, 33) notes that the author had to "maintain the attention of a potentially critical audience." This change of formula may have been a device used for that specific purpose.

96. Bloch and Bloch (*Song of Songs*, 189) note that a free translation of this verb is "dazzle." Longman (*Song of Songs*, 180) notes "overwhelm, excite, overpower, unsettle" as possible glosses. Longman's comments may fit the context better since the man's praise starts with "as awesome as an army" (6:4) and concludes with the same imagery (6:9).

fect of exalting her to the lofty position in which he holds her. The first person demonstrates that she becomes what he thinks of her.[97]

The fifth cycle concludes with a series of three verbs in first person from the male lover's mouth (7:9). His *wasf* of her (7:2–7) has the effect of not only praising her but of arousing him. He is so moved that he must tell her of his intention in detail: "I said, 'I will climb the palm tree, I will take hold of its fruit stalks'" אָמַרְתִּי אֶעֱלֶה בְתָמָר אֹחֲזָה בְּסַנְסִנָּיו (7:9). This use of the first person POV from his perspective shows her total desirability and his passion for her. The first person POV does not simply report his excitement. It allows the readers to feel its heat and hopefully motivate them to experience it in their own relationship.

Sixth Cycle (7:11—8:4)

In the sixth cycle all the instances of the first person pronouns are from the mouth of the woman. The section opens with the first person independent pronoun and the second half of the first cola begins with the genitive case first person pronoun. The section opens with the first person independent pronoun and concludes with the author's use of the second. These pronouns function to make the case that she is the object of his desire and he is the object of hers. Echoing his invitation (2:10), the woman invites her beloved to an early morning tryst in a secluded vineyard (7:12). The singular verb "come" לְכָה. quickly becomes a series of three verbs with first person plural pronouns that demonstrates her desire to be with her lover: "let us rise early" נַשְׁכִּימָה, "let us go" נֵצֵא, and "let us lodge," נָלִינָה. Once the lovers are together and alone, she promises him something special: "there I would give you my love" שָׁם אֶתֵּן אֶת־דֹּדַי לָךְ. There is a word play in the first person in this section. He is "my beloved," דּוֹדִי (7:11), but she wants to give him "my love" דּוֹדַי. The use of the first person plural "and over our doors" וְעַל־פְּתָחֵינוּ is reminiscent of the use of the first person plural in 2:16, 17 and the verb form in 5:2. This plural usage functions to show the continuing mutuality of their relationship.[98]

---

97. Keel (*Song of Songs*, 225) notes that this section (6:12) is the most difficult for exegetes to determine speaker and meaning.

98. Grab ("Song of Songs," 24) may go too far when she states, "The use of the personal pronouns express reciprocity of emotion and equality of status." While I see reciprocity in this verse, I do not see nor do I believe that the author intends to make a statement concerning gender equality.

In 7:12—8:2 the first person nominative forms are all prefixed to imperfect verbs that have the second person "you" as their objects through suffixed pronouns (e.g., "I found you" אֶמְצָאֲךָ, 8:1) or by preposition (e.g., "I will give my love to you" אֶתֵּן אֶת־דֹּדַי לָךְ, 7:12). Three lines of 8:1–2 begin with the imperfect verb and the direct object "you" ךְ. These verbs and objects run over each other. This intentional grouping conveys her intense desire for her beloved.[99] Whereas she is his desire in 7:1–9, he is now her desire in this section. The interplay between the first and second person allows for this exchange.

The woman's desire to have her lover as "my brother" כְּאָח לִי. provides her with the opportunity to fulfill her desire to enjoy physical contact with her lover and to do it publicly without societal ridicule or personal embarrassment (cf. 1:2). Without the "my," which denotes the familial relationship, she believes she would be open to reproach for such a public demonstration of affection. The use of the possessive pronoun "my" as in "my brother" כְּאָח לִי (8:1), "the house of my mother" אֶל־בֵּית אִמִּי (8:2), and "my pomegranate" רִמֹּנִי (8:2), builds the intimacy of this section. She wants to enjoy familial intimacy with him. She brings her lover into the intimacy of her mother's home, and finally she offers him her own intimate, sexual delights as evidenced in "my pomegranate" רִמֹּנִי (8:2).

Seventh Cycle (8:5–14)

The final cycle of the Song contains three nominative case pronouns, one accusative case singular pronoun, and four genitive case singular pronouns spoken by the female lover. There is one instance of the first person pronoun in the accusative case from the mouth of the male. Two nominative case plural pronouns and two genitive case plural pronouns come from the voices of the daughters of Jerusalem.

The first use of the feminine nominative case in 8:5 ties it to the refrain in 8:4 by the use of the root עור. In the adjuration refrain, the

---

99. It should be noted that the concentration of the first person is not simply a poetic device that draws the attention of the reader (which it does). This concentration is used by the biblical author to stress the message of the section or even the book. Wendland ("Discourse Analysis of Hebrew Poetry," 16) observes in biblical Hebrew poetry that poetic intensity "serves to attract the reader / listener's attention—not simply for their own sake (i.e., a purely artistic function), but in order to stress some important aspect of the text's wider meaning. The latter refers to its essential theological message." This theological dimension will be noted in a later section of this work.

female lover charges the daughters "not to awaken" תָּעִירוּ. In 8:5 she declares, "I awakened you" עוֹרַרְתִּ֫יךָ using the same root. The second and third use of the nominative case features an affixed verb and an independent pronoun (8:10). The use of the independent pronoun introduces a metaphor, "I am a wall" אֲנִי חוֹמָה, which may depict her self-control in the matter of physical purity.[100] Because she is sexually pure, she can say, "I became in his eyes as one who finds peace" הָיִיתִי בְעֵינָיו כְּמוֹצְאֵת שָׁלוֹם (8:10). This use of the first person may serve a didactic function to highlight the positive consequences of sexual purity (finding *shalom*) and for the audience not to hear the consequence but actually feel the woman's experience of peace, שָׁלוֹם. The genitive case in 8:14 "my beloved" דּוֹדִי, has been noted previously.[101] The genitive case in 8:10 heightens the wall metaphor by the use of the simile "and my breasts were like towers" וְשָׁדַי כַּמִּגְדָּלוֹת. Instead of her breasts being the object of illicit sexual play, they are the watchtowers over her sexual purity.[102] Her breasts as towers could also signify that just as an impregnable wall and guard tower could not be breeched nor scaled, neither could her sexuality as represented by her breasts. However, since the female lover is well fortified, שָׁדַי כַּמִּגְדָּלוֹת, she does not need the same embellishment or protection as the aforementioned little sister. Exum remarks, "In contrast to the aforementioned little sister, she requires neither reinforcement to protect her from suitors or ornamentation to attract one. She possesses her own enhancement, an erotic one, her breasts."[103] In contrast to the little sister who needs protection against unwanted male intruders, the female lover has no such need. She has already been "conquered" (2:4 cf. 6:4). Her lover scales her prominent "walls" and takes complete possession of her once she surrenders herself to him. With her self-capitulation

---

100. G. L. Carr (*Song of Solomon*, 172) recognizes the translation "I am a wall" instead of the past "I was a wall" because she "is proclaiming her maturity and readiness for love and marriage." Longman believes the woman "asserts her chastity" by the use of the wall metaphor (*Song of Songs*, 218). Hess (*Song of Songs*, 243) suggests that the brothers are concerned with the physical immaturity of their sister, i.e., "no breasts" (8:8) and thus not ready for marriage. Bergant (*Song of Songs*, 101–2) remarks that the female lover has no need of her brothers' direction for her future. She states, "As has been the case throughout the Song of Songs, she needs no one to direct her future, to assess her potential, to attend to her needs. At least where the love she shares with the man is concerned, she is in control of the circumstances of her life."

101. See p. 28.

102. Ezek 23:8.

103. Exum, *Song of Songs*, 258.

of her "towers" to her lover comes peace (8:9). That her body is her own to be "conquered" by whom she chooses is seen in the next cola as well.

The three genitive case pronouns that introduce the cola of 8:12 ("my very own vineyard" כַּרְמִי שֶׁלִּי לְפָנָי) highlight the fact that the vineyard, which is the woman's body, is without question her own. It is at her disposal to open to whomever she wishes. There is an emphasis that this vineyard is without doubt hers. This first person genitive construction כַּרְמִי שֶׁלִּי לְפָנָי takes this cycle back to the opening cycle, כַּרְמִי שֶׁלִּי (1:6).

The nominative case plural pronouns and two genitive case plural pronouns may proceed from the mouth of the daughters of Jerusalem who are interested that their sexually immature sister would handle love well when it came to her time to marry.

> We have a little sister, and she has no breasts; what shall we do for our sister on the day when she is spoken for? If she is a wall, we shall build on her a battlement of silver; But if she is a door, we shall barricade her with planks of cedar. (8:8–9)

The use of this group at this juncture may function to bring this last cycle full circle to the beginning, similar to the function of "my vineyard" (8:12; cf. 1:6).

The use of the accusative case from the voice of the female, "place me" שִׂימֵנִי (8:6), begins as Longman notes, "arguably the most memorable and intense verse of the entire book."[104] It is clear that the woman desires to be the object of her husband's affection both privately ("over your heart") and publicly ("on your arm").[105] This may function to bring the reader back to the first cycle. In 1:13 her beloved was a "pouch of myrrh which lies all night between my breasts." Now in 8:6 she wishes to be over his heart all the time as evidenced by the seal. Both lovers desire to be at that very special place of intimacy: over each other's heart. Murphy comments that this verse summarizes what the Song is about: "the desire of the lovers for abiding union."[106] The first person accusative case allows the reader to feel the intensity of the female's desire to abide with her lover always and not simply read about it. In addition, the use of the first person accusative case pronoun (from the female) places her as the object that wants to enjoy his intimacy always.

---

104. Longman, *Song of Songs*, 209.
105. Gledhill (*Song of Songs*, 227) notes the public and intimate aspects of the seal.
106. Murphy, *Song of Songs*, 196.

RECOGNITION OF SIGNIFICANT SHIFTS IN THE AUTHOR'S USE OF THE FIRST PERSON

Unlike the ancient love songs of the Egyptians, which were composed as monologues, the majority of the Song of Songs is dialogue. Westenholz observes that the speakers of Egyptian love songs "do not exchange words or affect each other by speech."[107] Since dialogue is the main vehicle for the message of the SoS, it is important to recognize the relationship between the author's use of the first, second, and third person.[108]

The Relationship between the First, Second, and Third Persons

If the Song follows the monologue pattern of the Egyptian love poetry, the first person would be the primary point of view without interaction from the other points of view. The lover would always be describing what she is feeling, thinking, or doing in the first person. In a monologue the object of her love would not answer but would simply be there in the third person as the object desired, or the lover's object may respond in a soliloquy. Westenholz remarks, "While the girls in the Egyptian love songs frequently address their lover in the second person whether or not they are present, the boys never address the girls in that way, even when their presence is implied."[109] Murphy concurs when he notes that in Egyptian love poetry "even in the integrated cycles, where both male and female speakers are represented, there is no true dialogue between the parties. Their respective speeches are, rather, juxtaposed soliloquies."[110]

In the Song, there is never any monologue. There is always a dialogue.[111] The woman lover is the main speaker but she never speaks

---

107. Westenholz, "Love Lyrics," 2480. Although Egyptian love poetry is basically monologue, not all ancient love poetry follows suit. Westenholz (2474) notes that some of the Mesopotamian love poetry (Sumerian and Akkadian) has dialogue like the Song of Songs.

108. Fokkelman (*Reading Biblical Poetry*, 208) believes that understanding the identity of the "I" or "we" is critical to understanding biblical poetry. He states that the first question a reader should ask of the text is, "Who is speaking the 'I' or a 'we'? and does it change in the course of the poem?" Since the focus of this paper is on the first person, the relationships of the second and third person will be viewed from their relationship with the first person. It may be profitable in the future to look at the author's use of the second and third person individually.

109. Westenholz, "Love Lyrics," 2480.

110. Murphy, *Song of Songs*, 47.

111. Fokkelman (*Reading Biblical Poetry*, 199) states, "The entire Song of Songs is a dialogue between a male and a female voice." Although I agree that the majority of

alone. She addresses the daughters of Jerusalem (e.g., 1:5–6; 2:3–7, 8–9) or her lover as "you" (e.g., 1:7, 16). In the Song the first person always interacts with the second or third person. For instance, in 1:5–7 where the female lover engages in self-criticism, the first person appears thirteen times in various forms. This section could be mistaken for a monologue except she addresses her lover with a question in the second person in 1:7 (which is a definite continuation of the previous verses) and except for the change of speaker in 1:8 in which he responds to her question. Instead of him answering her question in the first person (i.e., "I pasture down the path by the other shepherds"), the male lover coyly answers her question by providing some general directions, "Go forth on the trail of the flock, and pasture your young goats by the tents of the shepherds" (1:8). In another instance the first person is heard from the lips of the male lover (2:13–14). His desire is not to see "her" (third person) but to see "you" in the second. "Let me see your form, let me hear your voice; for your voice is sweet, and your form is lovely." In 7:2 the man is the first person speaker (cf. 7:8) and his description is mostly in the second person.[112] For instance, it is "your hips" יְרֵכַיִךְ, "your navel" שָׁרְרֵךְ, "your breasts" שָׁדַיִךְ that arouse his passion and make him want to "climb" her and partake of her fruits (7:9).

The first person point of view also interacts with the third person. In the section comprising 2:2–7, the female lover uses the first person point of view twelve times. However, in this section her lover is no longer the "you" (second person) of 1:16 but is now the third person "beloved," "his," and "he." The same is true from her perspective in 3:1–4. The interaction between the first and third person is seen at the end of the first line: "I sought him but did not find him" בִּקַּשְׁתִּיו וְלֹא מְצָאתִיו. In the *wasf* of 5:10–16 the female's perspective of the male lover is "my beloved" דּוֹדִי and "my friend" רֵעִי. But her description of her beloved is all in the third person. It is "his head" and "his locks" that are wholly desirable, וְכֻלּוֹ מַחֲמַדִּים (5:16).[113]

---

the Song is a dialogue, I would not limit the verbal exchange to only the male and female. For Elliott (*Literary Unity of the Canticle*, 240) states, "Every word that is spoken is directed to a specific audience and elicits a response." This is contra G. L. Carr ("Song of Songs," 285) who believes the "speakers even when they are addressing each other, do not carry on conversation. The speech units are essentially monologues."

112. There is one instance of the third person (7:9), which will be dealt with in the next section.

113. The first word of the section is first person, דּוֹדִי, and the last is first person, רֵעִי (if one eliminates the direct address of the daughters of Jerusalem). All the third person

Since the Song is not a monologue, the above observations are not unusual or unexpected. To make the observation *alone* that the first person interacts or has a relationship with the second and third person in this piece of biblical love poetry does not necessarily bring additional clarity to the Song. However, what is significant and unusual is the unexpected instances in the Song where the interactions between characters shift in relationship to the point of view.[114] Normally, a reader would expect that if an author begins an interaction between his characters in the first and second person in the first line of Hebrew poetry then that interaction would continue in the second line. For example, in 1:9 the author uses the first person "me" and "my," which explains how he, as the male lover, is feeling towards his darling: "To me, my darling, you are like my mare among the chariots of Pharaoh." Then there is the expected shift to the second person "you" and "your cheeks" as he speaks to his female lover. This is expected because it is a dialogue between the two lovers. In a dialogue there is always the "I" and the "you." However, there are a few situations where there is an "unexpected" shift. For instance, in 1:2a the author states: "May he kiss me with the kisses of his mouth!" In this first line the third person pronouns "he" and "his" are used to indicate her desire to be kissed by him. To be consistent one would expect the next line

---

descriptions fall between these two words. One wonders if the first person is acting as an envelope structure for the third person description.

114. The term "unexpected" may be misleading (but it is readily used by modern scholars of the Song). The shifts are only "unexpected" from the modern, Western perspective. These shifts are not unexpected to the original author (or his audience) of the ancient poetry. These unexpected shifts were part of the author's bag of rhetorical devices that he could use to engage his audience. For instance, Pss 23, 52, 55, and 91 show evidence of shifts in person that the modern reader would not necessarily expect. Watson (*Classical Hebrew Poetry*, 21–22) notes the shift of person in Prov 23:29–35. In this proverb, the third person is used in verses 29–32. Then there is a shift to second person in verses 33–34 and another shift to first person in verse 35. Murphy (*Song of Songs*, 125) comments that "the pronominal shift in v. 2 with reference to the male lover, from the third to second person . . . does not require emendation in the interest of consistency; such shifts (enallage) are well attested in Hebrew poetry . . . and elsewhere in the Song." In the Dumuzi-Inanna love poetry of the ancient Sumerians there is evidence of "unexpected" shifts in person as well. Sefati, *Love Songs in Sumerian Literature*, 136–37. Even though it is mainly monologues, Egyptian love poetry also evidences "unexpected" shifts. For instance, in "A Cycle of Seven Stanzas" from the Chester Beatty papyrus 1 collection, the woman speaks in the first person to a male lover in the third person in most lines. But there are some lines where the "him" becomes a "you." He is no longer the object being spoken about; he becomes the addressee. Lichtheim, *Ancient Egyptian Literature*, 182–83.

to read: "for his love is better than wine." What one finds, however, is this "unexpected"[115] shift to the second: "for your love is better than wine" כִּי־טוֹבִים דֹּדֶיךָ מִיָּיִן.[116] Grossberg recognizes the importance of these shifts. He believes they represent centripetal and centrifugal forces. Speaking of those forces, he writes concerning their combined effect on the whole composition:

> Shifts of perspective and speaker are also two-directional forces. They may loosen the text by their multiplying of the frames of reference. They may replace the single tone, speaker and vantage point which serves to concentrate a literary work. The shifts may thus change the focus and expand the range of the text. Paradoxically, the new multivalence resulting from perspectival shifts and shifts of grammatical person may impart a sense of wholeness also. Each shift is an additional piece of stone producing the patterns in the poem's mosaic. Moreover, the shift may formally signal a subdivision of the text which gives delineation and hence centripetality to the whole.[117]

Stern states that this "oscillation" is "one of the most striking literary features of the Song."[118] Longman defines this shift as "enallage."[119] Fox notes that enallage "is a deliberate literary device, one also used in Egyptian

---

115. Kinlaw ("Song of Songs," 1215) describes this shift as "a fascinating shift of persons." Elliott (*Literary Unity of the Canticle*, 44) calls such shifts "disconcerting." Grossberg (*Centripetal and Centrifugal Structures*, 60) recognizes the change in pronouns and labels such an abrupt shift as "an incongruent progression."

116. Kravitz and Olitzky (*Shir Hashirim*, 2) recognize the change from third to second person between 1:2 and 1:3. However, they ignore the biblical author's use of enallage and emend the third person to second person. For instance, they translate 1:2 as "Kiss me with the kisses of your mouth, for your caresses are better than wine." Their rationale for such an emendation is that they believe that the second person is the primary view point of the Song.

117. Grossberg, *Centripetal and Centrifugal Structures*, 11–12.

118. Stern, *The Jewish Study Bible*, 1564.

119. Longman, *Song of Songs*, 89 n. 14. Bullinger (*Figures of Speech*, 490, 511) lists it more specifically as "*heterosis*." Bullinger (490) defines enallage as "a change of one part of speech for another." He (524) notes this shift in person is used to "make what is said more emphatic."

love songs."[120] The next section will identify the author's use of enallage or these "unexpected" shifts.[121]

Identification of Shifts in Person

In the first cycle (1:1—2:7) there is a shift from the third to second person in 1:2 as noted previously.[122] In 1:4 there is a shift from second to third. In the first line the female is asking the male lover to "draw me after you and let us run together" מָשְׁכֵנִי אַחֲרֶיךָ נָּרוּצָה. One would expect that either the second person would be used in the second line, which would continue her desire to be with her lover, or the first person plural would be used. But neither is the case. The author uses the third person "the king has brought me into his chambers" instead of the second person "you have brought me," which would have been expected.[123]

After the daughters of Jerusalem speak in 1:11, there is a shift from the dialogue between the lovers to a third person description in 1:12–14 by the female lover. After this third person description, there is a shift back to dialogue and the use of the second person in 1:15–17. A subtle shift occurs beginning at the third line of verse 16 and continues through verse 17. In these lines the shift from second person is absorbed into first person plural.

> How handsome you are, my beloved,
> *And* so pleasant!
> Indeed, our couch is luxuriant!
> The beams of our houses are cedars,

---

120. Fox, "Scholia to Canticles," 200. Berlin (*Dynamic of Biblical Parallelism*, 40) states that these shifts in person in Hebrew poetry "should not be viewed as isolated 'poetic' devices, but as examples of morphologic parallelism."

121. Stoop-van Paridon, *Song of Songs*, 23. She is correct to note that enallage is not an uncommon stylistic feature in BH. While this feature may not need, according to her, any "special grammatical explanation" in her philological analysis, it is important to recognize the rhetorical role it plays in the Song. See also Murphy, *Song of Songs*, 125.

122. This section will identify these "unexpected" shifts between individual lines and within the stanzas of each individual cycle. These "unexpected" shifts may be from first to second, second to third, or first to third. However, since the thrust of this paper is primarily on the importance of the first person, the next section will only pursue the significance of the shifts from first person to either second or third.

123. Grossberg (*Centripetal and Centrifugal Structures*, 60) believes this section evidences "a rich sampling of sudden jumps of several kinds: of person (1:2), of speaker (1:4, 5), of addressee (1:4, 5), of sense of domains (throughout), and of scene (1:4)."

Our rafters, cypresses (1:16–17)

The use of the first person plural then gives way immediately to the first person singular in 2:1, which could be mistaken for a monologue except for the man's response.

I am the rose of Sharon,
The lily of the valleys (2:1)
Like a lily among the thorns,
So is my darling among the maidens (2:2)

The use of the word "lily" (שׁוֹשַׁן) (2:1) and "as a lily" (כְּשׁוֹשַׁנָּה) (2:2) shows the reader that dialogue is intended although the second person is not used. In the following verses (2:3–6) one would expect that the compliments would continue to flow between the lovers. But that is not the case; there is another shift. Instead of a second person dialogue (or a first person dialogue as in 2:1–2), the woman describes her beloved in the third person. Except for the one use of "my beloved" דּוֹדִי, all the other references to the man are in the third person, such as "his shade" בְּצִלּוֹ. and "his fruit" פִּרְיוֹ. It is not "your shade" but "his shade" בְּצִלּוֹ. (2:3). It is not "your fruit" but "his fruit" פִּרְיוֹ (2:3). This perspective is used throughout these verses. What is unusual is that when the woman expresses her desire to be held and caressed to ease her "love sickness," it is not "*Let* your left hand be under my head and your right hand embrace me," which one would expect because her lover is the only one able to relieve her "disease." Instead she requests, "*Let* his left hand be under my head and his right hand embrace me" שְׂמֹאלוֹ תַּחַת לְרֹאשִׁי וִימִינוֹ תְּחַבְּקֵנִי. The third person is used consistently throughout 2:1–7.

The second cycle (2:8–17) begins with the woman speaking about the imminent arrival of her beloved (2:8–9). Although the man is "my beloved," she still refers to him in the third person through the use of a number of Hebrew participles: "he is coming" בָּא, "he is standing behind our wall" עוֹמֵד אַחַר כָּתְלֵנוּ, "he is looking through the windows" מַשְׁגִּיחַ מִן־הַחֲלֹּנוֹת, and "he is peering through the lattice" מֵצִיץ מִן־הַחֲרַכִּים (2:8–9). In the beginning of this cycle among these participles, there is an unexpected shift to first person in 2:9. In 2:9b it is "our wall" כָּתְלֵנוּ. This is an interesting shift since the article הַ, is used in 2:9c, d. It is "the windows" הַחֲלֹּנוֹת, "the lattice" הַחֲרַכִּים, not "our windows" or "our lattice." One does not expect a first person possessive pronoun when the perspective has been shaped by third person common nouns and the definite article "the."

In the second part of this cycle (2:10–14) once the male lover arrives, the perspective is first person but not directly from the male's lips. This section is a report from the woman of what he had said to her, עָנָה דוֹדִי וְאָמַר לִי (2:10). Other than this "second hand" report, there are no unexpected shifts. The first person interacts with the second person throughout verses 10–14. In 2:15 the first person singular of the preceding verses shifts to first person plural. In this verse the two lovers are now a couple, not separate individuals. Although the dialogue is continuing from the previous section, now the "my darling," "my dove," "your form," and "your voice" become the plural "us." The foxes are not only a threat to each as individuals but to them as a couple; it is "our vineyard" כְּרָמֵינוּ. The need to catch these threatening creatures is a benefit to both of them: "catch for us" אֶחֱזוּ־לָנוּ ((2:15).[124] Although there is a shift from first person singular to first person plural, the shift is not unexpected. The same type of shift occurs in the first cycle when the lover's dialogue collapses into the first person plural: "our couch" עַרְשֵׂנוּ, "our houses" בָּתֵּינוּ, and "our rafters" רַהִיטֵנוּ (1:16–17). What is unusual and unexpected is the reverting back to the third person by the female lover in 2:16: "My beloved is mine, and I am his." One would expect the first clause, "My beloved is mine" דוֹדִי לִי, but not the second clause, "and I am his" וַאֲנִי לוֹ. One expects something more intimate such as "you are mine and I am yours." This is the expectation since the couple is together and engaged in intimate conversation (2:10–14). Once the shift from first person plural to third person is accomplished, it maintains that perspective in 2:17 which ends the second cycle.

The third cycle (3:1–5) which is the shortest of the seven cycles in the Song exhibits no unexpected shifts, or any shifts whatsoever. The section begins with the woman sharing her dream in the first person. Her dreams concern the one whom she loves deeply, שֶׁאָהֲבָה נַפְשִׁי. The male lover is always the object of her desperate search and is always referred to as "him": בִּקַּשְׁתִּיו וְלֹא מְצָאתִיו. He is never "you." In this cycle, all the

---

124. Paul ("Shared Legacy," 492) points out another possibility that "catch the foxes" may be a euphemism for sexual intercourse. "'Catch us, foxes,' thereby inviting them to engage in amatory delights with her since Akk. *aḫāzu* is also employed as a euphemism for intercourse." This is unlikely since the foxes are a danger to the blossoming vineyard.

characters—the male lover, the town guards, and her mother—are all third person. Only the daughters of Jerusalem, בְּנוֹת יְרוּשָׁלַםִ, are spoken to in the second person (3:5).[125]

The fourth cycle (3:6—5:1) contains three sections (3:6–11; 4:1–7; 4:8—5:1). In the first section, 3:6–11, there are no unexpected shifts although the section itself has a different perspective. Up to this point the woman or the man has verbally led the reader through the Song through the first person perspective. In this section of this cycle the speaker, whose identity is unknown, takes the perspective of a detached but omniscient narrator.[126] He (or she) knows, sees, and smells the fragrance of the unknown object (to the audience) coming up from the wilderness. Only in 3:11 are the daughters of Jerusalem addressed.

In the next section of the fourth cycle (4:1–7) the male lover begins his *wasf* of "my darling" רַעְיָתִי. In this extended physical description she is always depicted in the second person. For instance it is always "your eyes" עֵינַיִךְ, "your hair" שַׂעְרֵךְ, and "your teeth" שִׁנַּיִךְ. In this section the male lover never portrays his female lover from any other perspective.[127] There are no shifts in this section, unexpected or otherwise.

The next section of the fourth cycle (4:8–15) continues the man's praise of his lover. It begins with his invitation to her to leave her inaccessibility and to join him. She evidently acts on his invitation positively because he continues to praise her various attributes that would only be possible if she is near him.[128] All of his praise of the various aspects of her person and beauty are in second person. Again, there are no shifts in person in this section of this cycle.

In the last section of this cycle, there is a change of speakers (4:16—5:1). In this section, thus far the female lover has been present but silent

---

125. Even though there is no shift, one could suggest that the use of the third person is significant because she could have easily addressed this cycle to her male lover in the second person. The first verse could have read: "On my bed night after night I sought you whom my heart loves; I sought you but I did not find you."

126. For instance, the NIV notes it is the woman, while NASB attributes 3:6–11 to the man.

127. This is true throughout the book as well where the male is the speaker. The only exception is in 6:9. In this verse the male lover refers to her in the third person a number of times (i.e., "she" and "her"). It is not unusual for the female lover to refer to her beloved in the third person (e.g., 2:3–6; 3:1–4; 5:10–16).

128. He sees her eyes (4:9). He can smell the aroma of cedar on her garments (4:11). He tastes the honey and milk under her tongue (4:11).

(4:1–15). Now she responds to her lover's ever-increasing passion with her own invitation for him to enter "to his garden" לְגַנּוֹ (4:16). He responds by stating, "I have entered my garden" בָּאתִי לְגַנִּי (5:1). It is in this exchange between the two lovers that an unexpected shift in person occurs. In 4:16 the "garden" גַּן is described as "his garden" גַּנּוֹ.[129] This is third person. However, in 5:1 this same "garden" גַּן: now reveals itself to be "my garden" גַּנִּי from the male's first person perspective.

In the fourth cycle there has been a steady stream of interaction between the male and female lovers. Dialogue has been the prominent feature. But at the beginning of the cycle (3:6–11) and at the end of the cycle (5:1e, f) there is an unexpected shift to a third person narrator. In the verses previous to 3:6–11 the woman shares her reoccurring dream, which is replete with the first person (3:1–5). Immediately after the woman's adjuration not to awaken love, the POV shifts to a narration of a wedding procession in third person, which begins the fourth cycle (3:6–11). After the procession is described, the male lover once again takes center stage and compliments his beautiful companion. After the passionate exchange between the lovers is complete (4:1–15) and their love is consummated (4:16—5:1d), an unknown speaker addresses the couple in three successive commands: "Eat, friends; Drink and imbibe deeply, O lovers" אִכְלוּ רֵעִים שְׁתוּ וְשִׁכְרוּ דּוֹדִים.

The fifth cycle covers 5:2—7:11. This cycle, which is another report of her dream (cf. 3:1–4), opens with a dialogue between the woman and her late-night lover. The testy dialogue alternates between the two frustrated lovers until verse four. At this point there is a change from dialogue to narration. From this point forward (5:4—6:3) in this cycle, her third person vocabulary of "beloved," "he," and "him" reveals to the reader that she is talking about him, not to him. The shift is interrupted by the woman's dialogue with the daughters of Jerusalem (5:8–9) but is resumed once more in her *wasf* of him in 5:10–16.[130] The third person is broken once again by another dialogue with the daughters of Jerusalem (6:1–2) and her answer to the daughters' question of the whereabouts of her lover. The woman's answer, "I am my beloved's and my beloved

---

129. In actuality the garden is her body, which she is readily offering to her lover.

130. Her descriptions of her male lover are all in third person (3:3–6; 5:10–16). However, his extended descriptions of her are almost always in the second (2:10–14; 4:1–7; 6:4–9; 7:2–11 [7:1–10 English]). The only exception is 6:9. The description shifts to third person.

is mine" לִ֔י לְדוֹדִ֖י וְדוֹדִ֥י אֲנִ֨י (6:3), is a shift. She is not speaking to him (which would be evidenced by the use of a second person pronoun) but is speaking about him.

This statement is also a pronounced shift from the first use of this sentiment in 2:16. In this verse (2:16) she declares, "My beloved is mine, and I am his" ל֔וֹ וַאֲנִ֣י לִ֔י דּוֹדִ֥י. Here "my beloved is mine" דּוֹדִ֥י לִ֔י begins the line whereas in 6:3 it ends the line, לִ֔י וְדוֹדִ֥י. In 2:16 she sees herself as belonging to him (third person), but in 6:3 she sees him as belonging to her in the first person.

The male lover begins the next section of this cycle (6:4–12), describing the woman in the second person. Although she has previously described "his head," "his eyes," and "his hands," he paints a picture of her in the second person. For him it is "your hair" שַׂעְרֵ֖ךְ and "your teeth" שִׁנַּ֨יִךְ. The use of the second person by the male lover is not at all unusual. What is unusual is the shift in verse 9. This is when the man chooses to talk about her in the third person instead of talking to her as he had done in the previous verses (6:4–8). One would expect him to continue the dialogical use of the second person by saying, "*But* my dove, my perfect one, you are unique: you are her mother's only *daughter*; you are the pure *child* of the one who bore her." But instead he states, "*But* my dove, my perfect one, is unique: She is her mother's only *daughter*; she is the pure *child* of the one who bore her" אַחַ֥ת הִיא֙ יוֹנָתִ֣י תַמָּתִ֔י אַחַ֥ת הִיא֙ לְאִמָּ֔הּ בָּרָ֥ה הִ֖יא לְיֽוֹלַדְתָּ֑הּ (6:9).

The last section of this cycle (like the previous cycle) again highlights the man singing the praise of his beautiful companion. On this occasion the man praises his dancing lover in the second person (7:1–11). The first shift in this section is in 7:7–9. The man compares his love's stature ("your stature" קֽוֹמָתֵ֖ךְ) to a "palm tree" תָמָ֔ר. He continues the agricultural metaphor expressing his desire to climb the "tree" and enjoy its "fruit." The shift from second to third is not unexpected since he uses the palm tree and its accompanying metaphor to describe what he would like to enjoy on her body. The second shift however, is somewhat unexpected.[131] In this intimate scene where the female lover is seductively dancing for her love and he is complimenting her beauty, one would expect her response to him to be in the second person. But her response

---

131. The reason for the qualifier is that in reality the woman, when she uses similar expressions in 2:16; 6:3 and 7:11, never uses the second person. A modern reader would still "expect" it to be used.

is not specifically to him at all. It is a generic declaration to no one in particular: "I am my beloved's, and his desire is for me" אֲנִי לְדוֹדִי וְעָלַי תְּשׁוּקָתוֹ (7:2–10). Because of the intimacy of the scene, one would expect, "I am yours, and your desire is for me."

The sixth cycle (7:11—8:4) exhibits one "unexpected" shift, which occurs in 8:3. This cycle begins with the woman's invitation for her lover to join her for a morning tryst in the fertile fields (7:12–14). The woman's invitation "to come" לְכָה is quickly followed by her desire: "let us go" נֵצֵא. She offers him the opportunity to enjoy themselves physically. The cycle concludes with a shift from talking to him (second person), "Oh that you were like a brother to me" מִי יִתֶּנְךָ כְּאָח לִי (8:1), to expressing her desire for him to caress her, "Let his left hand be under my head, and his right hand embrace me" שְׂמֹאלוֹ תַּחַת רֹאשִׁי וִימִינוֹ תְּחַבְּקֵנִי (8:3). This almost identical verse is used in 2:6; however, there is not the same shift in person as there is in the surrounding context of 8:6.[132]

The seventh and concluding cycle covers 8:5–14. A rhetorical question from the mouth of the man opens the cycle and dialogue quickly follows in 8:5c–7. The lover's conversation follows a declaration presumably from the brothers of the female lover. They speak from the first person about the need for purity in their preadolescent sister (8:8–9). The woman picks up the wall metaphor and employs it in explaining her sexual purity. Because of her moral purity, she finds *shalom*, שָׁלוֹם (8:10). She then tells about a vineyard that Solomon enjoys as an absentee landowner from the third person POV (8:11). This discussion shifts to a direct address to Solomon in 8:12. This is a unique shift in the book since no proper names are used nor is any character called by his or her proper name. The last cycle (and the Song) ends with a brief dialogue between the man (8:13) and the woman (8:14). There are no significant shifts other than the woman directing her speech to Solomon.

Suggested Functions of Shifts

As has been noted in the preceding section throughout the Song, there is an "unexpected" shift of POV. For instance, her wish "may he kiss me" becomes the motivation in "for your love is better than" in 1:2. Exum states that enallage is part of the biblical author's poetic arsenal to "challenge

---

132. Although these verses (2:6 and 8:3) are identical in English (for instance, see the NASB), 2:6 has an additional לְ preposition in לְרֹאשִׁי that is absent in 8:3.

the intellect and imagination" of the audience.[133] This shift is interesting because one expects the third person to continue throughout the line: "May he kiss me with the kisses of his mouth! For his love is better than wine." Clines makes this noteworthy suggestion concerning the significance of this shift between the first person and the third person. "Let him kiss me with the kisses of his mouth! It is 'him,' 'his,' for *he* is not present. When lovers are together, or when they are writing poems to one another, they speak the language of 'thou.' Here they are not together. In his absence . . . she conjures him up."[134] In the Song the use of the third person indicates absence while the first and second evidence the presence of the beloved.[135] Exum summarizes well this poetic process of absence and presence that occurs throughout the SoS.

> Throughout the Song, speech embodies desire by calling bodies into being and playing with their disappearance in an infinite deferral of presence. Conjuring seeks to make immanent through language what is absent, to construct the lovers as "real" (that is, present before us) and endow them with meaning. This is how it begins, with the woman conjuring up her lover: "let him kiss me with the kisses of his mouth for your love is better than wine" (1:2). She begins by speaking of "him" and "his mouth" as if he is not there with her, and in the next breath she addresses him directly. . . . One might think of "let him kiss me with the kisses of his mouth" as an incantation, and the shift from "let *him* kiss me" to "*your* caresses" an act of conjuring. As if in response to articulated desire, the lover materializes, brought into being . . . by poetic imagination.[136]

One of the main functions of these "unexpected" shifts or enallage is to bring the characters of the Song onto the imaginative stage of the reader.[137] While Snaith recognizes the presence of enallage in 1:4 he sees the

---

133. Exum, "How Does the Song of Songs Mean?" 48.

134. Clines, "Why is There a Song of Songs?" 11.

135. This is contra Stoop-van Paridon (*Song of Songs*, 49), who states, "This passage contains no indications that the two lovers are together." The author's use of the rhetorical device, enallage, lends evidence to the fact that the couple is indeed in each other's presence.

136. Exum, *Song of Songs*, 6–7.

137. Speaking of the "odd juxtaposition of pronouns as she shifts from referring to Solomon in the third person . . . to the second person," Estes (*Handbook of the Wisdom Books*, 405), following the Blochs, believes that the rhetorical purpose of this literary device is that "a person of higher social standing is being addressed. Thus, Shulammith

device as a "mere change of persons."¹³⁸ However, he does acknowledge that the king is being introduced onto the stage. What Snaith misses is the use of enallage as the literary device the author uses to introduce the character of the king to the imagination of the readers.

Othmar Keel observes the change of address by the woman in 1:2 and attributes it to her lover being present as well: "She is no longer calling on a longed-for lover but one who is actually present."¹³⁹ Another example of this dynamic is the pericope that spans 1:12–17. Here "the king was at his table." He is removed from the immediate presence of his beloved (1:12). This is third person. In 1:13–14 there is a shift to the use of the first person as evidenced by the repetition of the four "my's" and the revelation of the inner thoughts of the woman. Then (almost by magic, but actually by the author's shift from third to first person) the beloved appears. His appearance is confirmed by his speaking to his darling in the second person, "How beautiful you are, my darling, how beautiful you are! Your eyes are *like* doves" (1:15). His being in her presence is further confirmed with her verbal recognition of him (1:16a) and the fact that he is lying next to his female lover on "our couch" (1:16b).¹⁴⁰

This use of enallage to identify presence is also seen in 2:1–7. The chapter begins with a dialogue between the lovers but without the use of the second person "you" (2:1–2):

I am the rose of Sharon,
The lily of the valleys. (The female lover)

Like a lily among the thorns,
So is my darling among the maidens. (The male beloved)

This first person dialogue between the lovers shifts quickly to the woman talking about the man in the third person (2:3–7):

Like an apple tree among the trees of the forest,

---

is speaking imaginatively to Solomon her king." While this is a possibility, there is no evidence in the rest of the SoS that there is any difference in social position between this couple. On the contrary, there is a mutual equality between the sexes that permeates the book.

138. Snaith, *Song of Songs*, 16.

139. Keel, *Song of Songs*, 44.

140. This shift of POV in relationship to "absence" and "presence" may be evident in 2:1–14, 15, and 6:2, 3, 4–10 as well.

So is my beloved among the young men.
In his shade I took great delight and sat down,
And his fruit was sweet to my taste.
He has brought me to *his* banquet hall,
And his banner over me is love.

Based on Clines and Keel's observation concerning the significance of the author's use of enallage, the reader would surmise that the male lover is not present.[141] And that is precisely so. He is not in her presence. This is why she declares herself to be lovesick. Her only remedy is his presence and his love (2:5–6):[142]

Sustain me with raisin cakes,
Refresh me with apples,
Because I am lovesick.

Let his left hand be under my head
And his right hand embrace me.

Evidence of his absence is further strengthened by 2:8–9. In these verses she is listening for the sound of his approach. That he is present with her once again gains support by his dialogue with her that she reports in 2:10–17. Generally speaking, the use of enallage by the biblical author is a literary device used to bring the characters onto the stage of the reader's mind. Elliott observes that "this transition from desire to union, often from absence to presence" is also evident in 2:8—3:5; 3:6—5:1; 5:2—6:3; 6:4—8:4.[143]

Marcia Falk suggests that the shift in person functions to indicate the different types of poems that compose the Song. "The presence or absence, and relative prominence, of the I-Thou relationship may provide a means of distinguishing different types of love lyrics in the Song."[144] The difficulty with Falk's suggestion is that it is contingent on the Song being

---

141. He would have been present in 2:1–2 to hear and respond to his lover's self-deprecation in 2:1.

142. Hess, *Song of Songs*, 8. He remarks that the food of these verses "represent a call for her lover to come and provide the refreshment and revival. Above all, she wishes to taste him." If the lover has to "come" to be in her presence, then it is assumed that he is not there.

143. Elliott, *Literary Unity of the Canticle*, 54.

144. Falk, *Love Lyrics*, 72.

viewed as an anthology of love poems and not a single, unified poem. Her suggestion for the significance of the various shifts is lost if one holds that the Song is actually one unified love poem. Falk does recognize that in the dream section of 3:1–5 the female lover "cannot address her beloved explicitly because he is absent, but the longing she expresses can be satisfied only by him."[145] Following Clines, the reason the reader knows that the male lover is not present is because of the absence of the "I-Thou" language of Falk and the presence of the third person.

Kinlaw recognizes that enallage or the "change of persons is not unusual in Hebrew poetry"[146] and thus it is not completely unexpected when it is encountered in a BH poem or the Song. However, one wonders if another function of the change in person is to hold the audience's attention. Watson writes that "the listening audience needs aids to attention, and assistance in following the movement of the poem especially when long or difficult. It must be charmed by the familiar, yet aroused and captivated by the unexpected."[147] The "unexpected" change of persons would encourage the audience (or the reader) to follow the reading of the Song very carefully. They would have to follow along closely because they would never quite know when the male beloved would appear by the side of the main voice of the poem, the female darling, through the author's use of enallage.

Another function of the shift from first person to third person may be a literary device the biblical author uses to communicate his opinion about what is happening in the text without stating explicitly what conclusion he wants his audience to draw. For instance, at the conclusion of the consummation scene in 5:1, there is a significant shift from first person to third person.

בָּאתִי לְגַנִּי אֲחֹתִי כַלָּה
אָרִיתִי מוֹרִי עִם־בְּשָׂמִי
אָכַלְתִּי יַעְרִי עִם־דִּבְשִׁי
שָׁתִיתִי יֵינִי עִם־חֲלָבִי
אִכְלוּ רֵעִים
שְׁתוּ וְשִׁכְרוּ דּוֹדִים

---

145. Ibid., 74.

146. Kinlaw, "Song of Songs," 1216. Although Kinlaw recognizes enallage, he fails to explain its significance in Hebrew poetry.

147. Watson, *Classical Hebrew Poetry*, 33.

> I have come into my garden, my sister, *my* bride;
> I have gathered my myrrh along with my balsam.
> I have eaten my honeycomb and my honey;
> I have drunk my wine and my milk.
>
> Eat, friends;
> Drink and imbibe deeply, O lovers.

The proliferation of the first person is clearly apparent even in the English translation. The first person perfect verbs are in the first position in four out of five lines and there are eight, first person possessive pronouns ("my") within the first four lines as well. But the fifth line evidences an abrupt shift to three imperatives addressed to the lovers themselves. An unknown voice in such an intimate scene as the consummation of the couple's marriage is a significant change. Although Dillard and Longman are speaking about biblical narrative, their comments provide insights for the significance of the author's use of enallage in 5:1. They observe that "The voice of the narrator is often the authoritative guide in the story, providing the point of view. The narrator directs the reader in his or her analysis and response to the events and characters of the story. It has been pointed out that readers react to the third-person omniscient narrator with unconscious submissiveness."[148] In the Song the voice of the narrator at this moment of sexual intimacy serves to sanction and bless the entire sexual process between this couple. The reader noticing the enallage would follow the third person omniscient narrator's lead.[149] The reader would find him- or herself agreeing with the unidentified narrator that the couple in the Song should enjoy the ecstasy of the moment completely, as suggested by the eating and drinking metaphors. It may be that the function of the author's use of enallage in this specific instance is to emphasize the message that sexual intimacy is to be enjoyed by all

---

148. Dillard and Longman, "Song of Songs," 33.

149. Surely it is the narrator who is the speaker (and is omniscient) because no one would be privy to such intimacy between the couple. Davidson ("Literary Structure of the Song," 61–62) believes the unidentified voice is Yahweh himself who "extends divine approbation, summoning the bride and groom to 'drink deeply' in the consummate experience of sexual union." He further says in note 44 that "the 'omniscient' narrator/poet at this high point in the Song seems to have the ring of divine authority and power—to be able to bestow a blessing and approbation upon the consummation of the marriage of the bride and groom."

married couples.¹⁵⁰ Elliott observes that "the Poet himself steps forward for a brief moment from his anonymity and offers a summarizing word" in 5:1e, f. She further suggests that the function of the poet stepping into the scene may be to address "the universal audience of all Spouses [sic] everywhere, at all times."¹⁵¹

Another function that may be tentatively suggested for the author's use of enallage is that of structure.¹⁵² Dumbrell believes there are seven units that compose the Song.

He divides the book as follows:

First unit (1:1—2:7)
Second unit (2:8–17)
Third unit (3:1–5)
Fourth unit (3:6—5:1)
Fifth unit (5:2—7:10)
Sixth unit (7:11—8:4)
Seventh unit (8:5—14)¹⁵³

He also observes that each of these units or cycles is composed of the following sequence: lover separated, expression of desire, and lovers united.¹⁵⁴ He believes this sequence is evident in every cycle except the last.¹⁵⁵ If Dumbrell's observations are accurate and this sequence is traced out, one discovers that the separation of the lovers can be recognized by the use of enallage by the biblical author and thus each cycle's composition is structured around and recognized by this shift in person.

---

150. Bullinger (*Figures of Speech*, 524) recognizes that enallage, or more specifically heterosis, is used "to make what is said more emphatic." At present it is difficult to ascertain the significance of the biblical author's use of the third person. It also lies outside the scope of this paper because there is no interaction with the first person.

151. Elliott, *Literary Unity of the Canticle*, 119.

152. Scholars have noted and the literature suggests that there is no consensus concerning the structure of the Song of Songs. Therefore, the relationship between enallage and structure needs further investigation and dialogue.

153. Dumbrell, *Faith of Israel*, 279–81.

154. Ibid., 279. Although Elliott (*Literary Unity of the Canticle*, 40) does not follow Dumbrell's outline of the book, she does recognize the theme of separation. This theme begins each of the six parts in her outline.

155. Although it is outside the scope of this paper, I would suggest there is an additional element in Dumbrell's sequence. There is an obstacle that must be overcome by the couple in each of the cycles. For a suggested outline based on thematic elements, see appendix 2.

For instance, after the title is expressed in 1:1, Dumbrell notes that "the lovers are apart."[156] The reason the lovers are recognized as absent from each other is because of the use of the third person in 1:2a. The lovers are brought quickly together as evidenced by the female lover talking to her beloved in the second person in 1:2b. The use of enallage may provide the opening structuring element of both the book and the first cycle. The couple resists being separated (which is created by enallage) as they strive to be together. For it is only as this couple is together that they experience shalom (8:10) which is evidenced in celebration (5:1) and sleep (7:10).

The second cycle opens with the couple not together because she is listening for his approach (2:8). The use of the "he is coming" (which highlights their separation and is third person) transitions to "he is standing behind our wall" (2:9). This clause gives evidence that the couple's separation is nearly over. The shift to second person dialogue tells the reader that the couple is once again together (2:10–17). Again, enallage may be used to provide a structural element that tells the reader that a new cycle is beginning.

The third cycle (3:1–5) is also introduced by the third person. This change of POV from the end of the previous section demonstrates that the union the pair enjoyed in 2:10–17 has changed for whatever reason. The couple (if only in her dream) is not together.[157]

The fourth cycle begins with a third person narration (3:6–11) which alerts the audience that the couple is separated. The change to second person dialogue (4:1—5:1) and the metaphors of sexual consummation give ample evidence that the couple is once again together.

In the beginning of the fifth cycle the first person dominates, which would lead one to believe the couple is together. The context suggests that this is another dream. In this dream she pictures herself inside a room in bed (5:2a) and her lover outside (5:2b–f). Since this is a dream, it may be that he is lying right next to her in the same bed. She is dreaming that she is alone. As the dream progresses, the reader realizes that the couple is not together since the POV changes from speaking to her lover in the first person to speaking about him in the third person, because she feels they are separated from one another (5:6—6:1). Enallage occurs

---

156. Ibid.

157. Further investigation is needed in this unit (3:1–5). There is no evidence of enallage. A shift in persons may have been expected to demonstrate that the couple has reached their desired union in 3:4.

again in this unit once he begins to sing her praises, which demonstrates that they are once again a couple (6:4—7:10).[158]

In the first five cycles the first element of the sequence has been the lovers' separation from one another as evidenced by the author's use of the third person POV or the context. Enallage develops the beginning structure of each cycle. As the pair comes together, there is a shift away from the third person. But in the last two cycles the sequence is reversed. The sixth cycle begins with the couple obviously together, evidenced by the use of the first person plural and her speaking to him (7:11—8:4). The female lover is suggesting an overnight getaway for just the two of them. But at the end of this unit there is an indication that, because of the author's shift back to the third person in 8:3, the lovers are once again separated. Here the structure is reversed.

The last cycle begins with the same reversal in sequence. The lovers are together in 8:5–9 as indicated by the second person dialogue. Then there is a shift to speaking about "a little sister" in 8:8–9. The woman resumes speaking about her sexual purity but to no one in particular. The cycle and the Song conclude with a dialogue between the two lovers, but there is a sense that they are not yet together. First, he pleads for her:

> O you who sit in the gardens,
> *My* companions are listening for your voice—
> Let me hear it!

She then passionately requests his presence to end their separation.

> Hurry, my beloved,
> And be like a gazelle or a young stag
> On the mountains of spices.

The Song concludes the same way it begins: the lovers are separated but cannot wait to be together. Only as they are joined do they find peace.

In summary, enallage is a literary device that is not only used for bringing literary characters onto the reader's mental stage but may also be utilized for emphasizing a particular theological viewpoint. It also may provide a significant clue to the structure of this book.

---

158. Dumbrell (*Faith of Israel*, 281) observes, "The unit begins with the lovers separated and ends with them united."

THEOLOGY AND EXEGESIS

It is important to recognize the relationship between theology and exegesis. Schultz is worth quoting at length because he captures the importance of recognizing the relationship between the two. He believes exegesis includes, among other pursuits, recognizing various literary devices, identifying the function of those devices, and articulating the theology that flows from such an endeavor.[159]

> Exegesis is incomplete if it does not lay bare the theological thrust of a text, seeking to identify words, phrases, motifs, images and even structural elements that reveal aspects of God's will and work in the world as it places demands on or otherwise affects Israel, the nations and/or all humankind. These elements should be analyzed in terms of their function within the given text and synthesized in terms of their participation in and contribution to the theological emphasis of the book as a whole, whether structural or thematic in nature.... Moreover, an exegesis that is consciously theological will also result in greater clarity regarding the contemporary implication and application of a given text.[160]

Wendland recognizes that the "theological sense is not overtly stated in the SoS; it is rather generously implicated by its poetic style and structure."[161] This observation that there is theology in the SoS is contra

---

159. Murphy recognizes the need for such a work on the Song: "It is a striking fact that the Song of Songs has largely been neglected in studies of biblical theology.... The Hebrew Bible thus provides a coherent framework within which one can interpret the Song as expressing a theology of human sexuality" (*Song of Songs*, 100–101). That the ancient SoS has a message on human sexuality should not be surprising. Writing on the purpose of the Sumerian Bridal Songs of the third millennium in Mesopotamia, Leick (*Sex and Eroticism*, 68) suggests the writing of those songs were morally purposeful for that culture. She writes concerning these love songs, "They enforce the traditional values of harmonious marital relations, based on sexual fulfillment. By stressing the positive experience of conjugal happiness, the Bridal Songs may serve to alleviate feelings of ambivalence and anxiety on the part of the bride."

160. Schultz, "Integrating Old Testament Theology and Exegesis," 195; cf. Bright, *Authority of the Old Testament*, 170. This endeavor to do complete exegesis cannot be overstated in light of some current work on the SoS. It is vitally important for the church to get the theology of the divinely inspired love song right and to get it from the text! For instance, Stephen Moore, a New Testament professor at the Theological School at Drew University, studies the book from a "queer theory" perspective. Boer ("Repetition and Insatiable Desire," 297) states, "The whole Song may be read allegorically as a series of sexual episodes, a poetic porn text: group sex in 1:2–4; a male-female combination with some extras, including shepherds and a bestial phantasy, in 1:5—2:7." (I fear to quote more would offend the reader.) See also Burrus and Moore, "Unsafe Sex."

161. Wendland, "Seeking the Path," 51.

The Use of the First Person

House (as well as Clines, Garrett, Campbell, and others), who states that when read in isolation, the "Song of Songs is artistically and thematically lovely but not particularly theologically enriching."[162] Clines, also joins House by stating, "And it is by now no doubt too late for the Song to have any major impact on societal change," although in the same paragraph Clines does relent: "Only perhaps in communities that are both essentially patriarchal and committed to the authority of the Bible may the Song still have a liberating effect and be able to suggest a vision of an alternative style of being"[163] Campbell, who interprets the book in an allegorical sense, states rather dogmatically," If the Song's meaning is exhausted as a celebration of human love, it is difficult to attach any theological significance to it."[164] In a recent article Hess asserts, "The Song is also not about theology."[165] While one may agree halfheartedly with this statement at face value, one must maintain at the same time that the purpose of this love song is theological.

Writing on the entire OT, Bright observes quite correctly the theological import of all texts: "All biblical texts are expressive of theology in that all are animated, if at times indirectly, by some theological con-

---

162. House, *Old Testament Theology*, 469. This endeavor will help Garrett ("Song of Songs," 98) and others who have a "problem finding a theology in the Song" because "the name of God and the word for God never appear in the book" recognize the theological weight this ancient love song does carry. Although Garrett exhibits this malady of theological shortsightedness, the introduction to his commentary does contain a chapter entitled "Implications of the Theology of the Song of Songs." A possible reason for theologians such as House and Garrett not appreciating the full theological relevance of the Song may be due in part to how they define theology. If theology is simply "the study of God," and if God is not mentioned in a biblical text, then there may be little theology to glean from such a text. However, if theology is defined more broadly as to include not only the study of God himself but also the study of his revelation (i.e., the Bible), then theology is both possible and profitable even when God's name is not mentioned. Waltke (*Old Testament Theology*, 39) believes that "because the Bible mediates the revelation of God, it is possible to do biblical *theology*" (italics are original). Since the Song is part of God's revelation, it has a significant theological voice. Garrett ("Song of Songs," 107) does believe that "the Song portrays an experience of transformation of great theological significance." However, he fails to meet his own requirement of elucidating its theology by suggesting that "there is an analogy between yearning for God and yearning for another person." As this thesis will demonstrate, there is no need to resort to analogy to get to the theology of the SoS.

163. Clines, "Why Is There a Song of Songs?" 117.

164. Campbell, "Song of David's Son," 21.

165. Hess, "Song of Songs," 34.

cern." Earlier he states "there are no nontheological texts in the Bible."[166] Certainly, Goulder, if not blunt, is correct when he states, "Manufacturers of motor-cars know that you must have a genuine product to sell as well as a naked girl on the bonnet; and the primary reason for the Song's success was not its supposed authorship, or its poetry, or its erotic appeal, but its implied theology."[167] Osborne concurs and writes succinctly, "Theology is central to biblical poetry."[168] In the SoS, theology is in the guise of poetry. One manner in which theology is revealed is through the author's use of the first person as a rhetorical device.

While it is important to recognize the theological import of the SoS, it is equally important to rein in those who want the theology of the Song to go deeper or past a literal theology of human sexuality to a theology that pictures the love between God and his people. For instance, Lyke believes, "While always the poetry of human love, it simultaneously can be understood in terms of the ancient idiom that understands humans' relations to God via the same metaphors. It is this expansion of the collective intuitions about its language that leads to the sense that the Song, as a whole, can be read allegorically."[169] Walton and Stuart recognize this movement to idealize sex. Comparing what is happening in academic circles to what is happening in the church, they write, "Sex is not abstracted but rather idealized. An increasingly common theological assumption is made that our human sexual activities are merely symbolic representations of a deeper sacred reality."[170] Even Murphy, whose work on the plain reading of the Song is admirable, is inclined to move past the literal sense and its theology related to human sexuality and embrace the *Nachleben* of the text. He observes most correctly,

> Human sexual fulfillment, fervently sought and consummated in reciprocal love between woman and man: Yes, that is what the Song of Songs is about, in its literal and theologically relevant meaning. . . . Nevertheless, as modern expositors we should be open to the possibility that our predecessors, despite their foibles,

---

166. Bright, *Authority of the Old Testament*, 170 and 143.
167. Goulder, *Song of Fourteen Songs*, 78.
168. Osborne, *Hermeneutical Spiral*, 186.
169. Lyke, "Song of Songs," 223.
170. Walton and Stuart, "Editorial," 119.

may have caught a glimpse of theological reality that is not exhausted by a literal sense of the Song's poetry.[171]

Sousan reads the Song allegorically as well. However, in his interpretation the woman of the Song is actually a metaphor for the royal city of God after it has repented and returned to him.[172] Even a conservative scholar such as Archer advocates a typical interpretative view of the Song. He writes, "Understood in this way, the Song is rich in spiritual overtones which have proved a comfort and an encouragement to devout students of Scripture throughout the ages of church history. And yet it requires a really mature soul to appreciate the spiritual beauties which are latent in this book."[173] Similarly, while recognizing the "profound theological value" of the Song, Merrill adds, "It is not exegetically or theologically inappropriate to understand the Song as a paradigm or template by which to gain access to a greater love and intimacy, that of the Lord for his creation and, in particular, for mankind created in his image."[174]

In a similar vein, those who seek a biblical relationship between the sacred and the sexual as in the Tantra tradition need to be reined in theologically as well.[175] For instance, Bullis, writing on the comparison between tantric sexuality and the sexuality in the Song, supposes that tantric ideas are expressed in the Bible and that the SoS "is powerful poetry in pursuit of embodied presence of God."[176] Without the Tantric influence, Vargas believes the erotic and sensual images in the SoS "express in a positive manner the human longing for union with the divine."[177] However, there is no hint of this theological relationship in the SoS.

Theological Observations Suggested by the Use of the First Person

The first person is part of the poetic style of the biblical author of the SoS. Thus, there are a number of theological observations that flow natu-

---

171. Murphy, *Song of Songs*, 103. Also see Mitchell's massive tome of thirteen hundred pages, *The Song of Songs*, which is a "theological exposition of sacred scripture" in the Concordia Commentary series.

172. Sousan, "Woman in the Garden of Eden."

173. Archer, *Survey of Old Testament Introduction*, 543.

174. Merrill, *Everlasting Dominion*, 639.

175. In short, Tantra is an expansion of consciousness through the ordinary acts of life such as eating or even lovemaking.

176. Bullis, "Biblical Tantra," 108.

177. Vargas, "Textual Analysis of the 'Song of Songs,'" iii.

rally from the author's use of the first person.[178] It should be noted that literary devices or figures of speech do not in and of themselves have a theology. As Osborne rightly notes concerning metaphor as a figure of speech, "Theology rarely stems from the metaphor itself but rather from the whole context of which it is part."[179] What is true of the metaphor as a part of speech is also true of the author's use of the first person. It is only in context that theology flows from the utilization of the first person in the Song.

It is important to recognize that the theological observations that flow from this rhetorical device specifically and from the book generally are not, as Lavoie would suppose, from a particular theological bias. She suggests that only an "essentially anthropocentric" reading will give the woman of the SoS her rightful place.[180] This endeavor will demonstrate that a thorough exegesis of the text will place all the voices of the Song in their proper context before God—thus demonstrating a clearly biblical theological reading without the prejudice of an androcentric vision or any other theological bias.

The first part of this section will suggest some general theological observations that arise from the biblical author's use of the first person. The second will offer some theological observations that flow from the use of the first person singular personal pronouns as it pertains to the

---

178. The formulations of the theological statements in this chapter will look different from theological reflections in most systematic theology books. Even the classic categories of theology such as God and sin are not present. What will emerge from this section are theological observations that concern the love relationship between a man and a woman. As a man and a woman live by the theology of this book, they will enjoy the gift of sex that God has graciously given to his human creatures. By living this theology, a couple will be pleasing God, which should be the ultimate goal of all theology. It should be noted that this segment of this project does not seek to distill all the theology of the Song but only those theological observations that arise from the author's use of the first person.

179. Osborne, *Hermeneutical Spiral*, 188.

180. Lavoie, "Woman in the Song of Songs," 76. While this thesis does not look at every rhetorical device that contributes to all of the theology of the Song, surely Lavoie (78) is reading against the natural grain of the text through the lens of her feminism when she writes, "by prizing sexuality only as difference and relation, the Song frees woman from the patriarchal stranglehold." Could it be that by reading with the "grain" of the biblical text the Song actually presents normal male-female relationship and the rest of the OT that deals with that relationship has been misread? Reading with the grain of the entire OT demonstrates that the Song does not subvert but complements what surrounds it in the canon.

female voice in the Song. The third will suggest observations that arise from the use of the first person personal pronoun singular in regard to the male lover that have not already been mentioned under part one. The fourth will offer some theological observations that concern the plural use of the first person.

General Theological Observations

The first and most obvious theological observation that can be made from the author's use of the first person is that there is a *masculine* first person and there is a *feminine* first person.[181] The celebration of marital pleasure that is sung in this song is between a man and a woman.[182] The man is the object of her desire (1:2), and the woman is the desire of the man (7:10). The God-designed order for romantic pleasure is between a man and a woman.[183] Weems goes too far when she remarks that even though "the drama appears to center around the heterosexual, erotic exchange between a woman and a man, Song of Songs is not in

181. Although the first person pronoun is not marked for gender in BH, the context of the Song does give the reader enough information to determine the gender of the first person in most cases. It is in this manner that the concept of first person masculine or first person feminine is used.

182. Davidson (*Flame of Yahweh*, 21) uses pronouns (and nouns) to make the same theological argument for monogamy in Gen 1–2. He writes, "The usage of singular nouns and pronouns throughout is significant.... the phrase 'a man ... and ... his wife ...' with both nouns in the singular, clearly implies that the sexual relationship envisioned is monogamous, to be shared between two marriage partners." Phipps ("Plight of the Song of Songs," 83) writes, "It would be anachronistic to interpret the Song of Songs as infatuations and sexual experimentation of promiscuous youth. In the tradition of Semitic culture marriage was covenanted near the age of puberty and intimate male-female association was not sanctioned prior to marriage." This is contra D. M. Carr (*Erotic Word*, 119), who states, "These lovers belong to each other, but they do not appear to be married. Most of their meetings take place outdoors, the prime trysting place for unmarried lovers in an ancient world with no separate bedrooms, cars, or motels."

183. The observation that heterosexuality is God's design in the Song (and was his design from the beginning (cf. Davidson, *Flame of Yahweh*) argues against Moore's contention that heterosexuality is an "invention" of the modern era. He believes, "The 'invention' of heterosexuality seems to have coincided approximately with the invention of electricity, photography, automotive engineering and other indispensable appurtenances of the modernity." He further suggests that rejection of the allegorical interpretation of the SoS is due to the "homosexual panic in twentieth-century Western culture." Moore, "The Song of Songs," 348–49. For those unfamiliar with Moore, he is writing from a "queer theory" perspective. This theory supposes "that gender identity is purely performative, the product of a compulsory set of social rituals and conventions" and not God-given (ibid., 328n1).

the end about heterosexual sex. Instead, it teaches us about the power and politics of human love."[184] Walton remarks dogmatically about the sexual orientation of love in the Song: "The love is certainly heterosexual, there is no question of this."[185] Garrett adds, "The sexuality of the Song is heterosexual; a 'gay reading' of the Song is the most violent kind of imposition of extrinsic values on the Song."[186] Even the feminist scholar, Athalya Brenner, agrees that the text puts forth a heterosexual orientation. "I find it implausible that . . . the SoS text is anything else but what it declares itself to be by its contents: songs of love and love-making between heterosexual humans."[187]

A second observation is that this physically passionate relationship between the man and the woman is not purely tactile. The Song reveals that the relationship is one saturated with communication, which is evidenced by the grammatical interchange between the first and second persons and the third person praise descriptions. Although all the physical senses are used in this love song, it is the sense of speaking and hearing that are set center stage by the author.[188] The majority of the Song is set as a dialogue between the couple in which they talk and listen to one another. While it is true that the male lover will clear any obstacle to enjoy the physical beauty of his lover (2:8, 14), he also wants to hear her voice (2:14; 8:13). This suggests that a vibrant and passionate physical relationship involves a healthy dose of communication.[189]

A third observation is that there is a theology of desire and sexuality in the Song. For example, she craves kisses and lots of them (1:2). She desires to be caressed and held often (2:6; 8:3). He wishes to climb her

---

184. Weems, "Song of Songs," 371.

185. Walton, "Theology of Desire," 33.

186. Garrett, "Song of Songs," 103.

187. Brenner, "'My' Song of Songs," 162.

188. This observation is contrary to Landy ("Song of Songs," 310), who states, "Sight and smell are the dominant sensations in the Song." On the contrary Landy believes "the discourse of the lovers separates them. It is a displacement of love, in which foreplay—seduction, sweet-talk—repeatedly defers fusion" (ibid., 316). The prevalent exchange of "I" and "you" dialogue, cumulating in sexual intimacy in 5:1 and 7:10, precludes Landy's observation from being accurate.

189. Christian sex therapist Rosenau (*Celebration of Sex*, 98–99) remarks, "Intimately connecting, feeling and enjoying a sense of partnership, is what a one-flesh marriage is all about, and dialogue is at the heart of this process. Sex is not the most crucial part of the relationship. Communicating and building a loving fulfilling companionship are the core needs. The more you communicate, the more intimately connected you will feel."

body as though she was a mountain ridge (4:6) or a fruit-filled palm tree (7:9). Desire is overtly evident and thoroughly enjoyed between the two "I's" of the Song. The theology of the Song does not stop with desire but continues to fulfillment (5:1).[190] A literal reading of the Song celebrates the multidimensional aspects of the physical relationship between a married couple. Marriage is the only arena in which the festivities of the sexual relationship are to occur. Bloch and Bloch do not flinch when they concur: "Sex is sanctioned only in marriage; on this point the Old Testament laws are unequivocal. Outside the pale of marriage there are only crimes and punishments, catalogued in exhaustive detail."[191] They both enjoy the physical oneness of sex where her "my garden" becomes his "my garden," and she is glad to grant him access to it (4:16—5:1). The author's use of the first person evidences sexual playfulness (2:10-14), sexual longing (2:5-6), sexual vocabulary (5:10-16; 7:1-11), and the physical consummation of the couple (5:1; 7:10). These sensual activities are sought after by the lovers (7:10-13) and approved by the author of the Song as divinely legitimate (5:1). Although God is never mentioned

---

190. This is contra Walsh who believes the lovers never consummate any of their sexual desire. Walsh (*Exquisite Desire*, 97) states, "Sexual love remains a yearning throughout the Song of Songs and is never consummated." Also Hess (*Song of Songs*, 35) observes, "Although anticipated and sometimes almost achieved, it is not possible to find a clear and certain description of coitus taken place." See also D. M. Carr (*Erotic Word*, 115), who states rather indelicately that "the man and the woman never actually 'make it' in this poem ... much of the rest of the Song of Songs is a tease."
While it is true that the Song is clear in its theology of desire (and fulfillment), that desire should only be sought to be satisfied within the proper time, i.e., the confines of marriage (2:7; 3:5; 8:4 cf. Gen 2:24; Prov 5).

191. Bloch and Bloch, *Song of Songs*, 6. While the marriage status of the couple is not mentioned in the SoS (if chapter 3 is not their wedding), it assumed based on the antecedent theology of the rest of the OT (Lev 18; Prov 5; Job 31:1; etc.) which precedes the Song. Preuss (*Biblical and Talmudic Medicine*, 450) is correct when he states, "For the unmarried, chastity is an obvious requirement." This is contrary to D. M. Carr ("Gender and the Shaping of Desire," 241), who states, "There is no sign throughout the Song that the lovers of the Song of Songs are married." Hess ("Song of Songs," 34-35) waffles when he states, "We do not even know whether the couple is married.... The Song puts no restrictions on their activities.... On the other hand, the book does not aim to deny the importance of theology or marriage or procreation. All such matters are left behind in sweeping passion." If Hess is correct, then the Song is a "dirty little book" because it advocates sex outside of marriage, which all of Scripture prohibits. In addition, if the couple is not married, that fact would mitigate against Hess' theme of commitment, which he sees as a major theme along with desire.

in the Song by name, his approval is always felt.[192] God is the creator of man, woman, and sex (Gen 2; Prov 5). It is his desire as evidenced in the Song that the physical relationship be enjoyed to its fullest within the confines of a married, heterosexual relationship.

Theological Observations concerning the First Person Pronouns with Reference to the Female Lover

An observation that may be suggested from the author's use of the first person in reference to the female lover is that the Song offers a detailed theology of female sexuality.[193] Carey Ellen Walsh remarks, "A woman's sexuality is developed, sustained and celebrated, not as object, but from a woman's perspective and that of her male lover(s). Throughout the book, in first person voice, the woman retains control of her fate, of her pleasure."[194] This book celebrates feminine desire and sexuality as normal, proper, and only to be fulfilled within the confines of marriage (2:7; 3:5; 8:4). As the main speaker in the Song, it is the female voice that often expresses a passionate desire for sexual affection.[195] The first person in reference to the female communicates the woman's desire for kisses, caresses, sexual union, and an outdoor tryst with her lover (1:2; 2:6; 4:16—5:1; 7:11–14). The female initiates all of these sexual activities, and

---

192. Gledhill, *Song of Songs*, 37. Gledhill asks and answers his own rhetorical question: "Where is God in the Song? He is nowhere explicitly mentioned, everywhere assumed." God's place in the Song will be investigated in chapter four.

193. While it is outside the scope of this work to develop this topic, it is important to note for further study. Also, the Song does not only inspire females to enjoy the physical relationship within marriage but it also instructs males as to a proper and biblical theology of female sexuality. Such theological observations correct such notions as "women don't desire sex" or "women do not like sex." Tennant ("Nice Yet Naughty," para. 8.) writes, "After all, women are the ones who aren't even supposed to like sex. We're the ones with the proverbial headaches."

194. Walsh, "Startling Voice," 133. Throughout her article Walsh uses the singular for the male lover. It is only here that she allows for more than one male lover. She, herself, recognizes this theological observation as a "benefit for feminist appropriation" (ibid).

195. This theological observation should not be overlooked or taken for granted as though this was normal for all ancient societies. God has always desired that women enjoy physical intimacy and desire it. Hunter ("'Sweet Talk,'" 232) makes the observation that "explicit expressions of female sexual desire are notoriously rare in Greek literature of all periods." Even in the present sex-saturated society of the Western hemisphere, women need to know that God has created them with sexual desire. While one may disagree with Neufeld's ("'Sex'tet on Love," 46) desire to "identify a new feminist sexual ethic," she does allow her search to take her to the Song. She (48) believes that "this ancient's message is both clear and necessary for us today."

her sexual initiative is communicated to the audience in the first person.[196] The first person communicates her desire or her "lovesickness," which is female fervor unfulfilled (8:3). She tells her audience in the first person about two of her erotic dreams of her lover (3:1). She shares freely (in the first person) her arousal for her lover (5:4). The female lover of the Song is a woman who enjoys the erotic relationship and is free to initiate sex (4:16). She is also a creative lover who promises her love erotic outdoor adventures.[197] This outdoor escapade offers both new and old sexual adventures (7:13).[198] As creative and free as this woman is as a sexual being, she personally guarded her purity before marriage (8:10). After her marriage her love is exclusively for her beloved, דּוֹדִי. This term, used twenty-four times, demonstrates her exclusivity towards her lover. This was and is her *only* lover. Hubbard notes well the theme of exclusive love in the book but without noting the specific literary devices, which makes it so. The theme of exclusiveness in the relationship is communicated, in part, by the author's use of the first person.

> No effort is spared, no literary device is left idle in making clear that the partners are pledged fully to each other and only to each other. *Metaphors* of exclusiveness (4:12—5:1; 4:4; 7:5), *vows* of exclusiveness (8:8–9), *yearning* for exclusiveness (8:6–7), *boasts* of exclusiveness (she: 8:10; he 8:11–12)—these combine to form a theme so dominant that it can be rightly called the main melody of the poems.[199]

This couple's love is exclusive and it is also permanent.[200] These poetic lines in the first person ring of permanency and not a one-night fling, "My beloved is mine, and I am his דּוֹדִי לִי וַאֲנִי לוֹ; "I am my beloved's

---

196. This is a valuable theological insight for Christian females contemplating the physical relationship in marriage. Sex therapists such as the Wheat and Wheat (*Intended for Pleasure*, 109) and Rosenau (*Celebration of Sex*, 242) point out that the reason many women do not experience orgasm is due to psychological problems. Some of these problems stem from an unbiblical view of desire and sex. Understanding the theology of feminine sexuality is a needed exercise in Christian homes and churches.

197. Bloch and Bloch (*Song of Songs*, 208) and others note that דּדַי means love-making.

198. Since fruit is used as a sexual metaphor throughout the book, the same metaphorical sense applies here as well. The "old and new" seem to indicate that this tryst will hold some new romantic overtures as well as some good old standards.

199. Hubbard, *Ecclesiastes, Song of Songs*, 262.

200. Hess ("Song of Songs," 35) observes that this theme has the same attention that the theme of desire has from scholars.

and my beloved is mine" אֲנִי לְדוֹדִי וְדוֹדִי לִי, and "I am my beloved's, And his desire is for me" אֲנִי לְדוֹדִי וְעָלַי תְּשׁוּקָתוֹ (2:16; 6:3; 7:11).²⁰¹ These verses, combined with the climacteric verse of the book (8:6), suggest an extremely strong and enduring permanency in the relationship. This pinnacle verse of the entire Song has as its object the woman who expresses her desire for permanency in the first person.

> Put me like a seal over your heart,
> Like a seal on your arm.
> For love is as strong as death,
> Jealousy is as severe as Sheol;
> Its flashes are flashes of fire,
> The *very* flame of the LORD. (8:6)

The author's use of the first person also demonstrates a mutuality of love. Both the male and female lovers are totally committed to their relationship. This mutuality is seen in first person phrases such as "my beloved is mine and I am his" דּוֹדִי לִי וַאֲנִי לוֹ (2:16; also 5:16; 6:13; 7:11). In the Song there is no "power struggle" between the sexes. There are no inequities between the two. They feel the same about each other (his: רַעְיָתִי, 4:7; hers: רֵעִי, 5:16).

The first person also reveals reciprocity in the relationship. Both lovers seek to meet the desires and wants of the other through their mutuality (3:4; 7:8). The female lover believes that the relationship is reciprocal as noted in the phrase, "my beloved is mine and I am his" דּוֹדִי לִי וַאֲנִי לוֹ. They both belong to each other equally and both desire each other equally as strong (2:16; 6:3). Elliott remarks that the /i/ sound in 2:10 "accents the aspect of his possession of the beloved" and "the mutuality of their possession" is found in 2:16.²⁰² Elliott furthers observes that the mutual possession of the couple as evidenced in 2:16 is demonstrated by the author's use of the "possessive suffixes."²⁰³ They both desire to be together and they take turns inviting each other out to be alone (his invitation: 4:8; her invitation: 7:12).

The use of the first person also communicates an intense level of friendship between the two lovers. Yes, they are lovers, but they see

---

201. Murphy, *Song of Songs*, 77. He refers to these three occurrences as "possession refrains."

202. Elliott, *Literary Unity of the Canticle*, 69.

203. Ibid., 75.

themselves as friends as well (4:7; 5:16).[204] Friendship between the sexes is not a modern, Western concept imposed on the Song. This friendship is nurtured by shared experiences (2:14; 7:11–14), mutual admiration (5:10–16; 7:2–11), physical attraction (1:2; 2:14), abundant praise of each other (5:10–16; 7:2–11), and demonstrations of physical affection (2:6; 5:1; 7:9). This intense friendship enjoyed by this couple is communicated to the reader by the author's use of the first person.

Thus far, all of the theological observations of the first person have been positive. However, there is one example where the use of the first person demonstrates a characteristic that is devastating to any relationship: selfishness. In the dream sequence of chapter five in verse three, there are four verbs in first person which state the woman's reasons not to meet the nocturnal advances of her lover. Four first person personal pronouns function as nominatives that highlight her own reluctance. The author draws attention to her subsequent discipline by paralleling the pronouns of her reluctance with four first person pronouns functionally accusatively to show that she is the object of the chastisement (5:6). The author might be making the case that the discipline inflicted by the watchmen was in direct response to her negative response to her lover. This "negative" theological observation should not be missed. When a spouse fails to respond to the other unselfishly, the marriage relationship suffers.

The author uses the voice of the female lover to make the theological point through the use of the first person personal pronouns that when one is devoted to purity (8:10), devoted to the expressions of love at the proper time (2:7; 3:5; 8:4), and devoted to one other person, *shalom* is found (8:10). Because she was devoted to such an extent, the female lover found peace in the eyes of her husband, אָז הָיִיתִי בְעֵינָיו כְּמוֹצְאֵת שָׁלוֹם. The term, *shalom*, שָׁלוֹם, according to Carr generally means "entering into a state of wholeness, and unity."[205] In the Song this wholeness (or oneness) can be (and should be) found in the marriage relationship.

These theological observations are evidenced by the use of the first person personal pronouns as they relate to the female speaker in the Song. This rhetorical device gives strong evidence that God approves of a woman's passion and intensity in sexual matters.

---

204. The same root for "friend," רֵעַ, is used to show the friendship between Judah and Hirah (Gen 38:12) and between Hushai and David (2 Sam 15:37). BDB 945.

205. G. L. Carr, "שָׁלַם," 930.

Theological Observations concerning the First Person Pronouns with Reference to the Male Lover

Some theological observations might be suggested concerning the author's use of the first person pronouns as it concerns the male lover that have not been previously stated. Generally, in the Song it is the man who is the responsive creature. The male lover responds passionately to the sexual invitation of the female. She requests him to come into her garden and he responds by stating, "I have come into my garden" בָּאתִי לְגַנִּי (4:16—5:1). The use of four epithets with the first person possessive pronoun, "my sister" אֲחֹתִי, "my darling" רַעְיָתִי, "my dove" יוֹנָתִי, and "my perfect one" תַמָּתִי (5:2) indicates his exclusive claim to enter the garden.[206]

Although he is generally the one who responds to the sexual invitations of the female lover (7:13–14, he is the one who initiates the verbal praise of her (4:1). The male lover has a high view of his female lover as his own friend, רַעְיָתִי (e.g., 1:9; 1:15). He considers her as "my beautiful one," יָפָתִי (2:10). He finds her arousing (4:9), and awesome (6:5) when he is the object of her gaze, הָסֵבִּי עֵינַיִךְ. Although not expressed in first person (because he is not the speaker), she is his desire: "I am my beloved's, And his desire is for me" (7:11).

The use of the first person as it refers to the male also demonstrates his complete enjoyment and fulfillment in the physical relationship. The four nominative case first person pronouns give evidence that her garden is a complete delight for him (5:1). Also, the four nominative case pronouns are doubly paralleled by the eight genitive case pronouns that demonstrate that her garden's "plants and spices" (4:13–14) have become "my" plants and spices (5:1). This morphing of "my garden" from her perspective to "my garden" from his perspective demonstrates the woman's pleasure in giving herself to him and his possession and enjoyment of her. Their enjoyment of each other is mutual and complete.

It is from the mouth of the male lover in the first person that the theological observation may be proposed that this couple revels in their nudity with each other.[207] They are naked, but without shame (cf. Gen 2:25). It is he that requests of her, "Let me see your form" (2:14), and it is he that is so moved by her alluring dance that he says, "I will climb the

---

206. Elliott, *Literary Unity of the Canticle*, 124.

207. Depending upon how one reads 2:2–6, it is possible that the female lover is "taking great delight" in her lover's nude body; so Longman, *Song of Songs*, 65.

palm tree, I will take hold of its fruit stalks" (7:9). These verses express his deep delight of her nude body and his complete pleasure with her.[208]

Theological Observations concerning the First Person Plural Pronouns

It is the first person singular personal pronouns in both genders that morph into the first person common plural. For instance, the male and the female "I" or "me" becomes "our" (1:16–17). Through the use of the singular pronouns the reader experiences the two individual lovers becoming one couple as the author shifts to the first person plural (cf. Gen 2:24). The use of the first person plural also shows that the two lovers share everything in their relationship. Neither holds anything as his or her own. It is not "my couch, my rafters," etc. It is "our couch, our rafters, our cypresses" (1:16–17), "our land" (2:12), and "our doors" (7:14). As Bloch and Bloch observe, "both of them delight in the sound of the first person plural . . . taking possession of the world around them."[209]

They share activity, as in 7:12–13 "let us arise and go." They also share ownership of solving the problems that crop up in their budding vineyard ("catch the foxes for us," 2:14–15). God intends a married couple to experience this two-becoming-one and mutual sharing from the beginning (Gen 2:24).

Conclusion

While personal pronouns in the first person have not enjoyed complete recognition by scholars of the Song, this chapter suggests a number of important functions for this generally nondescript part of speech.[210] The first person pronouns serve a number of functions in this love song: (1) they provide structure for certain portions of the Song as well as providing structural cohesion that unites the different cycles together

---

208. This verse gives biblical evidence for this being normal and acceptable masculine behavior within the confines of marriage. Rosenau (*Celebration of Sex*, 189, 195) notes the obvious: "Often, what he sees he also wants to touch," and "Your husband wants to touch what he visually enjoys." This observation contradicts Black's position ("Beauty or the Beast?" 318) that while "we might expect the descriptions of the woman to flatter her, but really they ridicule or worse, are repulsive, and as such they indicate something of the lover's unease about his love's body and her sexuality."

209. Bloch and Bloch, *Song of Songs*, 8.

210. This chapter proves Trible's assessment (*Rhetorical Criticism*, 104): "Little words in Hebrew often have big functions." While Trible is referencing particles, her dictum works for the often-overlooked personal pronouns.

into one unified song; (2) the repetitive use of the first person personal pronouns shows their overall importance to understanding the message of the Song;[211] (3) the shift of person from first to second or third, enallage, is an important rhetorical device that among other functions allows the author to bring various characters onto the imaginative stage of the audience or reader; and (4) the first person pronouns play a vital role for uncovering and understanding the theology of the Song. The first person pronouns are some of the rhetorical building blocks of the author's theology.[212] Through this rhetorical use of the first person perspective in direct discourse, the author of the Song invites every future generation of readers to become the lovers, to take their places in their own gardens, and to enjoy their own celebration of love. Through this rhetorical persuasion, every married couple is encouraged by the Song's intimate and erotic celebration to take the place of these biblical lovers. The Song establishes a model that every couple would be wise to emulate.[213]

This exercise in seeing how the theology of the biblical author flows from his use of the first person is important for seeing God's emphasis in the book. Although Nicole is writing about the institution of marriage, he notes well the need for communicating to this culture God's viewpoint on the physical relationship, which is a major component of God-honoring marriage. "God's concern for the institution of human marriage, and his hostility to all that disrupts it, must be emphasized today as he himself emphasizes it in the Bible."[214] The author's use of the

---

211. Fokkelman, *Reading Biblical Poetry*, 173. Fokkelman notes, "Interpreting a poem is a search for order and structure in a heap of language signs that at first sight seem impossible to penetrate. The order emerging from the apparent chaos is based on many and highly varied devices, themselves distributed on virtually all levels of the text. Most of the devices, however, are forms of repetition."

212. A survey of books of theology such as House, Childs, Merrill, and Zuck shows that they make profitable and accurate theological observations but they do not demonstrate *how* they came to those observations. For instance, while it is accurate to state that the relationship of the couple is mutual, the recognition of the first person shows *how* the biblical author used first person personal pronouns rhetorically to communicate a practice and theology of mutuality.

213. It is a goal of this chapter to fill the need that Parsons recognizes when writing about the Song. He ("Guidelines," 400) states, "Insufficient information is available concerning how to utilize this book for the church."

214. Nicole, "Wisdom of Marriage," 291. If this theology of married sexual relationship were to be preached (and practiced) in the twenty-first century, it would at least present for believers a healthy and biblical view of sex. There is a need for such a theology that places physical intimacy between a married couple in the proper bibli-

first person as a rhetorical device surely emphasizes God's pleasure in physical intimacy within the marriage bed.

---

cal perspective. Nicole gives evidence that marital intimacy is not viewed as highly as it should be today. "Today, erotica, coarse language, pornography, promiscuity, prostitution, nudism, pedophilia, rape, and other perversions—not to speak of the spirit of sexual titillation and indulgence that mark so many of our public spectacles, our TV programs and advertising, our popular songs, our contemporary literature, and our magazines and newspapers—combine to drag sex into the gutter" (ibid., 292). Penner and Penner (*Counseling for Sexual Disorders*, 3) concur concerning the frankness of sex in society and lament an uninformed approach to the topic by the general populace: "The sexual revolution has not necessarily made people better informed about how to function as healthy successful sexual partners. Rather, it has made people more comfortable in viewing sexual activity and hearing sexual terms used boldly. It also has made society more tolerant of a great range of sexual activity. But it has not helped the average married couple, churched or unchurched, experience a comfortable informed approach to sexuality." McBurney and McBurney (*Real Questions*, 25) surveyed more than a thousand couples in their counseling center and found that forty-six percent indicate a problem with sex. There is a present-day need for a thoroughly biblical theology concerning sexuality.

3

Rhetorical Questions

THIS CHAPTER WILL INVESTIGATE the literary use of the rhetorical questions (RQs) in the SoS and the theological significance of the author's use of this rhetorical device.[1] Abraham Mariaselvam observes that RQs are one of the rhetorical devices in the SoS. However, he does not identify them nor does he suggest their individual function.[2]

While studying the use of rhetorical questions in Jeremiah, Brueggemann notes the importance of understanding RQs since these "provide an important tool for understanding the poetry of Jeremiah."[3] Pursuing the significance of this rhetorical device is a worthy endeavor for, as Stuart Creason notes in his review of De Regt's work on rhetorical questions in Job, "Rhetorical questions are generally neglected by those interested in Biblical Hebrew."[4] To help correct this oversight, this section will first identify and classify all the interrogatives of the SoS. Second, it will define and explain the general use of rhetorical questions. Third, it will suggest the rhetorical function of the various RQs in their individual contexts and demonstrate how RQs aid the author in his purpose. It will conclude with some theological observations that flow naturally from the author's use of this literary device.[5]

---

1. "Rhetorical Patterns" (*Dictionary of Biblical Imagery*, 720–27) lists rhetorical questions as a main feature of biblical rhetoric.

2. Mariaselvam, *Song of Songs*, 69.

3. Brueggemann, "Jeremiah's Use of Rhetorical Questions," 358.

4. Creason, Review of *Biblical Hebrew and Discourse Linguistics*, 140.

5. Brueggemann ("Jeremiah's Use of Rhetorical Questions," 358) notes the validity of this theological endeavor in his study of the rhetorical questions in Jeremiah. He suggests that the rhetorical questions in Jeremiah are "employed in an intensely theological and perhaps even covenantal way." For another study of rhetorical questions in the OT, see Merrill, "Isaiah 40–55 as Anti-Babylonian Polemic," 3–18.

CLASSIFYING INTERROGATIVES

According to Waltke, biblical Hebrew has five uses of the interrogative: "questions of facts, questions of circumstances, alternative questions, exclamatory questions and rhetorical questions."[6] For the purpose of this thesis, the first three categories listed in *IBHS* will be summarized into one working category and labeled as "simple interrogatives." The reason for this grouping is because the first three classifications differ in function from exclamatory and rhetorical questions. The first group of interrogatives are questions of facts, circumstances, or alternative questions. These interrogatives are straightforward inquiries seeking information. On the other hand, exclamatory questions are interrogatives that function to make an exclamation, not gathering information. This category of questions (as well as the rhetorical interrogative), according to Waltke, "must be recognized in context."[7] The rhetorical questions are different from simple interrogatives because they too do not seek information. In fact, the biblical author uses the rhetorical interrogative to give information or provide a certain perspective to another character or reader. Ryken observes that the rhetorical interrogatives are used for a certain effect.[8] This effect is not to provide an answer to an inquiry or to seek information as is the case of a simple interrogative. The specific rhetorical purpose of each RQ will be pursued in a following section.[9] While Arnold and Choi list two types of interrogatives: "genuine" or rhetorical, this study will classify the various interrogatives three ways: simple,[10] exclamatory, and rhetorical interrogatives.[11]

---

6. *IBHS*, 316. This volume also lists polar questions (684). Polar questions are classified as questions of fact although some may function as rhetorical questions.

7. Ibid., 321.

8. Ryken, *Words of Delight*, 362.

9. In an unsigned article in the *Dictionary of Biblical Imagery*, "Rhetorical Patterns," the author notes two distinct ways the term "rhetorical" is used. "The adjective 'rhetorical' denotes two distinct features of discourse. It means either the persuasive strategy by which a written or oral discourse influences an audience or a set of conventional motifs or formulas that appear in a body of discourse" (ibid., 720). The discussion of rhetorical questions in this essay will encompass both aspects of the term. It will seek to identify the RQs in the SoS and will suggest how they aid the author in his persuasion of the audience or reader.

10. As noted previously, simple interrogatives are the author's designation of interrogatives that include questions of facts, questions of circumstances, or alternative questions.

11. Arnold and Choi, *A Guide to Biblical Hebrew Syntax*, 187.

Identifying Simple Interrogatives

The first two simple interrogatives are found in 1:7:

הַגִּידָה לִּי שֶׁאָהֲבָה נַפְשִׁי
אֵיכָה תִרְעֶה
אֵיכָה תַּרְבִּיץ בַּצָּהֳרָיִם
שַׁלָּמָה אֶהְיֶה כְּעֹטְיָה
עַל עֶדְרֵי חֲבֵרֶיךָ׃

Tell me, O you whom my soul loves,
Where do you pasture *your flock*,
Where do you make *it* lie down at noon?
For why should I be like one who veils herself
Beside the flocks of your companions?[12]

Stoop-van Paridon translates this verse as both an exclamatory and rhetorical question.[13] It could be argued that the interrogatives of 1:7 are rhetorical questions and not simple interrogatives. This would depend on how much the reader believes the woman actually knows about the coming and going of her beloved. If she is being coy and teasing, then these could be RQs. However, the beloved's answer in 1:8 may indicate that she did not know, but wanted to. Bergant states that "there is a mocking tone to the man's reply. The verb form suggests: 'If you do not know, you should have known.' There is no rancor in this response, just a tease."[14] While Bergant's observation concerning his mocking her is too strong, she might be correct in realizing that he is being coy to her simple inquiry. She is looking for a straightforward answer to his location so she could be with him. Longman recognizes her tease here and believes she is seeking directions and not making a statement (which would have to be true of a rhetorical question).[15] Hess recognizes that the female lover wants to be alone with her beloved and needs to know where he will lie down to escape the noontime heat. To accomplish that "she must know where he takes his flock."[16] Hess and Exum translate the

---

12. Translation is the author's.
13. Stoop-van Paridon, *Song of Songs*, 60.
14. Bergant, *Song of Songs*, 18.
15. Longman, *Song of Songs*, 100.
16. Hess, *Song of Songs*, 60. Exum (*Song of Songs*, 107) believes the female lover's question is a double entendre but is still a simple inquiry to his whereabouts at noon.

third interrogative in this verse as "lest I . . ." instead of "For why should I be like one who veils herself besides the flocks of your companions" שַׁלָּמָה אֶהְיֶה כְּעֹטְיָה עַל עֶדְרֵי חֲבֵרֶיךָ. This interrogative is functioning as a rhetorical question and will be dealt with in the next section.[17] Longman translates שַׁלָּמָה as an interrogative but does not suggest its function.

The second verse that contains a simple interrogative is in 3:3.

מְצָאוּנִי הַשֹּׁמְרִים הַסֹּבְבִים בָּעִיר
אֵת שֶׁאָהֲבָה נַפְשִׁי רְאִיתֶם

The watchmen who make the rounds in the city found me,
Have you seen him whom my soul loves?

The interrogative sentence "Have you seen him whom my soul loves?" has been understood by commentators to be an interrogative sentence although it is not marked in BH as interrogative. Stoop-van Paridon follows GKC when she states, "A question need not necessarily be introduced by a special interrogative pronoun or adverb. Frequently the natural emphasis upon the words is of itself sufficient to indicate an interrogative sentence as such."[18] Modern commentators including Longman, Exum, and Hess follow suit. Since the context surrounding this interrogative is the first "lost and found" section, it is assumed that the female lover's request of the night watchmen is a legitimate request for the whereabouts of her lost lover. Her frantic search is depicted in 3:1–2.

עַל־מִשְׁכָּבִי בַּלֵּילוֹת בִּקַּשְׁתִּי אֵת
שֶׁאָהֲבָה נַפְשִׁי
בִּקַּשְׁתִּיו וְלֹא מְצָאתִיו׃
אָקוּמָה נָּא וַאֲסוֹבְבָה בָעִיר
בַּשְּׁוָקִים וּבָרְחֹבוֹת
אֲבַקְשָׁה אֵת שֶׁאָהֲבָה נַפְשִׁי
בִּקַּשְׁתִּיו וְלֹא מְצָאתִיו׃

On my bed night after night I sought him

---

17. Exum (*Song of Songs*, 107) follows the LXX and the Vulgate and smoothes out the rhetorical question by providing the answer that the RQ assumes: "lest I be like. . . ." However, BDB (554) states that with an imperfect מָה often denotes a deprecating comment or it introduces a rhetorical question, i.e., "the reason why something should or should not be done." This reasoning will be expanded upon in the discussion of specific rhetorical questions.

18. GKC, 473.

Whom my soul loves; I sought him but did not find him.
I must arise now and go about the city;
In the streets and in the squares
I must seek him whom my soul loves.
I sought him but did not find him.

There is nothing in this context to suggest that her question is anything but a singular request for further information from those whose job it is to know who comes and goes in a city by night. This information is needed to aid in her search for her soul's object.[19]

The next interrogatives are found in a dialogue between the female lover and the daughters of Jerusalem (5:8–9). One מָה comes from the female lover and two interrogatives from the daughters as they endeavor to assist the female lover in her second search for her beloved.

הִשְׁבַּעְתִּי אֶתְכֶם בְּנוֹת יְרוּשָׁלָָם
אִם־תִּמְצְאוּ אֶת־דּוֹדִי
מַה־תַּגִּידוּ לֹו
שֶׁחוֹלַת אַהֲבָה אָנִי:
מַה־דּוֹדֵךְ מִדּוֹד
הַיָּפָה בַּנָּשִׁים
מַה־דּוֹדֵךְ מִדּוֹד
שֶׁכָּכָה הִשְׁבַּעְתָּנוּ:

I adjure you, O daughters of Jerusalem,
if you find my beloved,
What will you tell him?[20]
For I am lovesick.
What kind of beloved is your beloved,
O most beautiful among women?
What kind of beloved is your beloved,
That thus you adjure us?

On the chance that the daughters of Jerusalem find her beloved, the female lover asks and answers her own question. Her question is a simple

---

19. This is contrary to Provan (*Song of Songs*, 299), who takes the watchmen's silence in the text as meaning they did not know and could not know the answer to her question.

20. Based on the use of מָה I have chosen to insert a question mark although NASB, KJV, and NKJV do not. NIV does use the question mark.

request for information. She wants to be certain of what the daughters are going to say to her love (because of her recent refusal which separated the lovers in the first place).[21] To make sure there are no misunderstandings of her condition and her heart concerning her beloved, she answers the question herself. Stoop-van Paridon translates the interrogative and answer well:

> What will you tell him?
> That I (am) wearied by longing for love.[22]

Waltke suggests, "The indefinite use of מָה usually involves a clausal object,"[23] which in this case is the answer to her simple question introduced by the relative particle שֶׁ. Mitchell and Pope believe that this is a rhetorical question.[24] Pope references Hos 9:14 for support.[25] However, in Hos 9:14 and Song 5:8, the answer is given directly after the question. By the very nature of a rhetorical question, it expects no answer.[26]

Two more simple interrogatives are offered by the daughters of Jerusalem in this verse (5:9).

מַה־דּוֹדֵךְ מִדּוֹד
הַיָּפָה בַּנָּשִׁים
מַה־דּוֹדֵךְ מִדּוֹד
שֶׁכָּכָה הִשְׁבַּעְתָּנוּ

> What kind of beloved is your beloved,
> O most beautiful among women?
> What kind of beloved is your beloved,
> That thus you adjure us?

---

21. In her dream they were separated.
22. Stoop-van Paridon, *Song of Songs*, 283.
23. *IBHS*, 325.
24. Mitchell, *Song of Songs*, 1152.
25. Pope, *Song of Songs*, 528. Pope may be accurate in suggesting that the function of the question is for emphasis. Bloch and Bloch (*Song of Songs*, 183) state, "The question-answer format is purposeful, serving to emphasize the message." While emphasis may be the rhetorical function of the interrogative, this question does not seem to function as a rhetorical question.
26. Arnold and Choi, *Guide to Biblical Hebrew Syntax*, 187.

To aid in their search for the woman's lost lover, the daughters need additional information. So they ask the woman two questions that, when answered, will supposedly supply them with enough information for them to identify her lover from among all the other males they may encounter in their search. While Bloch and Bloch are correct that these two interrogatives serve a rhetorical function (i.e., they provide the woman with the opportunity to sing his praise in the following *wasf*, 5:10–16), this should not be mistaken as an identification of these interrogatives as rhetorical questions.[27] Leland Ryken defines a rhetorical question as "a figure of speech in which the writer asks a question whose answer is so obvious that it is left unstated; a question asked not to elicit information, but for the sake of effect, usually an emotional effect."[28] What the woman will say in answer to the daughter's question is far from obvious especially for the audience. This is especially true in light of their midnight conflict. While this interrogative is used emotionally, it is not a RQ. Exum notes well the rhetorical effect of their questions from the female lover's POV: "Their question is all the provocation she needs for her paean."[29] The lengthy *wasf* answers their question (5:10–16), and the context gives ample evidence that these inquiries from the daughters of Jerusalem are simple interrogatives.

The next and the last simple interrogative in the book is found again in a series of two questions and is once again heard from the mouths of the daughters of Jerusalem.

אָ֚נָה הָלַ֣ךְ דּוֹדֵ֔ךְ
הַיָּפָ֖ה בַּנָּשִׁ֑ים
אָ֚נָה פָּנָ֣ה דוֹדֵ֔ךְ
וּנְבַקְשֶׁ֖נּוּ עִמָּֽךְ׃

> Where has your beloved gone,
> O most beautiful among women?
> Where has your beloved turned,
> That we may seek him with you?

These two questions in parallel echo the two questions that began this lost/searching/found section (5:1—6:3). It is possible that the daughters'

---

27. Bloch and Bloch, *Song of Songs*, 184.
28. Ryken, *Words of Delight*, 362.
29. Exum, *Song of Songs*, 202.

question in 5:9 has helped the female lover find her beloved as evidenced by her answer in 6:2–3. At this point she knows where he is. While there is discussion as to the exact identification of the garden in which the male lover is found, it is obvious that the two location questions are answered. Thus, since the answer is given, these are simple interrogatives. Exum does not make such a distinction and labels 6:1 (and 5:9) as rhetorical.[30] Ogden and Zogbo observe, based on the context of these questions, that these are true questions and are not rhetorical in nature: "Even though the answer in verse 2 is not what we expect, this is a true question, not a rhetorical one."[31] While not classified as rhetorical questions, they do have a rhetorical function. Longman notes the rhetorical function of these interrogatives "as a catalyst to the speeches of the woman, so in the next verse she begins to describe the place where the man fled."[32] Roberts also believes the interrogative serves structurally to open this section and also perhaps as a marker for the change of speakers.[33]

A Rhetorical Word concerning Simple Interrogatives

Although these four verses (1:7b, c; 3:3; 5:9; 6:1) are classified as simple interrogatives, this does not mean they are of less literary importance than the RQs. These interrogatives not only seek information for the speaker but they demonstrate to the reader the woman's desire to be with her beloved in an imaginative way (1:7a, b). The woman could have simply said, "I want to be with you in the field." But the interrogative plays on the theme of desire without actually so stating. This veiling or double entendre is a common literary convention used throughout the Song and is accomplished by the author's use of metaphor, simile, and even here, the interrogative. The interrogative in 3:3 is an implied question. There are no interrogative pronouns or particles that signal the interrogative. The interrogative is implied by context.[34] Again, this interrogative is used to show the woman's desire for her beloved.[35] The

---

30. Ibid., 209–10.
31. Ogden and Zogbo, *Handbook on Song of Songs*, 169.
32. Longman, *Song of Songs*, 175.
33. Roberts, *Let Me See Your Form*, 422.
34. See NASB, NKJ, KJV, RSV, NRS. The LXX does have an adverb (μή) that expects a negative answer. This would suppose a question.
35. If Dorsey ("Literary Structuring in the Song of Songs," 86) and others are correct that there are separate sections in this song, and if Dorsey's structure is correct, then the

interrogatives in 5:9 and 6:1 are placed in the mouth of the "daughters of Jerusalem." The daughters' question in 5:9 allows the woman to begin the *wasf* of her beloved in 5:10–16. This question and answer provides a smooth and seamless transition from the woman's statement in 5:8 to the physical description of her beloved that follows. This question gives the woman ample reason to sing her beloved's qualities. The question in 6:1 indicates that the daughters of Jerusalem are persuaded to help her find him by the woman's physical description of her lover.[36] This man is worth searching for!

Although the simple interrogative seeks information, it functions within this Song deeper than simply gathering certain data. It is used for literary variety, to expose emotion, to transition from one point to another, and to provide structural elements. A deeper investigation of the "simple" interrogative could prove to be a productive avenue of future study, but this lies outside the scope of this work.

Identifying Exclamatory Interrogatives

The next classification of interrogatives found in the SoS is the exclamatory interrogative. According to Van der Merwe, Naude, and Kroeze, these interrogatives "function as exclamations to introduce the nature of a particular state of affairs or events. Speakers often use such constructions to express *their disappointment, satisfaction* or *amazement*."[37] As noted previously by Waltke and O' Connor, these interrogatives "must be recognized in context."[38]

The first two exclamatory interrogatives are found in 4:10.

מַה־יָּפוּ דֹדַיִךְ אֲחֹתִי כַלָּה
מַה־טֹּבוּ דֹדַיִךְ מִיַּיִן
וְרֵיחַ שְׁמָנַיִךְ מִכָּל־בְּשָׂמִים׃

> How beautiful is your love, my sister, *my* bride!
> How much better is your love than wine,

---

question of 3:3 is pivotal. Dorsey sees the interrogative of 3:3 as the middle of a chiastic structure of section 3:1–5.

36. The interrogative in 5:9 and 6:1 may be chiastic in form with the *wasf* in the middle being the highlighted section of this song.

37. Van der Merwe, Naude, and Kroeze, *Biblical Hebrew Reference Grammar*, 327. Italics are original.

38. *IBHS*, 321.

And the fragrance of your oils than all *kinds* of spices!

Here two parallel interrogatives are found in conjunction with two Qal perfect verbs that function adjectivally. Based on the context, it is clear in this verse that the male lover is not seeking information. Because of his intimate experience with his lover, he exclaims that her love is better than wine! While Stoop-van Paridon is incorrect in assigning this statement to sometime in the future, she captures the exclamatory aspect of the interrogative מָה.

> How pleasant your caresses will be,
> How delightful your caresses will be more than wine.[39]

Hess observes that the male is providing "an enthusiastic assessment of the lover's lovemaking."[40] Exum remarks that the male lover in this verse is intensifying his lover's remarks from 1:2–4.[41] Bloch and Bloch recognize the interrogative as a "common biblical formula of admiration."[42] Because her beauty and sexual prowess are more intoxicating than wine, the male lover uses the double exclamation with מָה to communicate his overwhelming emotions for his companion.

The second verse that has an exclamatory interrogative is 7:2.

מַה־יָּפוּ פְעָמַיִךְ בַּנְּעָלִים בַּת־נָדִיב
חַמּוּקֵי יְרֵכַיִךְ כְּמוֹ חֲלָאִים מַעֲשֵׂה יְדֵי אָמָּן:

How beautiful are your feet in sandals, O prince's daughter!
The curves of your hips are like jewels, the work of the hands
of an artist.

This occurrence is similar to the one previously noted in 4:10. However, this exclamatory interrogative is found individually and not in parallel with another. Stoop-van Paridon recognizes the construction as an exclamation and not a simple interrogative.[43] Bergant remarks that the man is "extolling the beauty of her feet." While there is much discussion and little consensus concerning the interpretation of פַּעַם, it is clear the

---

39. Stoop-van Paridon, *Song of Songs*, 225.
40. Hess, *Song of Songs*, 143.
41. Exum, *Song of Songs*, 172.
42. Bloch and Bloch, *Song of Songs*, 175. Also see 7:2, 7.
43. Stoop-van Paridon, *Song of Songs*, 364.

male lover is exclaiming that some part of the woman (or some activity she is doing) is beautiful. The disagreement over the interpretation of פַּעַם does not detract from the exclamatory use of the interrogative מָה. Hess observes, "The expression 'how beautiful' (*mah yāpû*) occurs only three times in the Bible, all of them in the Song and all used by the male to describe the love and beauty of his lover: 4:10; 7:2, 7 (7:1, 6 Eng.). Only in this occurrence, however, does the expression refer to a physical feature."[44] Ogden and Zogbo comment that this expression opens with the same exclamation as 4:10.[45] It is clear that this expression is one of amazement concerning her beauty and not an inquiry looking for information.

The third instance of the exclamatory interrogative is found in 7:7. Once again, the interrogative is paired.

מַה־יָּפִית וּמַה־נָּעַמְתְּ
אַהֲבָה בַּתַּעֲנוּגִים׃

How beautiful and how delightful you are,
Love, with your charms![46]

Once again, an exclamation escapes from the lips of the male lover. It is introduced by the interrogative מָה. According to Stoop-van Paridon, "the exclamation of Solomon in this verse ... shows his enthusiasm for the *shulammite*."[47] Hess observes the interrogative construction as two exclamatory phrases.[48] Ogden and Zogbo note the twofold repetition of the interrogative and suggest that they are "emphasizing how deeply the young man's feelings are affected."[49] Exum believes this is a summary exclamation of the male lover's detailed description of his female lover's body.[50] These exclamations with the introductory מָה are clear examples of exclamatory interrogatives.

---

44. Hess, *Song of Songs*, 212.

45. Ogden and Zogbo, *Handbook on Song of Songs*, 195.

46. I have chosen to drop the "my" (cf. NASB) since it is not present in the BH. Hess (*Song of Songs*, 219) suggests that אַהֲבָה is used as a vocative to address his female lover.

47. Stoop-van Paridon, *Song of Songs*, 389.

48. Hess, *Song of Songs*, 219.

49. Ogden and Zogbo, *Handbook on Song of Songs*, 202.

50. Exum, *Song of Songs*, 238.

The last exclamatory interrogative is found in 8:1.

מִ֤י יִתֶּנְךָ֙ כְּאָ֣ח לִ֔י
יוֹנֵ֖ק שְׁדֵ֣י אִמִּ֑י
אֶֽמְצָאֲךָ֤ בַחוּץ֙ אֶשָּׁ֣קְךָ֔
גַּ֖ם לֹא־יָב֥וּזוּ לִֽי׃

Oh that you were like a brother to me
Who nursed at my mother's breasts.
If I found you outdoors, I would kiss you;
No one would despise me, either.

This exclamatory interrogative is spoken by the female lover to her love. While Waltke and O'Connor note, "Exclamatory . . . questions in מי must be recognized from context," they do suggest that "There are patterns associated with each group. Exclamatory questions usually have a non-perfective verb and the sense is desiderative."[51] In this case the verb נָתַן is a Qal imperfect. The sense is clearly desiderative since she desires to have him as a brother and thus be able to kiss him in public without the fear of breaking cultural taboos. Stoop-van Paridon captures the exclamatory nature with her translation, "'O!, that you might'" or 'O!, that you were.'"[52] Bloch and Bloch note that this introductory phrase "is commonly used to introduce a fervent wish."[53] Once again, this is an example of an exclamatory interrogative and not a simple or rhetorical question.

A Rhetorical Word concerning Exclamatory Interrogatives

The exclamatory interrogatives of Song 4:10; 7:2; and 7:7 consist of the interrogative מָה and an adjective.[54] The exclamatory interrogative in 8:1 is made up of the מִי interrogative and an imperfect verb.[55] As Waltke explains, the exclamatory interrogative is recognized in context. It is clear from the context of these verses that the author intends the exclamatory use of the interrogative, not the simple or rhetorical use. Thus the man

---

51. *IBHS*, 321.

52. Stoop-van Paridon, *Song of Songs*, 414.

53. Bloch and Bloch, *Song of Songs*, 209. This construction is prevalent in Job to show strong desire: Job 6:8; 11:5; 13:5; 14:4, 13; 19:23; 31:31, 35.

54. Waltke notes that the exclamatory questions with מָה may involve either an adjective or verb (*IBHS*, 326).

55. Ibid.

in his strong declaration of his beloved's beauty and love spoke all these exclamations (4:10; 7:2, 7). The use of the exclamatory interrogative in these verses extols the beauty of his beloved and heightens the emotional feelings of the audience in such a way that readers vicariously experience her beauty and love above all others (and his deep emotion for her). The woman speaks the exclamatory interrogative in 8:1, and it too functions to heighten the emotional drama of the scene before the reader. Once the reader "hears" the exclamatory interrogative, he or she has an opportunity to agree with the character who makes the exclamation and thus is drawn deeper into the Song on an emotional level. A deeper rhetorical investigation of the exclamatory interrogative could prove to be a productive field for future study, but it lies outside the scope of this work.

DEFINING AND IDENTIFYING RHETORICAL QUESTIONS

Robert Koops distinguishes simple interrogatives from rhetorical questions by stating:

> In an ordinary conversation, then, a question is assumed to be a request for information. When it becomes evident to the hearer that the "information" in question is already well known to both of them, he understands that the speaker must be deliberately flouting the expected pattern, and thereby doing something else, namely, emphasizing a point.[56]

While Koops may state the purpose for a rhetorical question too narrowly as always emphasizing a point, he does correctly observe that RQs are literary devices that break the expected literary pattern. Thus, it is important to recognize the rhetorical purpose of the author when the expected literary pattern is broken by the unexpected. Although Ryken defines a RQ in light of a typical emotional impact, Wilfred Watson defines it without reference to the emotional component: "A rhetorical question is basically the posing of a question which requires no answer since either the speaker or the listener (or both of them) already knows the answer."[57] Based on these definitions, the RQ is actually a statement dressed as a question.[58] It is a question that covertly (and imaginatively)

---

56. Koops, "Rhetorical Questions," 418.

57. Ryken, *Words of Delight*, 362; Watson, *Classical Hebrew Poetry*, 338.

58. An emotional one. Waltke comments that the aim of a RQ is "not to gain information but to give information with passion" (*IBHS*, 322). As it has already been noted, Ryken recognizes the emotional tone of the RQ as well. De Regt ("Functions and Implications," 362) comments that the RQ makes an emphatic statement which I

makes a specific point by the author.⁵⁹ But the RQ is more than just a statement as Lénart J. de Regt notes: "An RQ is really something more than an emphatic statement: it includes the implication that the audience knows the answer, and not only the answer, but also that the audience will be fully cognizant of this implication."⁶⁰ The same dynamic is in play in Prov 5:20 in the area of sexual purity. Here the answer to the double RQ "For why should you, my son, be exhilarated with an adulteress, And embrace the bosom of a foreigner?" is obvious to the audience. According to Kaiser, the only question that remains is "Is the course of action obvious to the son who stands in the place of the reader when he finds him or herself confronted with sexual temptation?"⁶¹ De Regt observes that through the employment of the RQ "a speaker or writer may thus identify with the audience by implying that the audience will obviously agree."⁶²

It is important to consider this possibility regarding RQs in the Song of Songs to combine elements of these definitions. Ryken is insightful to note the emotional effect of the RQ. Watson has a good basic working definition of RQs, recognizing the fact that the answer is already known and, in fact, the question is really a statement. De Regt notes well the audience's cognizance of the implication of the answer to the RQ.⁶³

---

would argue is or could be an emotional statement. Whether an RQ *always* makes an emotional statement would be a matter for further study. With the possible exception of 8:8, it could be argued that all of the RQs of this song are emotional statements dressed as questions.

59. Brueggemann ("Jeremiah's Use of Rhetorical Questions," 371) notes the prophet Jeremiah uses the RQ "as a vehicle for confrontation of the most intense kind." This dynamic is seen clearly in the last chapters of Job where God overwhelms his suffering servant with over seventy RQs to demonstrate that Job should not be questioning the divine plan. Writing on the implications of the divine rhetorical dialogue (or monologue) with Job, Alter (*Art of Biblical Poetry*, 86) remarks, "The clear implication is that if you can't play in My league, you should not have the nerve to ask questions about the rules of the game."

60. De Regt, ("Functions and Implications," 362). Kaiser ("True Marital Love," 109) states that "the only logical conclusion that one can reasonably make" is " the God who has given the gift of human sexuality is the One who has the right to expect righteous living in that same area."

61. Ibid.

62. De Regt, "Functions and Implications," 362.

63. It may be important to note the audience's cognition of the answer to the RQ may only be fully realized *after* the question is made in context. This complete cognition is not something the audience possesses before the text in which the RQ is read or

In the SoS the biblical author uses RQs as a figure of speech (a declarative statement dressed as interrogative) for a variety of reasons. De Regt suggests, "A rhetorical question is used to convey or call attention to information, expressing the speaker's attitude, opinions, etc."[64] Rhetorical questions are also used to involve the audience emotionally in the Song. The use of RQs moves them to the author's point of view.[65] He desires to have his audience participate in this celebration of the physical aspect of love (in their own lives and at the proper time). This is the authorial purpose throughout the Song.[66]

While Watson is speaking about poetic devices in general, it is safe to assume (since RQs are part of the biblical author's poetic repertoire) that they also serve another purpose. Watson remarks, "The chief function of a repertoire of poetic devices is to facilitate smooth, imaginative verse composition and so maintain the attention of a potentially critical audience."[67] While the attention span of the original audience is unknown, Watson's observation about the audience may be another reason for the author's use of RQs. Watson writes that the audience "must be charmed by the familiar, yet aroused and captivated by the unexpected."[68] While not every RQ of the SoS may have been employed to "charm," "arouse," or "captivate," it is certain that some had those exact effects on the audience. Overall, the RQ is one of the poetic devices the author of the Song uses not simply to demonstrate his artistic ability but to encourage the biblical reader to adopt its theological message.[69] For as De Regt observes, "RQs are thus likely to be found in contexts where rhetoric is

---

heard. Brueggemann ("Jeremiah's Use of Rhetorical Questions") notes Jeremiah uses RQs to challenge his readers/listeners to an opposite opinion: the RQ functions to expose an existing deficiency in the heart and mind of Jeremiah's audience.

64. De Regt, "Functions and Implications," 362.

65. Writing concerning the genre of Amos, Bramer ("The Genre of Amos," 57) makes the point that the prophet uses rhetorical questions "to engage the thinking of his audience."

66. It is important to note that the RQ is only one of the literary devices that the biblical author uses to involve his audience in the Song and thus move them to his way of thinking and living.

67. Watson, *Classical Hebrew Poetry*, 33. While the emotional tenor of the original audience of the Song is unknown, it is clear that the prophets of Israel used RQs to direct a critical audience back to God. (cf. Jeremiah, Amos and Malachi).

68. Ibid.

69. Parsons ("Guidelines," 408) observes that rhetorical questions are part of the author's poetic repertoire of literary and rhetorical devices.

desired for accomplishing *persuasion*."⁷⁰ This would be especially needed in the SoS where there are no commands or appeals to torah. Persuasion to the divine author's theological point of view would have to come not from obedience to a set of commands or an instruction but from the art of persuasion, that is, rhetoric. Rhetorical questions are part of the literary arsenal of the biblical poet. There are eight verses in the SoS that contain questions that should be classified as rhetorical interrogatives: 1:7d; 3:6; 5:3; 6:10; 7:1; 8:4, 5, 8.⁷¹

Identifying RQs

In this section the various rhetorical questions will be identified. The identification process will suggest the identity of the speaker, the identity of the one being "questioned," the topic of the RQ, the answer to the RQ (either assumed or explained), and the form of the RQ.

THE FIRST RQ (1:7)

The first RQ is found in 1:7:

הַגִּידָה לִּי שֶׁאָהֲבָה נַפְשִׁי
אֵיכָה תִרְעֶה
אֵיכָה תַּרְבִּיץ בַּצָּהֳרָיִם
שַׁלָּמָה אֶהְיֶה כְּעֹטְיָה
עַל עֶדְרֵי חֲבֵרֶיךָ׃

> Tell me, you who my soul loves,
> Where do you graze?
> Where do you lie down at noon?
> For why should I be like one who veils herself
> Besides the flock of your companions?⁷²

The form of this first RQ is a single interrogative in series with the two simple interrogatives that preceded it. Although there is a difference in

---

70. De Regt, "Discourse Implications of Rhetorical Questions," 52.

71. While not arguing the presence of rhetorical questions in the SoS, Guillaume ("Rhetorical Questions," 16) questions the presence of RQs in Job 2:10 and Jonah 4:11, which are viewed by most scholars to contain RQs. Since these questions are unmarked by the introductory interrogative ה, he believes it is a "grave treachery" to translate those passages as such. Guillaume by his own admission is in the minority concerning this position.

72. Translation is the author's.

the types of interrogatives used in this verse (two simple interrogatives and one rhetorical), the tricolon structure of the interrogative is evident.[73] Stoop-van Paridon declares this interrogative to be a direct question but recognizes its rhetorical function as well.[74]

In this RQ the speaker is the woman, as indicated by the feminine Qal participle, כְּעֹטְיָה "the one who veils herself." She poses her question to "the one whom her soul loved" (1:7a), which is the male beloved throughout the SoS.

This RQ is preceded by two parallel interrogatives that seek to discover her beloved's noon resting location so she is able rendezvous with him (1:7c). The RQ is introduced with, שַׁלָּמָה which is translated with the interrogative phrase "for why." The male beloved answers her first two inquiries in 1:8, telling her to follow the footprints of the flock. But the third question, introduced by, שַׁלָּמָה is left unanswered. Ogden and Zogbo state categorically, "While the two previous questions are true requests for information, this one is a rhetorical question."[75] Longman notes that if the woman did not know the way, she would have to go out veiled and "she will have to go from shepherd tent to shepherd tent looking for him, and she assumes that he does not want her poking around the tents of his male friends and possible rivals."[76] This negative response is the unspoken answer to the RQ. Waltke comments, "In some cases the למה is used in a quasi-rhetorical way, introducing an undesirable alternative."[77] Waltke's observation regarding לָמָה supports Longman's interpretation of this verse. To have his beloved go searching for him among other males is definitely an undesirable alternative. Therefore, the unanswered answer to this rhetorical question in context would be from the woman's point of view something like "Of course you would not want me to go searching for you in some other guys' tents!" Ogden and Zogbo suggest that the woman may be trying to make her lover jealous and may be rhetorically asking in effect, "You don't want your friends to see me, do you? (Otherwise, they might be attracted to me!)"[78]

---

73. BDB (554) remarks that the interrogative with the imperfect often introduces the rhetorical question. The parallel tricolon is based on the interrogative.

74. Stoop-van Paridon, *Song of Songs*, 62, 65.

75. Ogden and Zogbo, *Handbook on Song of Songs*, 34.

76. Longman, *Song of Songs*, 100.

77. *IBHS*, 324.

78. Ogden and Zogbo, *Handbook on Song of Songs*, 35.

Hess chooses to answer the rhetorical question in his translation: "Lest I become like a cloaked woman, Besides the flocks of your friends."[79]

Despite the differences in the modern translation theory of various scholars (i.e., to either maintain the rhetorical question or to answer the rhetorical question in translation), there may be legitimate grounds to maintain the rhetorical aspect of the interrogative in this verse.

THE SECOND RQ (3:6)

The second rhetorical question is found in 3:6:

מִי זֹאת עֹלָה מִן־הַמִּדְבָּר
כְּתִימֲרוֹת עָשָׁן
מְקֻטֶּרֶת מוֹר וּלְבוֹנָה
מִכֹּל אַבְקַת רוֹכֵל׃

What is this coming up from the wilderness
Like columns of smoke,
Perfumed with myrrh and frankincense,
With all scented powders of the merchant?

It is a single interrogative not in any parallel structure. The contextual form is somewhat unique in that it introduces an extended simile.[80] There is spirited discussion as to who is the speaker in 3:6. The NASB has the RQ coming from the female chorus. The NIV believes it is the question of the young woman. There is some evidence to suggest that the NIV is correct. First, since it is the woman who is speaking in 3:5, there is no evidence to suggest that a change of speakers has taken place. Second, the woman addresses the chorus, the daughters of Jerusalem, at the end of this section in 3:11. No other speaker in the SoS ever addresses the daughters except the female lover. If 3:11 is a continuation of 3:6, then the woman is still the speaker. Third, in 2:7 the female lover makes the daughters of Jerusalem take an oath and then immediately speaks of her beloved coming to her as a ga-

---

79. Hess, *Song of Songs*, 59. Also Pope, *Song of Songs*, 330; Murphy, *Song of Songs*, 130; Goulder, *Song of Fourteen Songs*, 10. Ogden and Zogbo (*Handbook on Song of Songs*, 35) note this as a possible translation alternative. However, such a translation robs the literary device of its original rhetorical feature. It was written as a rhetorical question. On the other hand, De Waard ("Hebrew Rhetoric," 249) does suggest that answering the RQ may have to be the case if the receptor language does not share the implication of the rhetorical question. Exum makes no comment on the third interrogative in this verse.

80. Watson, *Classical Hebrew Poetry*, 260.

zelle (2:8–9). In 3:5 the daughters are again made to swear an oath, and there is another description of the male beloved coming, but this time as royalty. This evidence supports the view that the RQ is coming from the mouth of the female lover. Based on the woman's address to the daughters in 3:5 and the woman's command in 3:11, the audience of this RQ is the daughters of Jerusalem (3:5) or Zion (3:11).[81]

There is also discussion as to what the introductory מִי refers. Generally speaking, scholars see it referring to a thing or a person. Stoop-van Paridon believes that there are "no grammatical objections to applying מִי to both people and things."[82] So it could refer to either. Whatever the object or person being described, Stoop-van Paridon is correct to label the interrogative as a rhetorical question and to note along with Waltke that it is "a rhetorical question which 'aims not to give information but to give information with passion.'"[83]

The topic of this rhetorical question is the identity of the magnificent-smelling object that is coming up from the wilderness.[84] At first this object could only be described with a simile, namely, as columns of smoke. But sight is not necessarily important at this stage in attempting to identify the object. Sight is not important because it is the aroma of the object that grabs the attention of the woman (3:6). While the daughters may be clueless as to the identity of the object making its way up out of the wilderness (and to the forefront of the imagination of the reader), the identity of the object is already known. The object's identity is apparently obvious since the answer is introduced with the Hebrew הִנֵּה (3:7).[85] A possible way to translate this answer to her RQ might be,

---

81. And by extension the reader. This concept of the reader as the audience of the rhetorical question will be covered in chapter 4.

82. Stoop-van Paridon, *Song of Songs*, 157.

83. Ibid., 159.

84. Bergant (*Song of Songs*, 38) and Hess (*Song of Songs*, 109) feel it is the woman. However, it would be difficult for the woman to be both the speaker and the object coming up from the wilderness. Bloch and Bloch (*Song of Songs*, 160) see Solomon's bed arising from the wilderness. Exum (*Song of Songs*, 145) believes that what is coming up from the wilderness is Solomon's litter, presumably with the woman's lover in Solomonic disguise in it. Hocking (*Rise Up My Love*, 221) surmises that both Solomon and his bride to be are coming up. While there is much dispute concerning the identities of people and objects from the wilderness, the central theme of this section is the anticipation of the lovers being united once again.

85. *IBHS*, 676. Berlin (*Poetics and Interpretation*, 91) observes that the "basic function of *hinneh* is as an attention-getter.... When it is used in direct discourse it helps the

"Of course, it is the couch of Solomon."[86] Some may argue that since the answer is given in the next verse, this interrogative is not a RQ but a simple interrogative. But as De Regt notes in his study of RQs in the book of Job, "RQs in Job are frequently followed by their answer, given by the speaker." Also, since the speaker asks and answers her own question, this gives ample evidence that this is a RQ. One could also argue that the woman already knows the identity of the object and is simply asking the rhetorical question to build suspense for the reader.[87] Pope comments, "The answer need not be given at all, on the assumption that it is obvious or well-known."[88] While the modern scholar may struggle with identification of a certain feminine pronoun, the original reader, according to Pope's observation, would have recognized the RQ and would have supplied a ready and correct answer.

THE THIRD RQ (5:3)

The third RQ is in a parallel series of two (5:3):[89]

פָּשַׁטְתִּי אֶת־כֻּתָּנְתִּי
אֵיכָכָה אֶלְבָּשֶׁנָּה
רָחַצְתִּי אֶת־רַגְלַי
אֵיכָכָה אֲטַנְּפֵם׃

I have taken off my garment,
How can I put it on *again*?

---

reader zero in on a particular person or event." It also functions to change perspective. Here, the reader's perspective shifts from the woman's adjuration (3:5) to Solomon's couch (3:7). While Berlin has the biblical narrative in focus, her observations hold true for biblical poetry, at least in this case.

86. De Regt, "Functions and Implications," 363.

87. This thought will be developed when the rhetorical aspect is discussed later in this chapter. It could be that the speaker in this section is neither the daughters nor the woman but the author/narrator of the Song. Roberts (*Let Me See Your Form*, 283) suggests, "This segment . . . appears to be narrated by an outside voice." If this is true, then the question is definitely rhetorical since the author or outside voice is omniscient. In addition, this unfolding scene is not an actual procession but a literary creation. Thus, whoever conjured this image (the author or the woman), he/she already knows the identity of the object coming from the wilderness and thus it is a RQ.

88. Pope, *Song of Songs*, 423.

89. The structure of 5:3a, perfect verb-DO-interrogative-imperfect verb, is paralleled in 5:3b. There is also parallelism of sound. Except for the last word of each colon, each word in each colon ends with the same sound.

> I have washed my feet,
> How can I dirty them *again*?

The stage for this RQ is set in 5:2. The speaker of this RQ is the woman and the one being addressed is her beloved. However, the dialogue is imaginary. It is taking place in the woman's mind as she relates her second dream (5:2–6:3; cf. 3:1–4).[90] In this dream the man requests the female to open to him and allow him access to her (5:2). Her response to his erotic request is her rhetorical question. The question conveys more than simply wondering about getting dressed (now that she has disrobed) and the danger of dirtying her freshly washed feet that are tucked into bed! Pope believes the woman is being coy with the intent of teasing her once-absent lover because he is not next to her in bed.[91] Longman conjectures that if coyness is her strategy, it fails because her lover leaves her with the wet latch in her hand (5:6)![92]

Stoop-van Paridon recognizes that the woman's double question is a rhetorical question, but she translates them as exclamations. She dismisses Clines' observation that the interrogative introduces rhetorical questions and may be translated as "how is it possible that? surely it is not possible that."[93] Clines' observation would be the natural understanding of the RQ in context.

These two interrogatives are not the woman's innocent inquiry as to how she should go about granting her lover access once she is in bed. These interrogatives are designed by the woman to dissuade the male lover from pursuing any intimacies with her when she simply did not feel like it (for whatever reason). Both Longman and Pope recognize the double entendre of these RQs.[94] These RQs are employed by the fe-

---

90. All of 5:2—6:1 is a retelling of a dream by the female's lover. In her dream her beloved calls late at night; she rebuffs him; in her dream she suffers for her actions, and still in her dream state she seeks him only to find him right in bed beside her (6:2–3). Provan (*Song of Songs*, 337) may concur when he writes, "the search is unnecessary and the fears that have come to expression in the dream are groundless. The woman knows where her lover is. He was never really lost to her. He is to be found in his own garden (6:2)"

91. Pope, *Song of Songs*, 515. Also Exum, *Song of Songs*, 194. She sees the woman's reply as erotic foreplay.

92. Longman, *Song of Songs*, 166.

93. Stoop-van Paridon, *Song of Songs*, 266. She also places this RQ in the mouth of the male. *DCH* 1:209.

94. Pope, *Song of Songs*, 515; Longman, *Song of Songs*, 166–67.

male lover, not to seek information, but to make a passionate statement. Zogbo and Ogden says of this interrogative, "How could I put it on? is a rhetorical question meaning that she is not willing to put it on again."[95] These RQs communicate the woman's flimsy excuses not to engage in physical intimacies with her amorous love. The woman's answer to her own questions could have been roughly, "Of course I can put my clothes on and walk across my dirty floor but . . . I do not really want to let you into bed with me! But I rather not say that directly." In this case her RQs are strongly worded, negative emotional statements dressed as a question. Her beloved's answer is his appeal to her to reconsider (5:4). However, when she finally jettisons her verbal excuses and decides to entertain her beloved's sexual advances, she discovers too late that her lover has left (5:5–6).

The audience's response to the woman's RQs would have been near incredulous based on the woman's expressed desire thus far in the Song. This is the effect the author desires to have upon his audience. He wants them to feel that the woman's RQs are a poor attempt to hide her reluctance to grant sexual access to her lover. Since the audience agrees that female's RQs are not the correct response to his request, they will not quarrel with the discipline that comes upon the woman at the hands of the night watchmen (5:7).[96]

---

95. Ogden and Zogbo, *Handbook on Song of Songs*, 147.

96. It is important to note that her discipline is not real. It never happens in reality; neither does her refusal occur. It is simply a dream, where she imagines that she refuses her lover. The discipline by the watchmen is part of the dream sequence and is the punishment her own mind inflicts on her for her selfishness. It could be argued based on 6:1–2 that the male lover is in bed with her while she dreams. Once awake they engage in physical intimacy and she is now not refusing! Thus she has no fear of discipline and can confidently exclaim, "I am my beloved's and my beloved is mine, He who pastures *his flock* among the lilies" (6:3). Exum (*Song of Songs*, 201) notes well the possibility of a "double entendre in both 5:2–7 and 6:1–3" and suggests, "She has never really 'lost him.'" Seeing the rhetoric of the RQs in this manner and the subsequent self-imposed discipline as part of the same dream sequence may help Exum recognize that this event may not be as "disturbing" as one thinks. The imaginary discipline is the expected internal response to the RQs (and is self-inflicted by the woman's self-consciousness). This provides the textual justification that Exum (*Song of Songs*, 198) cannot find in the text for such punishment. Also, since this discipline is self-inflicted and is imagery, this segment of the Song cannot be made to support a patriarchal system that suppresses women, nor can it be made to be a negative comment on the author's view of women.

The Fourth RQ (6:10)

The fourth RQ (6:10) is a single RQ:

מִי־זֹאת הַנִּשְׁקָפָה כְּמוֹ־שָׁחַר
יָפָה כַלְּבָנָה
בָּרָה כַּחַמָּה
אֲיֻמָּה כַּנִּדְגָּלוֹת

> Who is this that grows like the dawn,
> As beautiful as the full moon,
> As pure as the sun,
> As awesome as an army with banners?

This is a unique form, for according to De Regt and Brueggemann in their studies of RQs in Job and Jeremiah respectively, RQs are often found in pairs.[97] This RQ begins an extended simile. There are four similes introduced with the particle preposition כְּ, which follow and extend the question.[98]

The speaker of this rhetorical question is the male lover.[99] His topic is the awe-inspiring beauty of his beloved. The man begins to extol her beauty in 6:4 and continues through 6:10. The text does not reveal this woman's identity who rivals the sun and moon for beauty and like celestial bodies inspires a feeling of awe. The reason this unique beauty is not identified is that she does not need to be. It is his beloved! Longman remarks concerning this inquiry, "There is no question as to the answer; it is the woman, the unique one." The description is "mostly in astronomical imagery, which is appropriate because it places her in the heavens

---

97. These RQs in the Song are also single questions: 3:6; 7:1, 8:5, 8.

98. This *wasf* by the male lover of the female beloved begins with three similes in 6:4 and ends with four similes in 6:10. Verse 6:4 concludes with a reference to a "bannered army" and 6:10 ends with the same reference.

99. Stoop-van Paridon (*Song of Songs*, 333) believes the speaker is the female friend of the female protagonist. This is most certainly a minority position. For instance, Exum, Hess, Bergant, Bloch and Bloch, and Ogden and Zogbo all place this rhetorical question in the mouth of the male lover. Longman (*Song of Songs*, 182), Keel (*Song of Songs*, 220) and Murphy (*Song of Songs*, 178) hear this rhetorical question from the lips of the women of the previous verse (6:9). While the quotation of her beauty may be from the lips of the other women, the report of these women's words is from the mouth of the male beloved.

where she looks down on everyone and everything else."[100] She is that beautiful and that unique among all other women.

Since there is no need to answer the interrogative, this is truly a RQ. Ogden and Zogbo observe, "Who is this? introduces a rhetorical question. . . . the focus is on the young woman."[101] Everyone (including the reader) knows "who looks down like the dawn, beautiful like the moon, pure like the sun, awe-inspiring like a bannered army." It is the woman of the Song.[102] Ogden and Zogbo observe that this rhetorical question conveys wonder and amazement.[103] Exum rightly notes that the interrogative in 6:10 is used for "rhetorical effect."[104] Roberts is more specific concerning the rhetorical effect and suggests that the "rhetorical מִי־זֹאת continues the theme of the uniqueness of the woman."[105]

THE FIFTH RQ (7:1)

The fifth RQ (7:1) is a single question:

שׁוּבִי שׁוּבִי הַשּׁוּלַמִּית
שׁוּבִי שׁוּבִי וְנֶחֱזֶה־בָּךְ
מַה־תֶּחֱזוּ בַּשּׁוּלַמִּית
כִּמְחֹלַת הַמַּחֲנָיִם

> Come back, come back, O Shulammite;
> Come back, come back, that we may gaze at you!
> Why should you gaze at the Shulammite,
> As at the dance of the two companies?

The form of this interrogative verse is similar to other RQs of the Song in that it is a single question. What is unique about this RQ is the fourfold repetition of the imperative שׁוּב that introduces the first colon. The second colon begins with the interrogative מַה. The object of the RQ is

---

100. Longman, *Song of Songs*, 182.
101. Ogden and Zogbo, *Handbook on Song of Songs*, 184.
102. Following an allegorical interpretation of the Song, Jenson (*Song of Songs*, 66) believes this "feminine apparition" is Israel.
103. Ogden and Zogbo, *Handbook on Song of Songs*, 184. The authors also suggest to those who translate this text that "if rhetorical questions can convey wonder and amazement (in the receptor language), the translator is urged to preserve the question form."
104. Exum, *Song of Songs*, 222. She also notes the same function for 3:6 and 8:5.
105. Roberts, *Let Me See Your Form*, 463.

straightforward. Stoop-van Paridon recognizes that the interrogative pronoun מַה may be translated in a number of grammatically justifiable ways, one of which is the rhetorical question. She chooses to translate this verse in the following manner with the interrogative and subsequent answer: "*What will you observe in the shulammite? Undoubtedly, or indeed, a dance which concerns two (army) camps*"[106] While her translation may be construed as a simple request for information, it is a rhetorical question since the speaker (according to Stoop-van Paridon, it is the friend or the attendant of the female protagonist) asks and answers her own question. This asking and then answering of her own question is a marker for the rhetorical question (cf. 3:1). If the speaker of the interrogative is different than those calling for the return of the Shulammite in the first line (i.e., the speaker is the female lover), the interrogative is still a RQ since the reason for the gazing is because of her unsurpassed beauty, which has been the subject of the previous RQ in 6:10. Longman recognizes the ambiguities of the verse and suggests the speaker is the Shulammite herself as she questions the audience's desire to look at her: "What is so special about her that they want to gaze at her so intently?"[107] As it has been true throughout the Song, her question is one that needs no answer supplied in the text because it is so readily apparent. It is her beauty that causes all those who see her to gaze so intently and who want to maintain her in their gaze. Ogden and Zogbo remark that if the woman is the speaker of this RQ and the male lover her audience, then "she asks him this question knowing full well that he adores her and enjoys looking at her physical qualities."[108] The following *wasf* (7:2–9) spoken from the man could be the answer to her rhetorical question. One could also argue that the audience is in view since the interrogative is addressed by the masculine plural pronoun (you) and there is no masculine plural group in the Song in view in this cycle.[109] The reader knows full well why she holds the attention of all who behold her. The reply to the RQ is self-evident. "Why should you gaze at the Shulammite?" The unspoken retort is that everyone should gaze at the Shulammite because she is so beautiful to look at! The man's lofty praise of her physical beauty

---

106. Stoop-van Paridon, *Song of Songs*, 359. Italics original.
107. Longman, *Song of Songs*, 193.
108. Ogden and Zogbo, *Handbook on Song of Songs*, 193.
109. This concept will be further investigated in chapter 3 as the relationship between audience and the characters of the Song is analyzed.

previously in 6:4–10 and what follows in 7:2–9 convinces everyone that she is well worth the gaze. This also gives support for this interrogative being categorized as a RQ. While many questions remain concerning this section, there is contextual evidence for recognizing this interrogative as a rhetorical question.

The rhetorical question may come from the Shulammite. However, up to this point in the Song, the woman has not been identified by name or title except by various terms of endearment from her beloved. Here, she is called by the speaker (or speakers) the Shulammite, הַשּׁוּלַמִּית.[110] Stoop-van Paridon, Hess, and Ogden and Zogbo agree that the term *Shulammite* with the article, הַשּׁוּלַמִּית is not a proper name but a title of some sort which has not been explicitly identified as of yet.[111] Whatever the significance of this title, the woman uses it to speak of herself in the third person. This is not unusual since she evidences a self-deprecating attitude in various places in the Song. This self-deprecation allows the male lover to praise her, and/or it allows her to see herself through his eyes (cf. 2:1–2).

The Sixth RQ (8:4)

The sixth RQ is in 8:4. However, the NASB, NKJV, KJV, RSV, and NRSV translate the RQ as a declarative statement and not as an interrogative. For instance, NASB translates the verse:

> I want you to swear,
> O daughters of Jerusalem,
> Do not arouse or awaken *my* love,
> Until she pleases.

These English versions follow the translation pattern of the similar adjuration refrains found in 2:7 and 3:5.[112] In providing translation guidelines

---

110. Stoop-van Paridon (*Song of Songs*, 355) does not believe the Shulammite is the main female voice of the Song. She thinks the term refers to the young women being prepared for Solomon's harem. These women are in the "process of becoming the . . . shulammite." They become the Shulammite "at the moment they are presented to Solomon." This is a minority view.

111. Ibid. Also Hess, *Song of Songs*, 208; Ogden and Zogbo, *Handbook on Song of Songs*, 192. Ogden and Zogbo (ibid., 193) suggest that the Shulammite can be rendered as "your perfect one."

112. The Jewish *Tanakh* also translates the interrogatives as declarative statements as well.

for this verse, Ogden and Zogbo simply refer their readers back to their comments on 2:7 and 3:5.[113] They do not comment on the absence of the two interrogatives in the preceding refrains. The other various English translations follow suit by morphing the interrogatives into declarative statements.[114] In 8:4 there are two interrogatives.

הִשְׁבַּעְתִּי אֶתְכֶם בְּנוֹת יְרוּשָׁלָםִ
מַה־תָּעִירוּ וּמַה־תְּעֹרְרוּ אֶת־הָאַהֲבָה
עַד שֶׁתֶּחְפָּץ

Those who recognize the interrogatives (but do not translate them as such) follow the grammatical notion that מַה can be used to express negation (thus the strong negative command not to arouse or awaken love until the proper time). Longman recognizes the differences among the three refrains and suggests, "We have a *mah* of negation" which makes the "warning stronger and more urgent" by "using a stronger form of negation."[115] This is a legitimate grammatical interpretation. However, as Bergant notes, "Most commentators maintain that *mah* is used here as a negative, thus keeping the sense of the statement the same as the earlier passages. However, a few do insist that it be understood as an interrogative."[116] While Exum, along with Longman, recognizes the possibility that *mah* may be used as a strong negation, she also suggests another possibility:

> On the other hand, perhaps there is a subtle difference in this last adjuration before the climactic affirmation of love in vv. 6–7. If we understand *mâ* in the sense of 'why?' ... then 'why should you arouse or awaken love before it wishes?' becomes a rhetorical question, whose implied answer is, there is no need to since, when it is ready to be aroused, love overwhelms with its force.[117]

---

113. Ibid., 220. Hess (*Song of Songs*, 230–31) makes no observation concerning the double interrogative in 8:4. Garrett ("Song of Songs," 249) notices the absence of the gazelles in this verse but makes no mention of the presence of the interrogatives or the possibility of these being rhetorical questions.

114. While there are two interrogatives in this verse in the LXX (see τί twice), the English translation of the LXX renders them as negative declarative statements, although BDAG (1006) recognizes that τί is an interrogative and may be used in "direct, indirect and rhetorical questions."

115. Longman, *Song of Songs*, 206. Also Mitchell, *Song of Songs*, 1152. Pope, *Song of Songs*, 661.

116. Bergant, *Song of Songs*, 94.

117. Exum, *Song of Songs*, 248.

Concerning this final adjuration, Stoop-van Paridon states quite simply, "The interrogative clause which follows the request can be taken as a rhetorical question." At the same time, she recognizes that "the meaning of the rhetorical question introduced by the interrogative מַה may be loaded negatively."[118] Further she writes, "The formulation of this rhetorical question certainly has negative tendency."[119] With this combined insight of the rhetorical nature of the interrogative and the strong feeling of negation, the following may be a legitimate translation that recognizes the rhetorical dimension of the questions:

I want you to swear, O daughters of Jerusalem,
For why would you arouse or why would you awaken love
before it pleases?[120]

While the text provides no answer as to why love should not be aroused or awakened, the reader answers the rhetorical question with a resounding "No!" This emphatic response follows the expected answer to the negation present in the Hebrew interrogative. Such a strongly negative response is elicited from the reader because the reader has followed this Song from its beginning and recognizes that love is a most powerful emotion. The Song has proven that there is no valid reason to awaken love or arouse such passion before the proper time. While the first-time reader does not know what follows this double rhetorical question, love (because of its immense power, 8:6–7) should not be awakened or aroused until the proper time.

Although this point will be covered in greater depth in the next section, it should be noted that if the rhetorical interrogatives are translated

---

118. Stoop-van Paridon, *Song of Songs*, 422. Also *IBHS*, 326. They state that one of the uses of מַה rhetorically would be one where there is an expectation of a "strongly negative answer." Glickman (*Solomon's Song of Love*, 227) disagrees even though he recognizes that "grammars and lexicons suggest this new word (*mah*) may imply negation." He believes that the *mah* is not one of negation but of "adverbial intensity." He further states that the *mah* is "unlikely introducing the rare rhetorical question."

119. Ibid., 423.

120. While it may not be proper English to translate both interrogatives separately, I chose this manner to give credence to the biblical author's inclusion of this double use of the interrogative as a rhetorical device. Unlike the contemporary practice of morphing the interrogatives of this verse into declarative statements, Gordis (*Song of Songs*, 72) translates and maintains the interrogatives in his SoS commentary: "I adjure you, O, daughters of Jerusalem: Why should you disturb or interrupt our love until it be satiated?"

as declarative statements (even strongly worded negative ones), such a translation may rob the translator of a rhetorical device whose authorial function is purposeful, that is, to see if the reader is following and agreeing with his reasoning. If the double RQ is present (and not massaged into a declarative statement), then the reader has an opportunity to respond. If he responds to the RQ in the negative, then the author has made his point. In short, to ignore the RQs in this verse may be to miss an ancient pedagogical moment that still works today (and is the purpose of the biblical author).

There is little disagreement as to the speaker and audience of these RQs (although Stoop-van Paridon sees the motivation of the speaker differently than most). The RQs in 8:4 are from the lips of the female lover for the ears of the daughters of Jerusalem. To the readers of the Song this refrain has a familiar ring since it is similar to the refrain of 2:7 and 3:5, but the rhetorical purpose is much different.

The Seventh RQ (8:5)

The seventh RQ (8:5) is a single question:

> מִי זֹאת עֹלָה מִן־הַמִּדְבָּר
> מִתְרַפֶּקֶת עַל־דּוֹדָהּ
> תַּחַת הַתַּפּוּחַ עוֹרַרְתִּיךָ
> שָׁמָּה חִבְּלַתְךָ אִמֶּךָ
> שָׁמָּה חִבְּלָה יְלָדַתְךָ

> Who is this coming up from the wilderness,
> Leaning on her beloved?
> Beneath the apple tree I awakened you;
> There your mother was in labor with you,
> There she was in labor *and* gave you birth.

This RQ is not in parallel with any other. There is nothing significant about this form except to note that it stands alone. Keel does note, however, that the interrogative מִי "is emphasized by the repetition of its sound in מִן ('from') and in מִתְרַפֶּקֶת ('leaning')."[121] This RQ is similar to the RQ of 3:6 in form and point of view. In both of these RQs the speaker has the position of viewing an unidentified object coming up

---

121. Keel, *Song of Songs*, 266.

from the wilderness.¹²² The form of the RQ in 3:6 and 8:5 is singular as well. Ogden and Zogbo state succinctly, "At 8.5 we have a rhetorical question echoing 3.6."¹²³

The text does not identify the speaker of this rhetorical question; however, it is probably the daughters of Jerusalem. They are addressed with the female lover's adjuration in 8:4 and thus are the ones who respond. This makes sense, since the daughters are the speakers of other RQs in the Song in response to the woman's comments (cf. 5:9; 6:1). This would be possible as the speaker(s) see an unidentified person coming up from the wilderness "leaning" on her beloved. Since the two main speakers of the Song, the male and female lover, are the unidentified couple seen in the distance, they cannot be the speakers. In view of the fact that they are in the wilderness, they are not on the imaginative stage of the audience and thus cannot be the speakers. Since it is unlikely that the female lover is talking about herself and it is equally unlikely that the male lover is narrating a past event, the speaker (or, better, the speakers) of this RQ are בְּנוֹת יְרוּשָׁלָם. Exum believes this RQ fits best in the mouth of the women of Jerusalem since they are "the only other speakers in the Song" other than the man and the female lover.¹²⁴ Exum's observation also argues against Stoop-van Paridon, who conjectures that the speakers of this RQ are possibly "the guards of the walls."¹²⁵

That this is a RQ is without question since the speaker(s) already knows the answer to the inquiry. The answer to "who is this coming up from the wilderness?" מִי זֹאת עֹלָה מִן־הַמִּדְבָּר, comes in the description of the one who is "leaning on her beloved," מִתְרַפֶּקֶת עַל־דּוֹדָהּ. Ogden and Zogbo state clearly, "The latter phrase indicates that people already know who it is, otherwise they would not know that the person accompanying

---

122. Bergant (*Song of Songs*, 95) observes that the question in 8:5a is also similar to the question in 6:10. While the interrogative and the indefinite pronoun are indeed the same, the similarities cease from that point forward.

123. Ogden and Zogbo, *Handbook on Song of Songs*, 221. Stoop-van Paridon (*Song of Songs*, 425) claims that this verse opens with an "exclamatory interrogative clause." However, in the same paragraph she mentions that it is a rhetorical clause. Her translation of the interrogative clause seems to proceed along the lines of the rhetorical question, since she chooses to punctuate the interrogative with a question mark and not an exclamation point, which one would expect if the clause is truly an exclamatory use of the interrogative. For example, see her translation of the interrogative as exclamatory in 1:15 and 1:16 (ibid., 91–92).

124. Exum, *Song of Songs*, 248. cf. Longman, *Song of Songs*, 208.

125. Stoop-van Paridon, *Song of Songs*, 426.

her was *her beloved.*"[126] While there is no scholarly consensus concerning the speaker of the RQ, the object of the RQ is without a doubt the woman! Stoop-van Paridon argues that "the author clearly indicates that unlike SofS 3.6, here concerns a woman, . . . the female protagonist of the SofS."[127] Concerning the identity of the unknown person leaning on her beloved, Murphy asserts that "here it is clearly the woman who 'comes up from the desert.'"[128] Mitchell observes that the feminine singular demonstrative pronoun, זאת in the clause "who is this?" always refers to the Shulammite.[129] While the RQ is not answered in the text, the attentive reader would answer the interrogative easily: "Of course, the only possible identity of the 'who is this' is the female lover. She is coming up from the wilderness on the arm of her lover." As they leave the wilderness behind, they appear to the audience as a couple. Hess believes this RQ (as well as the one in 3:6) functions in a "theatrical sense."[130] One would assume this means the author uses the RQ as a rhetorical method to bring the couple back onto the stage of the reader. Roberts believes it also may function structurally to open a new section of the Song.[131] The adjuration refrain of 8:4, which closes the preceding section, also gives evidence that this RQ may function to open this new section of the Song (cf. the RQ of 3:6).

The Eighth RQ (8:8)

The eighth rhetorical question is in 8:8:

אָח֥וֹת לָ֙נוּ֙ קְטַנָּ֔ה
וְשָׁדַ֖יִם אֵ֣ין לָ֑הּ
מַֽה־נַּעֲשֶׂה֙ לַאֲחֹתֵ֔נוּ
בַּיּ֖וֹם שֶׁיְּדֻבַּר־בָּֽהּ׃

> We have a little sister,
> And she has no breasts;
> What shall we do for our sister
> On the day when she is spoken for?

---

126. Ogden and Zogbo, *Handbook on Song of Songs*, 223. Bold is original.
127. Stoop-van Paridon, *Song of Songs*, 425.
128. Murphy, *Song of Songs*, 195.
129. Mitchell, *Song of Songs*, 1171.
130. Hess, *Song of Songs*, 235.
131. Roberts, *Let Me See Your Form*, 626.

The form of this RQ is once again a nonparallel, single question. If Dorsey's structuring of the song is correct, this RQ forms the center of his final unit.[132] Longman does not see 8:8 as an obvious rhetorical question.[133] However, it is clear it is a RQ because the speaker already knows the answer. The speakers of the RQ in 8:8 express two options they will follow based on the response of their little sister. These two conditional responses are the possible answer choices to their own question as laid out in 8:9.

> If she is a wall,
> We shall build on her a battlement of silver;
> But if she is a door,
> We shall barricade her with planks of cedar.

While the action of the speakers has to wait for the activity of the "little sister," the fact remains that the speakers of the interrogative know that their response will be one of two options. They will either figuratively build upon her or barricade her. Either way their choice of actions is already determined. They are not seeking information. The speakers asking and then answering their own question is a defining characteristic of a RQ. While it is difficult to say how this interrogative is not "strictly a rhetorical question," Zogbo and Ogden recognize the importance of this interrogative as a literary device. They note that if this BH interrogative which "is not strictly rhetorical" is massaged into a declarative statement in a translation, "it does change the literary style slightly," and "in most languages it will probably be best to retain the question form."[134] While contrary to these authors' observation that such a transition from interrogative to declarative is a "slight change," this interrogative best serves the contemporary audience as a RQ since it is the intended rhetorical device employed by the biblical author.

Typically, scholars attribute this final RQ (8:8) to the brothers of the main female voice of the SoS. However, other potential speakers

---

132. Dorsey, "Literary Structuring in the Song of Songs," 91.
133. Longman, *Song of Songs*, 216.
134. Ogden and Zogbo, *Handbook on Song of Songs*, 236. It is interesting that these authors feel that this interrogative "is not strictly rhetorical, as it leads into and highlights an answer." The RQ of 3:6 surely functions in the same manner, for it leads to the answer in 3:7. They state that the interrogative of 3:6 is a RQ (ibid., 221).

are numerous.[135] Longman, taking the typical position, notes, "Here the brothers speak for the first time, although the woman mentions them in 1:5–6."[136] After eliminating other potential speakers, Stoop-van Paridon concurs and states categorically, "In view of the fact they speak of *our sister* it can only be the brothers of the female protagonist who are the speakers here."[137] Murphy takes a slightly different tack and feels the RQ is from the brothers but the woman quotes their words herself.[138] Garrett, however, feels that the brothers never function as speakers in the SoS:

> Nowhere else in the Song, however, does one find any indication that there is a male chorus functioning as "brothers." This is a result of thinking of Song of Songs as a drama rather than as a Song. . . . One should also add that the plural forms in Song 8:8–9 are fairly clear indicators that these lyrics belong to the chorus. . . . The first person plural forms imply that the chorus is singing.[139]

That the brothers are the speakers is an assumption because the term אָחוֹת "sister" is used in 8:8, which may imply brothers. However, it could as easily imply older sisters. Scholars have assumed that the female lover's brothers are the speakers of this RQ simply because of the single mention earlier (1:8). Since the male gender plays no major role throughout the Song up to this point (except for the male beloved), it is uncharacteristic of the biblical author to give them a speaking part at this critical juncture of the SoS. While there has been talk of shepherds (1:8), mighty men of Israel (3:7), city watchmen (3:3; 5:7), and the male lover's companions (1:7; 8:13), no speech is heard from any of their lips. Also, while there are examples of brothers caring for their sister's purity in the OT (cf. Gen 34), seeing such care in this chapter of the Song may be reading too much into the text of this love poem. Even the mention

---

135. Bloch and Bloch, *Song of Songs*, 214. They point out that various proposals for the potential speaker(s) of this RQ include: "the brothers; a group of suitors; the brothers in 8:8; and the suitors in 8:9; the girls of Jerusalem; the young man; the Shulammite, quoting an earlier speech by her brothers." Mitchell (*Song of Songs*, 1237) believes the speakers are brothers but not the brothers of the main female voice of the SoS. He thinks that "the most likely speakers of 8:8–9 are brothers that belong to a family other than the Shulammite."

136. Longman, *Song of Songs*, 215. cf. Bergant, *Song of Songs*, 100.

137. Stoop-van Paridon, *Song of Songs*, 445.

138. Murphy, *Song of Songs*, 198.

139. Garrett, "Song of Songs," 259.

of the "sons of my mother" is less than endearing (since she did not call them "my brothers," 1:6). This term does not communicate the familial feelings that demonstrate that she feels they are concerned with her purity since they sent her out to the vineyards alone. This would surely open her up to sexual attack (1:6; cf. Deut 22:25–27). Exum also believes the brothers cannot be the speakers of this RQ either as the direct speakers or as quoted ones:

> The problem with this view is that it appeals to a "story" that lies outside the poem in order to account for what is being said; it invents a plot where none exists. The woman's brothers appear in only one verse of the Song. Not only do they never speak, they are never spoken to. To assign to them a speaking part, even in the form of a quoted speech, is to give them an important role in the Song that the text does not warrant.[140]

Since the speakers are mentioned in the first person plural and the only speakers who are a plurality (other than the couple themselves) throughout the SoS are the daughters of Jerusalem, it is probably the simplest explanation to see the speakers of this RQ as the daughters. Since the daughters have spoken prior to this, it is not unusual to hear their voices near the conclusion of the Song. Having the daughters speak here allows this dialogue to be the concluding interaction between the woman and her entourage, which has functioned as her sounding board throughout the Song. While Exum does not hold to this position, she does state, "That the women of Jerusalem should speak now—at that very point when the poem has reached its climax in the affirmation of the strength of love (vv. 6–7)—is very much in keeping with the way they function elsewhere: to remind us, by their presence, that the poem is addressed to us."[141] Exum captures one of the rhetorical aspects of how the biblical author uses the daughters of Jerusalem: they stand in for the audience in the poem. Since the audience is not actually in the Song as a character or voice, the daughters are the ones who allow the woman

---

140. Exum, *Song of Songs*, 256.

141. Ibid., 257. Exum assumes the speaker is the woman herself and the "little sister" is a hypothetical example. However, Exum does not explain why the woman would apply the first person common plural when her lover does not seem to be on the imaginative stage of the audience. He is missing in these verses. His absence is evidenced in his response in 8:13. If the couple is together, he would not have to be listening for her voice (which signals her approach; cf. 2:8), nor would she have to ask him to hurry to her (8:14).

to share what she wants the audience to know and feel. In addition, the daughters function to change the direction of the Song (5:9; 6:1; 7:1; 8:5, 8). Since the Song may climax with the woman's speech in 8:5–7, then a change of direction may be a literary necessity to help move the Song to its conclusion.

If the speakers of this RQ are the daughters of Jerusalem, then they are also the audience in the Song, since they ask (8:8) and answer their own question (8:9). Mitchell observes well, "Since the verb is first person (plural), the speakers are also the subjects: they are asking what they themselves must do."[142] However, as Exum observes, their presence reminds the reader that the "poem is addressed to us," the audience.[143] This rhetorical usage of the daughters of Jerusalem will be investigated further in chapter 4.

Typically, scholars view the topic of this RQ (and its answer) as the sexual purity of the sister. The speakers are concerned with maintaining the sexual purity of their sister once she becomes physically and sexually mature. Seeing the brothers as the speakers of this RQ and the guardian of the woman's honor, Hess remarks, "The brothers remain watchful to guarantee that her honor is not compromised and that her beauty is adorned in the best way possible."[144] Stoop-van Paridon believes the brothers are not necessarily protecting their sister but their own pockets! She feels the woman (portrayed as the "little sister" in 8:8) is not ready for marriage and thus the brothers have to find a way to make her ready so they would not lose the bride price. She believes that putting the woman alone in the field was the plan of the brothers to get the fine stipulated in Deut 22:28. By her reasoning, the brothers of the Shulammite wanted her raped! The reason for such a despicable plan was because the woman was actually not physically or sexually ready for marriage (8:8). Thus, the brother might lose the bride price. However, all economic profit was not lost if she was sexually violated in the field.[145]

Garrett follows the same general theme of the sexual purity of the young girl except he hears the RQ coming from the mouth of the daughters. He sees the possibility of her being a door or wall as both positive

---

142. Mitchell, *Song of Songs*, 1238.

143. Exum, *Song of Songs*, 257.

144. Hess, *Song of Songs*, 244. Cf. Bergant, *Song of Songs*, 100. Mitchell, *Song of Songs*, 1239.

145. Stoop-van Paridon, *Song of Songs*, 446.

metaphors which refer to her guaranteed sexual purity.[146] Based on the textual evidence, it may be best simply to see the "little sister" as a literary creation of the biblical author and not in familial relationship with any character (or voice) in the Song. The "little sister" of the daughters is a rhetorical device that introduces the female lover's response in 8:10. "She" is also the object of the RQ to which the audience relates. Like the daughters, the audience would answer the rhetorical interrogative in the self-same way: they would seek to adorn their own daughters for their future marriage while at the same time seek to protect their virginity. When the audience agrees with the daughters' answer, it demonstrates that the Song has taught them well and that the rhetorical nature of the interrogative has worked for the author.

There is an unusual twist to this RQ because the woman in an offhanded way responds to the RQ as well in 8:10. The woman seemingly answers the RQ by putting herself in the place of the grown-up or sexually mature "little sister." She explains to the daughters that she is a "wall" and that she possesses "towers" (cf. battlement, 8:9), that is, her sexually mature breasts. Her choosing to use key words from the RQ (and answer) may signal a sense of irony in that the speakers' concern for sexual purity and adornment in her case is unfounded. She did keep herself as a "wall." Alternatively, her reply may suggest that when she was young, she was protected and adorned. Because of that loving oversight and her own desire to remain pure, she now reaps the rewards of purity and sensual beauty, the love of her committed lover.

RHETORICAL FUNCTIONS OF THE RQS

John Callow makes the point, "The author of the Song wrote *to communicate*; he had a purpose which he sought to achieve by writing the Song."[147] Callow further notes that the author achieves his purpose by employing dialogue between the man and the woman.[148] If the point of the author of the SoS is achieved by this intimate discourse between the couple, then one can reasonably assume that the literary devices in the dialogue such as RQs aid the author in making his point. The author's use of RQ in the dialogue of the Song is there for specific purposes. While not speaking

---

146. Garrett, "Song of Songs," 26.
147. Callow, "Units and Flow," 473. Italics are original.
148. Ibid.

concerning the importance of the RQ in the SoS, Brueggemann does make an excellent point of the use of the RQ in Jeremiah when he states that the RQ "is a conscious development and important to the intent of the prophet."[149] If such a literary device is important in communicating the intent of the author of this OT prophetic work, then it is a valid endeavor to pursue the importance of this literary device in the SoS. For the author of the Song also wishes to persuade his readers of his position and one of his tools of persuasion is the RQ. While Greenstein does not mention the RQ specifically, he does capture the importance of studying the manner in which the author of the biblical text endeavors to move his audience:

> The truly significant question is: In what ways do the devices of Biblical poetry control the audience's perception of the message? In what ways does Hebrew verse attract, appeal to, and move its audience? Certainly the ancient Hebrew poets sought to affect their hearers, perhaps to amuse them as well. If the use of parallelism, meter, word-pairs, and the like had chiefly served the needs of the bard and did not engage the audience, the poets and the prophets of ancient Israel would have played to an empty house.[150]

This observation demonstrates the need for the reader to be sensitive to the use of RQs in the Song as well as in other parts of the Bible. Since RQs are passionate, declarative statements dressed as questions, one needs to be aware that the author is not seeking information or simple answers to his inquiries but is actually using RQs for an emotional effect. He is seeking to make a specific point. According to Brueggemann, the author wants to move his audience to "assert a common ground of opinion."[151] The author desires that the audience would think and thus act like him.

Unlike the declarative, exclamatory, or even the simple interrogative, the RQ allows the reader of any generation a unique opportunity to enter into the ancient biblical action by answering the question being asked. McCabe notes the same dynamic in his study of another piece of OT wisdom literature, Ecclesiastes. He observes that Qohelet, by his use

---

149. Brueggemann, "Jeremiah's Use of Rhetorical Questions," 370.

150. Greenstein, "How Does Parallelism Mean?" 42–43.

151. Ibid. However, the RQs in Jeremiah function as part of the prophet's literary arsenal to dispute with his erring nation. In the SoS there is no use of the RQ as a form of disputation.

of rhetorical questions (and other "various genres"), "draws us into his world."[152] If this literary device is missed or translated out of existence, the reader is missing out on a rhetorical device that is meant to engage the audience in a personal way as they read or hear the biblical text.[153]

Occasionally the RQs in the SoS give evidence of functioning as structuring elements, either opening or closing a section of the Song. Although there is little agreement concerning the overall structure of the Song, there may be enough preliminary evidence to suggest that RQs (and interrogatives in general) play a structuring role in Hebrew poetry. For example, the role of RQs in Malachi and Amos as structuring devices is clear and should not be missed as one approaches these books.[154] In his study of the RQs in Job, De Regt notes numerous examples of RQs with a "structuring function, either starting a section or closing one."[155]

Other RQs provide emphasis. Since the RQ is a statement dressed as a question, it flies in the face of what is normal grammatical convention. The reader must note this use of the interrogative by the author. Koops notes that when the speaker deliberately flaunts the expected pattern, the author is emphasizing a point.[156]

While every writer employs various literary devices for the benefit of his readers, the RQ may be a unique rhetorical device that draws the audience into direct contact with the poem by involving them in the questions and subsequent answers they would provide. The biblical poet may also utilize RQs in a didactic manner. When the reader responds to a RQ in the author's intended manner, the author is thus successful in leading his audience to his way of thinking. If RQs are not accounted for in reading (or in the exegetical process), the exegete may miss an important tool that the writer has to persuade the audience of his purpose for writing. This section will suggest the various rhetorical functions of the specific RQs in the SoS.

152. McCabe, "The Message of Ecclesiastes," 100. McCabe also lists reflection stories, proverbs, comparative sayings, and autobiographical material as "various genres" along with rhetorical questions.

153. Pierce ("Thematic Development," 405) recognizes the same literary function of rhetorical questions in Zech 1–8. He states that the rhetorical questions in this biblical text are used "for the purpose of drawing the reader into the experience of the prophet."

154. Kaiser, *Toward an Exegetical Theology*, 74–75.

155. De Regt, "Functions and Implications," 371.

156. Koops, "Rhetorical Questions," 418.

First RQ (1:7b)

The function of the first RQ, 1:7b, (in combination with the first two simple interrogatives in the same verse) is at least threefold. First, this RQ allows a smooth transition to introduce the male speaker. Up to this point the male speaker has not uttered a word. He has been spoken about (1:2a) and spoken to (1:2b–4), but he has yet to utter a word himself. While the woman's use of the second person in verses 2–4 demonstrates that he is on the mental stage of the audience, he has not taken center stage. The simple interrogative in combination with this RQ allows the audience to focus on the man and allows him to speak for the first time. Although Hess does not distinguish between the types of interrogatives the author uses in this verse, he does note, "The command and question bring the female's concern to a conclusion and invite a response from her lover."[157] In essence the RQ allows the female lover to step back verbally (not offstage but to the side) while the man moves verbally forward to center stage and addresses her queries.

Second, this RQ may serve to demonstrate (and heighten) the suspense and sexual tension between the couple. The audience already knows she desires him completely and immediately. However, at this point in the SoS, the reader is not quite certain of his response. Does he desire her as much as she desires him? Does he want to be with her as much as she wants to be with him? These questions and others may run through the audience's mind as they listen to the one-sided dialogue of the woman from 1:2–6. Up to 1:7 all the reader has at his or her disposal are the deeply amorous feelings of the female. The reader does not know whether the object of her affection will return her love and, if he does, whether he do so with the same passion. His answer to the first two simple interrogatives assures the audience that he does indeed have strong feelings for her as well. He desires her to discover his whereabouts but he teases her with a less than full retort. The man answers her question in 1:8, but it may not be the response the audience is expecting. Instead of telling her exactly where he will be at noon so they can enjoy an afternoon tryst, he responds, as Bergant suggests, in a tease.[158] His response, if it is indeed a tease, heightens the sexual tension between the couple. It also builds the suspense of the Song and leaves the audience

---

157. Hess, *Song of Songs*, 60.
158. Bergant, *Song of Songs*, 18.

wondering if and when this couple will ever be together. While Walsh is incorrect in not recognizing the consummation of the couple in various places in the poem, she captures its theme of desire: "Desire remains the theme throughout its eight chapters.... For the Song is not about sex per se, but about sexual yearning."[159] She also observes the effect this unfilled desire in this section may have on the audience. "The two lovers want each other badly, achingly.... This is frustrating and almost unbearably erotic for the reader."[160] This "frustration" in the audience is created by the author's use of this rhetorical question.

Third, this RQ functions to draw the audience into the Song, into direct contact with its characters and, most importantly, with its author. At this point in the Song, the audience is on the edge of its seat listening to the sensual dialogue of the two lovers. However, listening is all they are doing. By the use of this RQ the author nudges the readers into contact with the characters by allowing them to answer the RQ themselves and feel the sexual tension of the couple and their desire to be together. Ryken captures the emotional aspect of the RQ when he writes that it is "a figure of speech in which the writer asks a question whose answer is so obvious that it is left unstated; a question asked not to elicit information, but for the sake of effect, usually an emotional effect."[161] Not only does the audience relate with the characters but to the author as well through the use of the RQ. De Regt observes, "A speaker or writer may thus identify with the audience by implying that the audience will obviously agree."[162] The audience is well aware that the male lover does not want his love poking into the tents of the other males as she searches for him! By answering the RQ in the negative, the audience joins the viewpoint of the author (neither he nor the male lover desires her to look into other tents). This connection with the Song's characters and author is a rhetorical effect of this RQ.

---

159. Walsh, *Exquisite Desire*, 29.

160. Ibid. While she is incorrect in seeing this frustration for the audience throughout the book, sexual tension (even self-imposed) seems to be obvious.

161. Ryken, *Words of Delight*, 362.

162. Ibid. It may be more accurate to suggest that the author does not identify with the audience through the use of RQs but through the answering of the RQ.

Second RQ (3:6)

While there is disagreement concerning the division of the SoS, Roberts' study concludes that 3:6–11 is "recognized as a unit by interpreters representing a wide variety of approaches."[163] This second RQ (3:6) functions structurally to open this new section.[164] The RQ introduces a narrative scene in which the speaker may be the female protagonist of the SoS.[165] Since the unit closes in 3:5 with the second adjuration refrain from the mouth of the woman, the male lover exits the reader's mental stage. To bring him back, the author structures his opening with a RQ which focuses the attention of the audience on something (or someone) that is "coming up from the wilderness." Up to this point the woman has always been present and the man moves in and out. As in 1:7 this RQ also functions to creatively return the male lover into the picture through a smooth and seamless transition so he is able to speak of his beloved's beauty in 4:1. That she is the object of his *wasf* (4:1–15) is readily apparent. In order to bring him back onto the stage for the audience to hear, there must be a smooth transition for the audience from watching the man come up from the wilderness (i.e., from out of their view) and then letting the man praise the object that has come into his view, namely, his beloved.

This RQ also functions rhetorically to involve the audience more deeply in the song. Longman remarks, "The question draws our attention and raises our curiosity as to what possibly could be on the horizon."[166] Exum concurs and writes, "By means of a question, the speaker calls our attention to what looks like columns of smoke on the horizon. The question that immediately arises is, who or what is the cause?"[167] Exum in an earlier article suggests, "The poet here draws the reader into the poem by not yet specifying the addressee; in the absence of an acknowl-

---

163. Roberts, *Let Me See Your Form*, 147. Also see Stoop-van Paridon, *Song of Songs*, 157.

164. That this is a new unit is supported by the adjuration refrain (3:5), which closes the preceding unit (3:1–5), and the adjuration refrain (2:7), which closes the first unit (1:2—2:7).

165. There is an ongoing debate concerning the speaker and the object of this section. Bergant (*Song of Songs*, 37) states, "While the Hebrew in which it is written is not difficult to translate, its precise meaning cannot be determined with certainty."

166. Ibid., 135.

167. Exum, *Song of Songs*, 142.

edged audience, the speakers seem to be addressing the reader directly."[168] While the description builds the suspense of the identity of the one who is coming up from the wilderness, the audience already knows it is the man. This is evident since the woman is the speaker (she is the only one that addresses the daughters [3:11]) and the man is the object of their gaze (4:11). This RQ makes the audience part of the Song. Again, Exum notes that the RQ is for the audience's benefit. She asks and answers her own question: "To whom is the question, 'What is this coming up from the wilderness?' (v. 6) addressed? As elsewhere, the audience is the women of Jerusalem ... and the poem's readers."[169]

This RQ may function rhetorically to heighten the listeners' suspense by asking the question to which the female lover (and the audience) already knows the answer. Bergant remarks, "The rhetorical question with which it opens is less a query seeking an answer than it is an exclamation with dramatic intent."[170] While the audience knows that what is coming up has something to do with the male lover, the description is different than previous descriptions of the male lover. While he has been previously described as a king (1:4, 12), in this instance the portrayal is much more regal and possibly unexpected. While the answer to the RQ is given in 3:7, the rest of the account (3:6–11) gives evidence that the person on the litter is the focus of the female attention. That he is not identified until 3:11 as Solomon functions to heighten the suspense of "who is coming up from the wilderness."

There may be a didactic purpose as well for this RQ. De Regt points out that RQs are used to "call attention to information, expressing the speaker's attitudes, opinions, etc."[171] It is possible that the author wants to call the reader's attention to the fact that love between a man and a woman certainly deserves the royal treatment.[172] This imperial metaphor is evident in the threefold references to Solomon (3:7, 9, 11) and the rich construction of his couch, מִטָּה. The woman also calls the daughters to appreciate the uniqueness of the day (3:11).

---

168. Exum, "Seeing Solomon's Palanquin," 303.
169. Exum, *Song of Songs*, 142.
170. Bergant, *Song of Songs*, 37.
171. De Regt, "Functions and Implications," 365.
172. Pun intended.

Third RQ (5:3)

The third RQ, 5:3, is a series of two. These two RQs in parallel structure may function to demonstrate the woman's reluctance to meet her beloved's sexual advances without actually stating it explicitly.[173] If the woman voices only one of these questions to her ill-timed lover, it might seem at face value a legitimate reason for her not to admit her beloved. Used together however, the RQs expose to the audience her reluctance without actually stating it. Stoop-van Paridon prefers to see this RQ as a "*non-perfective of deliberation*. . . . In this context the interrogative particle in a rhetorical question can be understood as an exclamation. This conveys the connotation of complaint and doubt."[174] The woman is complaining about her lover's nighttime desire for intimacy. But even used together these RQs are stated in such a way by the woman that at first blush (at least from her point of view), they seem reasonable and require an affirmative answer by the man. The answer the woman is expecting might be, "You are correct, dear. How could I expect you to get dressed or run the risk of dirtying your feet once again? How thoughtless of me to even ask." Although the woman may have thought that she had good excuses, the man and the audience read right through her. The audience knows the man does not believe her excuses are valid because he leaves (5:6). Here it is not only the man who is rebuffed in his advance—so is the audience! The reader knows what she really is stating by her use of the two RQs. The audience knows she is saying "no" to her lover's nocturnal advances. Waltke makes the point that "rhetorical questions aim not to gain information but to give information with passion."[175] This is seen clearly in the woman's use of these RQs in this verse. She is telling her beloved in no uncertain terms that she is not interested in being with him that night. These RQs allow the reader to be involved in the SoS and to make a judgment on the woman's behavior. The reader realizes the woman is wrong for not being open to her beloved. They would even

---

173. Some scholars believe these RQs are simply a tease; for example Murphy, *Song of Songs*, 170; Pope, *Song of Songs*, 516; Ogden and Zogbo, *Handbook on Song of Songs*, 147. Exum (*Song of Songs*, 191–92) suggests these verses are filled with euphemisms and that intercourse is actually taking place. In view of the lack of scholarly consensus concerning these verses, Stoop-van Paridon (*Song of Songs*, 266) reasons that the man is actually the speaker of these RQs.

174. Stoop-van Paridon, *Song of Songs*, 266. Italics are original.

175. *IBHS*, 322.

recognize and agree with the justified (but imaginary) discipline of the night watchmen in 5:7.[176]

These RQs may serve a didactic purpose as well. It is fairly certain the RQs highlight the woman's reluctance to meet her lover's advances. That she is wrong for such an attitude is evidenced by the discipline she suffers and endures without complaint. (There is also no judgment of the watchmen by the author or any character in the Song). This section demonstrates that failure to receive one's own spouse is wrong and selfish. While the SoS communicates the beauty of sexual love and desire throughout, there are dangers which are evident in this poem since it is on the fall side of the first garden. Concerning this pericope Schwab notes, "In very erotic language, fraught with double-entendre, she describes a scene that illustrates how emotionally complicated and self-contradictory love can be. Her lover calls to her. She is unsure how to respond, due to conflicting feelings."[177] Whatever her motivation or feelings, she is wrong in her refusal. This section may teach the reader what should be one's attitude to the sexual advances of his or her partner.[178]

Fourth RQ (6:10)

This RQ functions structurally to close the *wasf* of 6:4–9. While Dorsey views 6:10 as an interrogative that opens the section 6:10—7:1a, the listing of the three similes in the opening of 6:4, the listing of the four similes in 6:10, and the repetition of the "bannered army" in 6:4 and 6:10 argues that the RQ of 6:10 closes this section.[179] Roberts also thinks this RQ closes the section as well. He believes this closing component of 6:10, the rhetorical question, is linked in a number of ways with what has preceded it and thus closes 6:4–10.[180] While this RQ

---

176. To reiterate, all of 5:2—6:1 is part of the dream sequence.
177. Schwab, *Cautionary Message*, 67.
178. See 1 Cor 7:1–6 for the NT teaching on the proper response to sexual advances.
179. Dorsey, "Literary Structuring in the Song of Songs," 89. If Longman is correct that 6:11 presents a different speaker than the previous verses, then that would give evidence of 6:11 being the beginning of a new section (*Song of Songs*, 183). Callow ("Units and Flow," 463) notes that a change of speaker constitutes a change of semantic unit. While there is debate, it is clear that the RQ plays a key structural role. Kaiser (*Toward an Exegetical Theology*, 72) observes that the rhetorical question "could signal a switch to a new theme and section." According to Kaiser (ibid., 74), "The most celebrated of all cases where the rhetorical question is used to structure the whole book is Malachi."
180. Roberts, *Let Me See Your Form*, 243.

concludes this section, it may also provide the reason for the opening RQ of the next section (7:1–10.). Since the woman is so stunning and breathtaking in her beauty, it may be the reason that others would want to gaze at her (7:1).

The RQ also functions as a climax for the praise of the woman. This climax brings the reader to the same lofty conclusion that the man has of her beauty. She is awesome. The use of the RQ commands the reader's attention and compels him or her to answer the question in the same manner as the man. Exum recognizes the rhetorical effect and notes, "The question 'who (or what) is this?' is used for rhetorical effect three times in the Song (see under 3:6 and 8:5). The woman not only surpasses other women (vv. 8–9), she rivals the sun and moon in their splendor."[181] In short, not only does the man know that she is a unique beauty, the audience knows as well and answers the RQ along with the man: "who is this that . . . ?" It is the female lover who is matchless in her beauty among women and competes with the heavenly bodies in grandeur. But this gazing at such a beauty is not a voyeuristic or lustful look at the woman by the male audience but is an affirmation of her beauty by her lover.[182] Provan notes, "*Of course* everyone holds her to be a radiant beauty. How could it be otherwise? No other judgment can be contemplated, because she is the only woman for him."[183] By asking a RQ, the author engages the reader more personally in the poem.

Fifth RQ (7:1)

As was discussed in the previous section, there are a number of questions with little consensus concerning this next RQ in 7:1. Rhetorically, however, it may function to introduce the *wasf* of 7:2–10. Hess states that this interrogative "anticipates the male's description of her physical beauty in the following section."[184] The RQ sets up the reader to want to "gaze" through his mind's eye at the "dance" of the woman in 7:2–10. The following *wasf* allows the reader to "see" and appreciate the beauty of the male's beloved through the descriptive language of the man. Ogden and

---

181. Exum, *Song of Songs*, 222.

182. This is contra Clines ("Why Is There a Song of Songs?" 114) who suggests that the original purpose of the Song was to provide the ancient male population of the Song with pornographic literature.

183. Provan, *Song of Songs*, 340. Italics are original.

184. Hess, *Song of Songs*, 210.

Zogbo observe, "The question asked in 6:13 [Hebrew 7:1] as to why the young man would want to look at his lover is now answered by a *wasf* or description of her physical beauty."[185] If this RQ is from the mouth of the woman, it heightens the reader's appreciation for her character as well as her physical beauty because she did not see anything in herself that would make anyone want to gaze at her. This same self-deprecating position is expressed by the woman earlier in the poem (cf. 2:1). Roberts believes that the repetition of the interrogative in 7:2a links it with 7:1. "The most obvious structural link is the repetition of the interrogative מַה with a perfect form of the verb in 7:1c and 7:2a. This structural link supports the thematic link provided by the 'rebuking' interpretation adopted in 7:1. The beauty of the woman is not the beauty of the common camp dancer (1d), but a beauty that is appropriate to royalty."[186]

This RQ functions as do previous RQs, that is, to bring a character back onto the imaginative stage of the reader. While the female lover is the object of the male's praise from 6:4 through 6:10, she does not acknowledge the praise he heaps upon her. To give her voice again in the song, she answers demurely concerning being the object of such scrutiny (as in 2:1). She wonders aloud "why would you gaze?"[187] The inquiring response of the woman to the praise of her lover brings her to center stage and gives her a voice once again in the Song. Exum observes, "The woman returns through the power of the man's description" in 7:2–7. However, what Exum fails to realize is that the woman is already present in her rhetorical question.

Like preceding RQs, this one functions rhetorically to draw the audience into the story. This introductory RQ invites the reader into arguably the most explicitly erotic description of the female and her lover's desire in the entire Song. While this RQ introduces the description that invites the reader into certain intimate places, the author is careful not to allow the reader to venture too deeply into the couple's most passionate settings. Exum concludes: "The reader is invited to enter the lovers' private garden of eroticism yet is excluded from the most intimate moments. . . . The poem invites the reader to look by presenting inventories

---

185. Ogden and Zogbo, *Handbook on Song of Songs*, 194.

186. Roberts, *Let Me See Your Form*, 276.

187. Garrett ("Song of Songs," 234) believes the male lover is the speaker of this RQ. Mitchell (*Song of Songs*, 1030) thinks two different groups are speaking responsively to one another. In either case this RQ seems to function to open the *wasf*.

of the lovers' bodies, and at the same time it holds the reader off by clothing these bodies in metaphor."[188] While the RQ draws the reader into the couple's sexual foreplay, the metaphor maintains a safe distance between them and the audience. Nevertheless, in such places the Song arouses the amorous feelings of the audience by such intimate dialogue (of which rhetorical questions are a part) and draws them into the poem.

Sixth RQ (8:4)

The sixth RQ of 8:4 may play a vital didactic function in the Song. This verse is similar (but not identical) to the refrains in 2:7 and 3:5. This RQ reiterates the common theme of the earlier exhortations (2:7; 3:5). Since this repetitive refrain is in the concluding cycle of the Song, it would be appropriate to listen to the theme of this important refrain one last time (since it already bore repeating two previous times).[189] However, this refrain is in a different grammatical form than 2:7 and 3:5. The previous RQs are declarative statements from the woman to the daughters of Jerusalem. Conversely, this refrain in 8:4 is in the form of a rhetorical question composed of two interrogatives. The rhetorical purpose for this RQ in place of the declarative statement is to allow the audience the opportunity to demonstrate that it has learned the lesson that the author has been sharing throughout the Song. His lesson is that while love is something that should be desired, pursued, and celebrated, this emotion should not be aroused or awakened until the proper time. If the audience answers this RQ in a strongly negative manner (the way the author intends), they would respond to the rhetorical question something like this: "We will certainly not awaken or arouse love." If this is the reader's reply, then the author's caution has been accepted and he has communicated his point to the audience. Stoop-van Paridon would agree with such a conclusion. She states, "Keeping to a literal translation, which I have chosen to do, in itself, therefore helps the listener or reader already fill in the (negative) answer. Moreover, the context makes any other answer (sc. positive) implausible."[190] As stated in the previous section, a translation that ob-

---

188. Exum, *Song of Songs*, 230.

189. For instance, Exum (*Song of Songs*, 248) sees this last adjuration coming before the climactic affirmation of love in 8:6–7. Pope (*Song of Songs*, 226) states that 8:6 "has been generally recognized as the theme and message of the Song of Songs."

190. Stoop-van Paridon, *Song of Songs*, 423. While she does not translate this verse as an interrogative, Exum recognizes that the presence of the interrogative in this

scures this RQ may be missing a vital rhetorical device that enables the author to emphasize the Song's message one final time.[191]

Like other RQs, this one aids the author in drawing the reader into the Song at a crucial moment in the poem. If the writer has communicated his point well, this RQ will elicit a strongly negative response from the audience. When the reader responds negatively, he is agreeing with the author's intent implied in the RQ. Engaging the audience through this RQ may enable the author to maintain (or refocus) the audience's attention at this critical juncture of the Song as it begins to draw to its conclusion. Watson notes that the biblical author employs various poetic devices as aids to attention "when the poem is especially long or difficult" or as a method of maintaining "the attention of a potentially critical audience."[192] There may also be an element of self-discovery in the audience's answer to this RQ. If the reader or the audience responds to the RQ as the author intends but without the author's direct input, then the audience has reached the proper conclusion without the aid of the author. This is self-discovery (albeit the audience is led down a very narrow path by a creative author who wishes his reader to come to "his own conclusion" about love).

There is also a structural function for this RQ as well. According to Roberts, the adjuration refrain of 8:4 functions to close the section 7:12—8:4 in the same way the adjuration refrains of 2:7 and 3:5 did. While he does not mention the rhetorical question of 8:4, Dorsey concurs that this adjuration refrain does indeed close, according to his division, the sixth main section of the Song.[193] Bergant agrees and remarks, "A twofold refrain (vv. 3–4) brings this poem of yearning and indeed the entire unit to a close."[194]

---

verse may indicate a "subtle difference" with the previous refrains. If this is so, she surmises that it would be a rhetorical question whose answer is a negative (Exum, *Song of Songs*, 248).

191. Although he is studying RQs in Job, Koops ("Rhetorical Questions," 423) notes the need and potential problem of translating RQs: "Translating these devices literally may give us a picture of the way the Hebrew writers used language, but for many readers much of the meaning is lost because their own literary tradition uses different devices (or the same devices for different ends)."

192. Watson, *Classical Hebrew Poetry*, 33.

193. Dorsey, *Literary Structure*, 209.

194. Bergant, *Song of Songs*, 93.

Seventh RQ (8:5)

In contrast to the previous RQ (8:4), the RQ of 8:5 functions structurally to open the final section of the SoS. Bergant comments that this final unit "opens with a statement of admiration in the form of an unanswered question."[195] The unanswered question is rhetorical. While acknowledging the lack of coherence in the section 8:5–7, Roberts recognizes that the interrogative opens the section. Arguing that 8:5 does indeed open a new section, he states, "The use of the interrogative is a common marker of opening function in the Song already (3:6 and 6:10)."[196] Dorsey believes a new section is evident by the author's employment of a shift in scene, mood, speaker, and "the rhetorical question in 8:5."[197] He feels this RQ "has the effect of transporting the audience to a new scene."[198]

It is at the beginning of this new scene that the author feels the need to once again convey the two main characters to his audience's imaginative arena. This RQ from the mouth of the daughters of Jerusalem may function to bring the male and female lover back into the view of the listeners. Seeing the similarity between the introductory rhetorical questions of 8:5a and 3:6, Hess states, "In both cases it introduces a kind of theatrical sense in which the lover appears. As in 3:6, so here the 'desert' (*hammidbār*) sets the perspective for an approach from a distance."[199] As has been stated previously, some RQs may function to return the individual lovers to the reader's attention. With the possible exception of the rhetorical question of 3:6, this is the only RQ that serves the rhetorical

---

195. Ibid., 95.

196. Roberts, *Let Me See Your Form*, 320. Roberts argues against this being a rhetorical question because Fox asserts that rhetorical questions function to close sections of the Song. Since this interrogative is not closing a section, then according to Roberts it cannot be a rhetorical question. However, Fox is arguing that the RQ of 8:5 is somehow a response to the adjuration refrain of 8:4 and thus 8:4 and 8:5 are linked. Since adjuration refrains close the sections they are associated with previously, then 8:4 and 8:5 must close this section. Instead of rejecting Fox's closing structural function of the interrogative, Roberts could have rejected the supposed link between 8:4 and 8:5. This would maintain his proposed introductory structure function for 8:5 and would allow for this interrogative to be a rhetorical question as well. Fox, *Egyptian Love Songs*, 119.

197. Dorsey, *Literary Structure*, 209.

198. Ibid.

199. Hess, *Song of Songs*, 235. Ogden and Zogbo (*Handbook on Song of Songs*, 223) agree; they see the rhetorical question "as setting the scene for what follows by bringing the young woman back into the picture." Bloch and Bloch (*Song of Songs*, 159) note that the introductory phrase מִי זֹאת עֹלָה "is a stylized formula of dramatization."

purpose of bringing the couple onto the center stage for the final cycle of the poem.

This RQ may also serve the rhetorical purpose of the biblical author by setting a different tone for the final section of the Song. The previous six sections of the Song began with the lovers separated. In each cycle, there has always been a certain amount of tension to see if their individual desire for one another would be fulfilled as they strive to come together as a couple. As they verbalize their desire to be with one another, the author joins the couple together. The tension of the parted lovers is resolved in each other's loving embrace. At the beginning of this last cycle or section, the individual lovers are already together. The women of Jerusalem observe the female lover emerging from the wilderness. She walks into their view (and the audience's) leaning on the arm of her beloved (8:5). Since they are already a couple, there is no tension. There is no movement to union. There is no desire unfilled. On the contrary, the woman leaning on her beloved gives the impression that desire has indeed been fulfilled. They are seen as one. This is a different mood for the audience to experience and the RQ sets this different tone.

The reason for this different introductory mood in this section may be needed because the cycle concludes with the couple apart! As has been observed previously, each of the previous cycles begins with the lovers separated. Throughout each cycle, they endeavor to be united. However, in the cycle that encompasses 8:5–14, the sequence is reversed. The individual lovers begin together as a couple (8:5) and end with the couple calling to each other to be together once again (8:13–14). Bergant notes that the Song ends "not with final consummation ... but on a note of separation with a plea for union."[200] This reversal gives the sense that the book never actually ends.[201] The cycle of desire replays itself once again. There is always a desire on the part of these individual lovers to be together. Exum rightly concludes, "Far from being anti-climactic or mystifying as a conclusion, as many critics have observed, these verses provide an inspired ending to the Song. Rather than bringing the poem

---

200. Bergant, *Song of Songs*, 105.

201. Thematically this is a book without a beginning and without an ending, for it starts in the middle of a relationship already experiencing strong desire to be with (and enjoy) each other (1:2). And while the words of this Song may end (8:14), desire still drives the lovers to be with one another.

to closure, they lead us back into it."²⁰² While love may be fulfilled for a moment (cf. 5:1; 7:10b), desire is never ultimately fulfilled (cf. 5:2; 7:12).

Bergant captures the dynamic of the Song's conclusion: "As incomplete as this may sound, it is also quite true of authentic love. Human love knows no definitive consummation, no absolute fulfillment. Loving relationships are never complete; they are always ongoing, always reaching for more."²⁰³

Finally, this RQ may function to remind the reader of his involvement in the story. The answer to the RQ מִי זֹאת עֹלָה is no more difficult here than it has been in the past RQs. The reader knows conclusively that the answer to the question is the woman. There can be no other choice. Although on this occasion, the audience may be surprised to find that this time she is not alone: the lovers are together from the very beginning. The author's use of the rhetorical questions reminds the reader that the biblical author is mindful of their presence in the Song and he seeks to include their participation. Exum is correct in her observation that, "The poet once again reminds us of the presence of an audience, onlookers who participate in the unfolding of the lovers' relationship, and so encourages the readers' involvement. We do not only look, with them, to see lovers approaching from the steppe, we also listen." However, the audience's participation at least in relationship to this RQ is more than simply listening. They are actively responding to the author and his characters as they answer this RQ. Through the use of this rhetorical device, the audience is actively involved in the poem by answering the RQ either in verbal response to the reading or mentally as they read the book themselves.

Eighth RQ (8:8)

The last RQ is found in 8:8. Dorsey believes the verses that compose the context of this RQ constitute the chiastic center of this final unit.²⁰⁴ He bases his reasoning on the shifting of speakers throughout. Roberts disagrees since he suggests that the final section does not begin until 8:8 and continues until 8:14. He thinks there are "few if any structural

---

202. Exum, *Song of Songs*, 261.
203. Bergant, *Song of Songs*, 104.
204. Dorsey, *Literary Structure*, 211.

features that mark the opening of this strophe."[205] He remarks that the reason for a new section at this juncture is due to the recognition of a new theme rather than any structural evidence found in the verses.[206] Stoop-van Paridon states categorically, "All commentators are agreed that the preceding verse 8.7 forms a conclusion to a coherent passage in the SofS, and that a new passage begins in verse 8.8."[207] If this strophe is not connected to what preceded it (8:1–7), it may be possible to suggest that this RQ (like others in the Song in 3:6; 7:1; 8:5) does indeed function to open this section. This position may be strengthened if one sees the speaker of this RQ as the women of Jerusalem. The author employs them to open the previous unit of 8:5. This is only a suggestion since this section is notoriously difficult to determine the relationship between the separate units.[208] Bloch and Bloch note, "The great difficulty of this section is reflected in the widely differing interpretations given in commentaries. There is hardly any consensus even on essential questions."[209]

Once again, this RQ may function rhetorically to involve the audience in the Song. Exum surmises that verses 8–9 and 10–12 "have an enigmatic quality, as if the speakers wished to engage the audience in solving a puzzle."[210] Exum may be correct since the audience would recognize easily the power of love (8:6–7) and the need for purity before marriage (8:9–10). This recognition would cause them to respond that they would do everything in their power to protect and prepare their immature girls for the day they could marry and enjoy the pleasures of marital bliss. This is the same response the speakers recite in 8:9. Because the audience responds to the RQ in the same manner as the speakers in 8:9, they are drawn into deeper involvement with the Song. The reason for this involvement is because of what the poem has celebrated thus far and their own culture, which places a heavy responsibility on sexual purity (Lev 18; Deut 22).

---

205. Roberts, *Let Me See Your Form*, 342.
206. Ibid.
207. Stoop-van Paridon, *Song of Songs*, 444.
208. Roberts, *Let Me See Your Form*, 340. Stoop-van Paridon (*Song of Songs*, 444) concurs concerning the uncertainty of the following passages.
209. Bloch and Bloch, *Song of Songs*, 214.
210. Exum, *Song of Songs*, 255.

THEOLOGICAL OBSERVATIONS CONCERNING THE AUTHOR'S USE OF RQS

Various theological observations arise from the author's intentional use of RQs in the SoS. Articulating these observations is a valid biblical theological enterprise on at least two levels. First, as Bright explains, "All biblical texts are expressive of theology in that all are animated, if at times indirectly, by some theological concern. It is incumbent upon the interpreter to seek to discover what that theological concern is."[211] While not using the term "theology," Weems understands that the author of the Song has a theological purpose for his writing.[212] Weems states, "The fundamental assumption here is that poets, like ancient and modern speakers, design their messages with a specific audience in mind: to instruct, build upon, defend, challenge, or correct prevailing assumptions."[213]

The author's theological concern is in the literary devices he chose to communicate his message, in this case, rhetorical questions. Second, such an endeavor seeks to complete the exegetical process and produce a theologically sound application of biblical truth.

Again, to quote Schultz:

> Exegesis is incomplete if it does not lay bare the theological thrust of a text, seeking to identify words, phrases, motifs, images and even structural elements that reveal aspects of God's will and work in the world as it places demands on or otherwise affects Israel, the nations and/or all humankind. These elements should be analyzed in terms of their function within the given text and synthesized in terms of their participation in and contribution to the theological emphasis of the book as a whole, whether structural or thematic in nature.... Moreover, an exegesis that is consciously theological will also result in greater clarity regarding the contemporary implication and application of a given text.[214]

---

211. Bright, *Authority of the Old Testament*, 170.

212. While some scholars would disagree with Weems' purpose for the book, her recognition of the general intent of the author is accurate. Weems ("Song of Songs," *Women's Bible Commentary*, 166) states that the purpose of the book is persuasive. "Her audience needed to be persuaded of the suitability of this woman and this man's love for each other." Some scholars would also disagree with her position that the author of the Song may be female as well (thus the "her audience").

213. Ibid., 167.

214. Schultz, "Integrating Old Testament Theology and Exegesis," 195.

Travers concurs. He then asks and answers his own rhetorical question, "How, then, are figures of speech to be interpreted? They are to be interpreted like the rest of Scripture—in their appropriate contexts and their theology."[215]

However, while such a biblical theological enterprise is needful and desirous, Osborne makes an observation that functions as a cautious reminder in pursuing such an inquiry. Although Osborne is commenting on the study of the use of metaphors in Psalms, he offers a concern that applies to the relationship between theology and the study of other rhetorical devices as well: "Theology rarely stems from the metaphor itself but rather from the whole context of which it is a part."[216] Osborne's reminder is appreciated. Unlike the author's use of the first person where there are numerous theological observations, the theology that flows from the actual RQ itself is at best minimal if the exegetical study confines itself to the RQs themselves and not the surrounding context.[217]

The significant observation stemming naturally from the author's collective use of RQs that impacts the theology in the SoS is a fairly general one and is nondescript but it is important rhetorically nonetheless. As has already been attested in a number of RQs, the biblical writer uses certain rhetorical questions to persuade the audience of his point of view. Brueggemann believes the rhetorical questions in Jeremiah are in a didactic form and that "form is employed in an intensely theological . . . way."[218] For example, the introductory RQ by God, from the mouth of Jeremiah, Why should I pardon you? (5:7) "evokes an obvious, indisputable answer," according to Brueggemann.[219] He continues: "I should not pardon you!" Based on the evidence given by Jeremiah, the answer and "punishment is natural, normal, and to be expected."[220] The RQ allows Jeremiah's audience to agree theologically that their punishment

---

215. Travers, "Figures of Speech in the Bible," 290.

216. Osborne, *Hermeneutical Spiral*, 188.

217. Since this work is analyzing three particular literary devices and the theology that flows from their specific uses, it will confine itself to the theology that arises from the actual rhetorical question and not from the theology that emerges from the context in which they are employed. The one exception is the RQ of 5:3. The theology of this RQ will be studied in view of its larger context because the significance of its theology is not completed until 5:7.

218. Brueggemann, "Jeremiah's Use of Rhetorical Questions," 358.

219. Ibid., 366.

220. Ibid.

is divinely sanctioned and warranted. Because Jeremiah's readers would answer the RQ in the self-same way; their own words condemn them. The RQ moves them to agree with the theological position of both God and his spokesman, the prophet.

Writing on RQs in general, De Regt asserts that the "rhetorical question is used to convey or call attention to information, expressing the speaker's attitudes, opinions, etc."[221] The use of this type of rhetoric is clearly seen in Song 6:10:

מִי־זֹאת הַנִּשְׁקָפָה כְּמוֹ־שָׁחַר
יָפָה כַלְּבָנָה
בָּרָה כַּחַמָּה
אֲיֻמָּה כַּנִּדְגָּלוֹת

Who is this that grows like the dawn,
As beautiful as the full moon,
As pure as the sun,
As awesome as an army with banners?

The answer to מִי־זֹאת is without question the female lover. When the individual reader answers the RQ in his mind that it is indeed the woman, the author employs the RQ as a rhetorical device meant to persuade the reader of his position. The author already knows the woman is beautiful, now he knows the audience agrees with his assessment. The RQ has done its rhetorical duty.

The same dynamic is seen in the biblical writer's use of the RQ in 7:1. While agreeing with the author's opinion concerning the physical beauty of the woman may not carry any explicit (or implicit) theological weight, it does function to draw the audience into agreement with the author. The reader's mental assent at this juncture may allow the author to draw the audience one step closer to his position so as to make the assent "not to awaken or arouse love" as the response to the RQ in 8:4 that much easier.

While Exum's work on the Song is admirable in so many ways, she may have miscalculated the author's mastery of the rhetorical question when she asserts that the writer of the Song "is too subtle, and too good a poet, to preach or teach, and never addresses the reader directly."[222] On

---

221. De Regt, "Discourse Implications of Rhetorical Questions," 52.
222. Exum, *Song of Songs*, 249.

the contrary, it is the author's use of the RQ in 8:4 that allows him to preach and teach so subtly that the audience may not even be aware that it is happening. This subtle use of the RQ is not unusual. De Regt contends that since "the speaker implies more than the words as such and expects no response, the hearer is impressed by the thought processes that would logically lead to the kind of answer the speaker intends the hearer to reach."[223] Labuschagne stresses that "the hearer is not merely a listener: he is forced to frame the expected answer in his mind, and by doing so he actually becomes a co-expressor of the speaker's conviction."[224] According to Sternberg, when the reader, characters, and author share the same conclusion, they have reached the "stage of virtual synchronization."[225]

Thus it is with the RQ of 8:4:

הִשְׁבַּעְתִּי אֶתְכֶם בְּנוֹת יְרוּשָׁלָ͏ִם
מַה־תָּעִירוּ ׀ וּמַה־תְּעֹרְרוּ אֶת־הָאַהֲבָה עַד שֶׁתֶּחְפָּץ

I want you to swear, O daughters of Jerusalem,
Why would you arouse or why awaken love, before it pleases?

While Exum acknowledges the possibility that 8:4 may indeed be a RQ, she does not suggest what the rhetorical purpose would be for such a device at this point in the Song. It is possible that the purpose of this RQ is clearly didactic. Presently, the majority of scholars view the RQ of 8:4 in the same vein as the adjuration refrains of 2:7 and 3:5. This is evident in the declarative translation of 8:4 in most English Bibles. Because the wording is similar, scholars opt to answer the interrogative of 8:4 with the same negative answer that is present in the earlier refrains. However, the author is not only trying to communicate his previously held position (not to arouse or awaken love) but is now leading the audience to the same conclusion, albeit this time the audience is to supply the strongly negative response. Since the reader would answer the RQ of 8:4 in a strongly negative manner, it proves the author has persuaded his audience to the proper conclusion. Thus, the RQ is, as De Regt notes, a "persuasive device." The reader's strongly negative response to the RQ of 8:4 is conditioned by the author's use of the declarative refrains of 2:7

---

223. De Regt, "Discourse Implications of Rhetorical Questions," 52.
224. Labuschagne, *Incomparability of Yahweh*, 23.
225. Sternberg, *Poetics of Biblical Narrative*, 512.

and 3:5 that also express a negative adjuration. When the reader agrees with the writer, according to De Regt, he "may gain a position of power. ... RQs are thus likely to be found in a context where rhetoric is desired for accomplishing *persuasion*."[226] In this case the author wants to persuade his audience that it is not a biblically proper activity to arouse or awaken love until its proper time. This is the author's theological position, and it is the one that he persuades his reader to accept by his use of the RQ and their subsequent negative answer.[227]

Before the poet can achieve this, he must ensure that his audience is engaged in the Song. While not specifically theological, this may be the rhetorical use of the RQs in 3:6; 6:10; 7:1; 8:5. It may be that without these RQs to draw the reader into the book, the author would not be able to convince his audience of the theological impact of the RQ of 8:4.

The RQs of 3:6 and 8:5 refocus the audience's attention on the absent woman. These RQs introduce a new section in the Song as the female lover materializes before their very eyes. In the RQ of 3:6 she enters the mental stage of the reader alone, albeit in royal style.[228] In the RQ of 8:5 she comes up from the wilderness leaning on her beloved. In either case the answer to the RQ מִי זֹאת in these verses is the same and is unquestionable: it is the woman. The audience or the reader engages the poem as they answer the question mentally. Thus, there is an identification between author and reader. They both know

---

226. De Regt, "Discourse Implications of Rhetorical Questions," 52. Italics are original.

227. The audience's inclination to the theological position of the author of the Song is unknown. His audience may have been inclined favorably to his stance or they may have been antagonistic (or anywhere in between these two poles). Although Sternberg (*Poetics of Biblical Narrative*, 444) is writing about narrative in BH, this observation concerning the audience of the scriptural writer may be instructive for understanding the mindset of the audience of the Song. Sternberg writes that the Bible does not envisage "a homogeneous audience. ... We have already traced enough of the energy that the Bible invests in its rhetorical strategies ... to dismiss the idea that it implies a likeminded reader, whose attitudes can be safely presupposed. ... And the closer one looks, the more visible the signs of uphill work for consensus." If Sternberg's observations concerning the audience's contrary penchant are accurate in the Song, the importance of the RQ as a rhetorical device to attempt to persuade is of utmost importance.

228. It may be that the author wants to call the reader's attention to the fact that love between a man and a woman deserves the royal treatment. This royal treatment is evident in the threefold references to Solomon, who is recognized as king (3:7, 9, 11), and the rich construction of his מִטָּה. The speaker also calls the daughters to appreciate the uniqueness of his royal wedding day, חֲתֻנָּה (3:11).

the same information and agree to the answer of the RQ. This may function to move a potentially hostile (or indifferent) audience to the same position as that of the author.

The RQs of 6:10 and 7:1 remind the audience of the attractiveness of the woman without commenting on her beauty in simple declarative statements. This is a legitimate function of RQs. De Regt recognizes such a purpose: "A RQ functions as a reminder of information that the speaker considers relevant to the hearer."[229] Again, agreement between the reader and the author concerning the woman's beauty may be a subtle way of persuading the audience to join the author's opinion in a nonthreatening and nonpersonal situation. If the reader agrees with the innocent conclusion of the author concerning the beauty of the woman, he might be more easily persuaded to agree with the more strongly theological RQ of 8:4. While Gordis may be borrowing too much from Freud in some of his observations, he may have caught a dynamic between author and reader: "From earliest times, whoever has sought to gain the assent of his fellows to any proposition has to contend with a deep-seated, seemingly instinctive spirit of contrariness in his listeners."[230] The RQ concerning the woman's beauty may function to break down theological barriers that may exist between author and reader by allowing the author and the reader to agree.

There is no scholarly consensus concerning the purpose or the function of the woman's RQ of 5:3. Is it a tease, verbal sexual foreplay, or a thinly veiled rejection of her lover's ill-timed, nocturnal sexual advance? However, this RQ determines the theology that flows from this rhetorical interrogative in its immediate context, which includes the subsection 5:2–7. The larger context begins with 5:2 and ends with the announcement of her "found" lover in 6:3. It is this subsection that is most important to the discussion since it holds the author's evaluation of the woman's rejection of her lover.

Speaking of the watchmen's treatment of the woman, Exum believes, "The woman's harsh treatment at the hands of the watchmen is a disturbing event in the poem for which the text offers no justifica-

---

229. Ibid.

230. Gordis, "Rhetorical Use of Interrogative Sentences," 213. Gordis (ibid.) continues, "Or to put it in physiologic terms, the ego functions far more pleasurably when it asserts itself in opposition to its fellows than when it acquiesces in a judgment previously uttered by another."

tion, and however one explains it, it intimates that all is not well in the garden of erotic delights."²³¹ It is only Exum who is uncomfortable with the discipline because she accurately notes that the female lover of the Song "seems unaffected by this setback." The female lover of the Song is unaffected because she realizes that the imagined discipline (she is in a dream that begins in 5:2) is warranted because she has rejected her lover's advances.²³² The woman's lack of negative response to her treatment at the hands of the night watchmen should not be dismissed lightly.²³³ Rather, it should be seen as an approval of their treatment. It is her way of saying that she deserves the chastisement because of her previous lack of responsiveness to her lover.²³⁴ Exum is surely right to note, "All is not well in the garden." Indeed, all is not well in this couple's garden because the woman uses the RQs of 5:3 to hide her reluctance in opening to her love's sexual advances (even if untimely).

The theology of this subsection (including the RQ of 5:3) is not the poet's way of rewarding the woman's "successful defiance of and challenge to social restrictions," as Exum supposes.²³⁵ On the contrary, the theological principle that flows from this section is that rejection of a lover's sexual advances no matter how ill-timed should not be met with equally flimsy excuses.²³⁶ The poet may be advocating a sexual willingness even when the request comes at an inopportune time. While the Song's female character takes the blame on herself, this is not to insinuate that the female gender is the only gender that can be guilty of withholding sexual desires. Modern anecdotal evidence reveals an increasing

---

231. Exum, *Song of Songs*, 198.

232. She is unaffected verbally. As the speaker of this section, she does not miss a verbal beat. She is unaffected physically. Although she is struck, bruised, and without her shawl הִכּוּנִי פְצָעוּנִי נָשְׂאוּ אֶת־רְדִידִי, she still maintains the search for her departed lover.

233. This same woman is quick to point out that her sunburnt skin is the result of her brothers' anger (1:6). Her response lets the reader know if she has been treated correctly by those in the Song.

234. It should be noted that this "discipline" is inflicted only verbally on herself. The entire sequence of events is only her retelling of her dream, a literary creation of the biblical author. This section of the Song no way advocates physical discipline of either spouse no matter the gender.

235. Exum, *Song of Songs*, 199.

236. While the lovers of the Song did not have the New Testament, this theological principle is repeated in 1 Cor 7:3–5.

number of men are at fault for failing to "open the bedroom door" to their wives as well.[237]

The RQ of 1:7 gives divine approval to sexual, verbal teasing within a marriage relationship. Exum asks and answers her own question about this RQ. "Are they playful? The sexual innuendoes they contain suggest that they are."[238] This RQ contains sexual connotations implying that the woman of the Song desires to rendezvous with her lover for a midday tryst. His answer in 1:8 continues the sexual flirting by not providing her with the exact directions to his noontime whereabouts. This exchange between the two lovers with her RQ in the middle gives theological evidence of the appropriateness of sexual teasing within a marriage relationship. Provan recognizes the import of proclaiming and reclaiming such truth. "Christians are called, therefore, to proclaim a resounding 'yes' to sexual expression, in the context of a resounding 'yes' to God."[239]

Also in this RQ is the theme of desire. Inherent in her inquiry is the yearning to be with her lover and to enjoy him. Since a purpose of a RQ is to express the opinion or attitude of the author, it could be that desire (i.e., sexual yearning) is a God-approved emotion.[240] The biblical author strongly infers that the desire expressed by the woman is a good and biblically proper emotion and may be pursued. The author records no negative consequences of such an endeavor by the female lover, unlike the discipline she "suffers" at the hands of the watchmen in her dream (5:7). Without saying so explicitly, the author is making a theological state-

---

237. According to Weiner-Davis ("When Your Sex Drives Don't Match"), "Many sex experts believe that low sexual desire in men is America's best-kept secret." In another article Weiner-Davis ("Sex Starved Marriage") states, "And before you jump to conclusions that low sexual desire is a woman's issue, I am convinced low sexual desire in men is America's best-kept secret. Millions of men are not in the mood for sex. And when I say that, most think about men who have difficulty performing. This is not so. Men who turn down their wives' advances do so for many of the same reasons women do." Penner and Penner (*Counseling of Sexual Disorder*, 196) observe, "Men find it less acceptable to admit a lack of desire, but the dilemma may be almost as prevalent as in women."

238. Exum, *Song of Songs*, 106. The modern term would be sexual flirting.

239. Provan, *Song of Songs*, 252.

240. There is an ongoing discussion to define desire as an emotion. According to Gonzaga et al., lay people list sexual desire as an emotion. However, according to her study ("Romantic Love," 174–75), "Many emotion researchers, in contrast, tend not to treat romantic love and sexual desire as distinct emotions." While her study does not conclusively demonstrate that desire is an emotion, it does give documentation that this viewpoint is starting to change. Being a layperson myself in the area of psychology, desire will be defined as an emotion.

ment with divine credence that desire may be expressed and pursued within a marriage relationship. The biblical author is an accomplished poet who celebrates desire between his characters and at the same time moves his reader to crave desire themselves. Walsh is correct when she states, "A Song about desire winds up making its reader yearn for desire itself."[241] This yearning for desire is a divinely sanctioned emotion that may be consummated within the bounds of a biblical relationship.

CONCLUSION

RQs are more rhetorical than theological. Deep or elaborate theological statements (implicit or explicit) are not to be harvested from each individual RQ. However, that does not mean there is no theology expressed in RQs. The theology of the SoS manifests itself not from this one rhetorical device (RQs) but from the contribution of this literary device to the whole composition within the context in which they are used by the biblical author. Nevertheless, it is important to realize that rhetorical questions do function rhetorically, structurally, and theologically in the SoS.

---

241. Walsh, *Exquisite Desire*, 159.

4

Poetic Characters

THIS CHAPTER HAS AS its impetus the literary analysis of biblical narrative literature forwarded by David Gunn, Danna Nolan Fewell, Meir Sternberg, Rolf Jacobson, Adele Berlin, and Robert Alter. This section seeks to stand on their shoulders and analyze the characters of the SoS. However, it gazes in a new direction. It sets out to inquire how the Song's poet employs characters as a rhetorical device in biblical *poetry*, not in biblical *narrative* as these scholars have done so admirably. A goal of this analysis is to determine as Berlin,[1] Alter,[2] and Exum[3] suggest, "How does poetry mean?" In other words, how does the biblical poet communicate his message? What rhetorical tools does he employ to shape both his message and the response of his audience? Since the characters of the SoS play such a major role in this biblical composition, an analysis of their rhetorical function will determine their contribution to a proper understanding of the question "how does the SoS mean?"

To accomplish this goal this chapter will (1) survey how various interpretive schemes identify and view the characters in the Song throughout history, (2) seek to identify the participants of the Song,[4] (3) suggest the author's rhetorical use of those participants and, (4) propose what part the characters play in delineating the theology of this biblical author.[5]

1. Berlin, "On Reading Biblical Poetry."
2. Alter, *Art of Biblical Poetry*.
3. Exum, "How Does the Song of Songs Mean?"
4. According to Brenner (*Israelite Woman*, 47), the identification of the "*dramatis personae*" is one of the questions that still inspires scholarly debate concerning the SoS.
5. Although Waltke (*Old Testament Theology*, 106–12) is centering his attention on narrative theology, he recognizes the validity of analyzing the manner in which the author uses his characters to arrive at his theology. Since this method holds true for the

A SURVEY OF VARIOUS INTERPRETATIONS OF THE SONG AND THEIR ANALYSIS OF ITS CHARACTERS

R. K. Harrison recognizes the wide variety of interpretations that have plagued this biblical love song:

> Few books of the Old Testament have experienced as wide a variety of interpretation as the Song of Songs. The absence of specifically religious themes has combined with erotic lyrics and the vagueness of any plot for the work to furnish for scholars an almost limitless ground of speculation.[6]

Not much has changed since Harrison's almost forty-year-old observation. This chapter will survey the relationship between the various interpretations and how each scheme views the main characters of the Song.[7]

---

theology of biblical narrative, it is legitimate to pursue this method for biblical poetry as well in the hopes of exposing the theology of the biblical poet.

6. Harrison, *Introduction to the Old Testament*, 1052. LaCocque (*Romance She Wrote*, 2) laments, "There is no more regrettable example of a biblical text being tormented by its critics than this one."

7. The major interpretations that follow in the main text are presented in a roughly chronological manner in which each has developed and are recognized by the majority of Song scholars. The purpose is not to show development of each but to see how each represented the characters of Solomon's finest song.

These interpretive schemes are representative of the major interpretations of the Song. There are some variants within or across some of these positions. For instance, Phillips (*Exploring the Love Song of Solomon*) holds unapologetically to an allegorical interpretation (10); however, he also writes of a typological interpretation (10) and holds to a dramatic, three-character view (8).

This chapter will survey the primary interpretations of the Song. However, these are not the only interpretations. There are some tangent interpretations as well. Cainion ("Analogy of the Song of Songs," 221) believes the SoS should not be read as an allegory but as an analogy with Genesis. He surmises that the king of the Song, "the 'Beloved', is not God but Satan" (236). The Shulammite woman "represents Adam and Eve" (237) and the rustic lover is God (257).

Although not representative of all feminists, Arbel ("'My Vineyard,'" 90–91) considers the Song "a woman's inner and personal discourse.... the poetic expression of the inner dreams, emotions and thoughts of one individual woman. All these are presented in a variety of voices, and acted out in a range of settings and in parallel sequences." It is difficult to have a representative of the feminist interpretation since, according to Brenner ("Introduction," 17), "Feminist readers of this Best of Songs might do well to say to the ancient authors and traditionalists who preserved it for us, 'thanks for your text, and I'll decide how to read it.'"

While not an interpretative view per se, Moore suggests a reading that has a distinct homosexual flavor. He proposes that the reason the twentieth century has witnessed

Early Jewish and Christian Views

Treat observes that there is evidence of allegorical interpretation of the Song "as early as the middle of the first century C. E."[8] According to Fields, "By the time the Talmud was complete the allegorical interpretation of the Song was accepted."[9] Because of their uneasiness in dealing with the plain, erotic language and understanding of the text, these early Jewish interpreters opted to explain the book through allegory. For example, the various body parts of the female lover do not literally mean what the text states but they express a different or higher level of meaning. For instance, Fields quotes an early Jewish writing that believes the "navel" (7:3; 7:2 English) actually stands for the Sanhedrin. "By 'navel' is meant the Sanhedrin. And why were they named navel? Because they used to sit in the middle of the world (according to the Talmud, Jerusalem was the middle of the world and the Temple was the centre of Jerusalem)."[10] Because of the allegorizing of the text, the characters of the Song did not maintain their seemingly literal identities. For these ancient exegetes, the main characters, the male and female lovers, represent God and Israel respectively.[11] *Targum of Canticles* interprets the SoS as tracing the history of God's and Israel's stormy relationship from their deliverance from slavery in Egypt until the Messiah. Even the minor characters did not escape allegorizing in the Targum. For instance, according to Alexander's translation of the *Targum of Canticles*, it views the "sons of my mother"

---

a rejection of an allegorical reading of the Song is because of "the pervasiveness of homosexual panic in twentieth century Western culture." According to Moore ("Song of Songs," 349), the early allegorizers of the Song were more comfortable assuming the voice of the female lover pining after the male lover, God. Today, the male gender has "trouble throwing themselves into the role of a vivacious young woman in love; that the intrinsic queerness of the role sits too strangely in a culture that has scripted them to be superlatively straight at all times."

Bullis ("Biblical Tantra," 104) sees a connection between the Tantra sexual practices of the East and the Song of Songs. In Tantra there is a connection between the sexual and the sacred. In "the most transformative sex" of Tantra, the couple "respect, even adore, each other as physical expression of a divine power—even as god or goddess themselves." Bullis further writes, "The Biblical book of the Song of Solomon . . . is powerful poetry in pursuit of the embodied presence of God" (108) and "The Biblical literature also illustrates this (Tantra) and other tantric principles, particularly the *Song of Songs*" (114).

8. Treat, *Lost Keys*, 5.
9. Fields, "Early and Medieval Jewish Interpretation," 227.
10. Ibid., 227–28.
11. Tanner, "History of Interpretation," 24.

of 1:6 as false prophets and the "daughters of Jerusalem" as the Gentile nations (1:5).[12]

The majority of the early church exhibited no more comfort with the sexual frankness of the Song than her Jewish counterpart. Treat notes that "patristic catenae attribute allegorical interpretations to church writers in the late second century."[13] According to Tanner, allegorists had hoped to move the Song beyond its obvious sexual nature to discover the "spiritual message . . . that exceeds the supposed earthly theme of human sexuality."[14] The early church, according to Norris, "focused on the meaning of the Song for interior life of the faithful soul."[15] While early Jewish scholars viewed this love poem as the love of God for his chosen people, the church scrutinized the book as depicting the love between Christ and his bride, the church. Thus the two main characters of the SoS, the male and female lovers, symbolized Jesus and his church or, in Origen's words, the Bridegroom and the Bride.

Carr observes that the goal of the allegorical method is to find "some deeper spiritual truth."[16] Thus, the female breasts in 1:13 are not simply a reference to the woman's bosom. According to Bernard of Clairvaux, they represent a deeper spiritual meaning. For this twelfth-century monk, they were the place of the mediation of the suffering of Jesus Christ: "you will always retain in your memory all the bitter pains which he bore for you, and meditate upon them continually, so that you too may say with the Bride, *A bundle of myrrh is my well-beloved unto me: he shall lie between my breasts.*"[17] Jerome spiritualized the woman's

---

12. Alexander, *Targum of Canticles*, 83n48. For a modern commentary on the Song that views Israel as the female beloved, see Hocking, *Rise Up My Love*. Hocking (7–8) states, "For us, it becomes clear that the Song of Songs traces the love relationship between the Lord and Israel from its beginning of its history to the end, from the patriarch Abraham through to the grand messianic millennial reign." For a modern Jewish commentary that recognizes the literal meaning of the Song but seeks "to provide modern liberal readers with a more spiritual reading of the text, raising it once again beyond the carnal to the more sacred level," see Kravitz and Olitzky, *Shir Hashirim*.

13. Treat, *Lost Keys*, 5.

14. Tanner, "History of Interpretation," 26.

15. Norris, *Song of Songs*, xx.

16. G. L. Carr, *Song of Solomon*, 21.

17. Bernard of Clairvaux, *Song of Solomon*, 268. Italics are original.

longing for her lover in 3:1 as being a virgin longing for Christ whom she loved.[18]

Unlike the Jewish allegorists of the past who linked the Song to the history of the nation Israel, the church allegorists seldom established such a link with any historical events in the Old or New Testament. Thus, the interpretative results have been a variety of fanciful suggestions even within their own camp.

Typical View

The typical[19] or the typology[20] view is similar to the allegorical view. Carr states, "Typology recognizes the validity of the Old Testament account in its own right, but then finds in that account a clear, parallel link with some event or teaching in the New Testament which the Old Testament account foreshadows."[21] Tanner summarizes this view: "In the typical view there is a definite affirmation of the historical setting of the Song even though it ultimately transpires to a higher level of meaning. Hence, the poem is based on an actual historical incident in Solomon's life with the Shulammite country girl."[22] This view believes the love poem pertains to the historical personages of Solomon and his Shulammite *and* it depicts the love Jesus Christ has for each individual believer. Carr suggests that those who practice this view read each verse of the Song "through Christological eyes for what it can reveal about that relationship."[23]

This position recognizes the historicity of the characters of the book and typifies them into characters for today. Phillips, who states he does not draw "back from following typological truth to its logical conclusion," feels that there are three main characters in this book.[24] He suggests the "Shulamite represents the church, the betrothed of Christ. She also represents the individual Christian in the world today. The

---

18. Jerome, "Letter LXVI," 138.

19. This term is that of Tanner, "History of Interpretation," 31. Functionally this view (typical) is the same as the allegorical. The distinction is drawn simply to use the categories that are accepted today by Song scholars and to investigate how each represented the characters of the SoS.

20. This term is that of G. L. Carr, *Song of Solomon*, 24.

21. Ibid.

22. Tanner, "History of Interpretation," 31.

23. G. L. Carr, *Song of Solomon*, 26.

24. Phillips, *Exploring the Love Song*, 10.

shepherd pictures the Lord Jesus.... He is absent right now; however, He visits from time to time.... Solomon depicts the tempter, the enemy of our souls."[25] Brug, who also evidences leanings towards the typological position, suggests there is little evidence for the love-triangle view and therefore follows a two-main-character position.[26]

Mythological-Cult View

The mythological-cult view (or cultic-mythological view or the cultic view) maintains that the Song is, according to Garrett, a "mythic poem from the fertility cults" of the surrounding nations of Israel.[27] Kinlaw summarizes this view by stating, "The poem does not really speak about human love at all; rather, it is either the celebration of the sacred marriage of a goddess in the person of the priestess with the king, or else it is the celebration of the victory of the divine king over death and drought."[28] Pope suggests the Song be viewed as a funeral cult: "Certain features of the Song of Songs may be understood in the light of the considerable and growing evidences that funeral feasts in the ancient Near East were love feasts celebrated with wine, women and song."[29]

Generally, in this view the divine marriage is acted out by the king and queen or by the king and a priestess, who stands in place of the god-

---

25. Ibid., 17–18.

26. Brug, *Song of Songs*, 12. While Brug does not hold to a typological approach. He believes the Song has two levels of meaning: spiritual and the literal. For instance, concerning the daughters of Jerusalem who are part of the drama of the Song, Brug (24) comments that these female characters are to be understood figuratively as "the individual members of the church." He (19) does declare, "The Song declares that human sexual love is good. It must be, if it is to serve as a type of divine love."

For recent commentaries that espouse a typological view, see Jenson, *Song of Songs*. Jenson reads the Song in an "overt sense" (i.e. plain sense) and as "theological allegory." Also see Hess (*Song of Songs*, 35), who states that the Song's theme of "sex enables an experience of love whose intensity has no parallel in this cosmos and serves as a signpost to the greater love that lies beyond it." Mitchell (*Song of Songs*, 64) believes the Song "is about both relationships: the marriage of two individual believers, Solomon and the Shulammite, and implicitly also about the marriage of Yahweh to Israel—which foreshadows the NT church's betrothal to Christ."

For a recent article that argues strongly for a typological view based on the Davidic covenant see Campbell, "Song of David's Son."

27. Garrett, "Song of Songs," 82.

28. Kinlaw, "Song of Songs," 1205.

29. Pope, *Song of Songs*, 228.

dess.³⁰ Songs are sung that extol such a wedding, marriage, and sexual consumption. The sexual union represents the promise of spring and the hope for fertility of the land and its people. Pope remarks, "The sacred marriage of the king and priestess had as its purpose the magical fertilization of the earth and the renewal of the seasonal cycle."³¹ With this idea of the sacred marriage between the human king and a female deity, this position advocates two protagonists. The mythical origin of the Song from Israel's idolatrous neighbors is the force behind such an interpretation.

Dream View

Tanner recognizes that "some scholars have made the claim that a large portion of the Song of Songs is a dream rather than a reflection of actual experiences."³² This position holds two main characters: Solomon and his bride, the Shulammite. According to Tanner, "The book begins with the married state of Solomon and the Shulammite, but she is fearful and insecure in her new environment. The dream section (2:8—8:4) serves to purge the love relationship as it recounts crucial moments in the relationship."³³ Since dreams rarely follow a logical sequence, one would not expect to find a logical sequence in the Song of Songs. According to proponents, that is exactly what one finds in the SoS—no logical sequence. It is because the Song lacks such an orderly progression that Freehof suggests that the Song is a sequence of dreams and should be interpreted symbolically.³⁴

Literal-Historical View

It may be misleading to label this interpretation as a single view since it has given birth to a number of views that read the Song literally. This literal-historical interpretive scheme (or the plain or the literal view) follows the basic principles of a literal, grammatical hermeneutic. Tanner, who practices such hermeneutics, suggests that "the Song of Songs should be understood literally of the romantic and sexual relationship between

---

30. Longman, *Song of Songs*, 44.
31. Pope, *Song of Songs*, 202.
32. Tanner, "History of Interpretation," 37.
33. Ibid., 38.
34. Freehof, "The Song of Songs," 401.

two lovers."[35] This view is not new. Even while the early Jewish and Christian scholars allegorized their readings, Theodore of Mopsuestia (ca. 350–428) argued that the Song "should be read in its plain sense as an erotic song."[36]

The literal or plain reading of the Song has given rise to the dramatic, the literal-didactic, the love song, and the wisdom views. Each of these recognizes the plain sense of the text of the Song within the genre of ancient Hebrew poetry. All hold in common the erotic and sensual nature of the biblical love song. None of these plain readings blushes at the expression of sexual love between a man and a woman. They recognize the passion of sexual language within the Song's delicate metaphors and similes. Although they are similar in that they accept a literal reading of the text, they do differ in how they view the characters of the SoS.

Dramatic Views: Two or Three Main Characters

In this literal scheme the basic interpretive mechanism is the recognition of a plot that unifies the entire Song. As Carr notes, a drama is distinguished by "its narrow focus and essential unity."[37] To be an effective drama, he continues, it "must show elements of progression in the story, development of theme and character, and some sort of conflict and resolution."[38] Delitzsch recognizes such a unity and calls the Song a drama (although not a true theatrical piece). As an effective drama, the Song contains six acts of two scenes each.[39] Delitzsch observes two main characters in the Song: Solomon, himself, and the country maiden, the Shulammite.

To summarize this position, Solomon finds this humble maiden, courts her, brings her to Jerusalem, marries her, and they grow together in their relationship. As Parsons observes, this is truly a "Cinderella story"[40] for the Shulammite. Solomon rescues her from her overbearing brothers who made her work in their vineyard to her own physical detriment. The king exalts her by making her his wife and queen. This literal

---

35. Tanner, "History of Interpretation," 39.
36. Ibid.
37. G. L. Carr, *Song of Songs*, 33.
38. Ibid.
39. Keil and Delitzsch, *Song of Solomon*, 504.
40. Parsons, "Guidelines," 403.

interpretation of the Song is driven by the existence of a chronological plot that unifies the entire poetic piece.[41]

The dramatic view with three main characters (or the shepherd hypothesis) is similar to the dramatic, two-character interpretation. Both reading schemes are compelled by the notion that a story or plot unifies the entire composition. However, there are two differences in the three-main-character view that distinguish it from the two-main-character interpretation. First, there is an additional male player on the stage, a rustic shepherd. Second, Solomon is not "the knight in shining armor" but is actually the villain of the story.

In the three-character view, the second male is a country shepherd whom the Shulammite truly loves. Solomon, the king, tries to persuade the country lass to leave her rural vineyards (and shepherd lover) and return with him to the metropolitan capital of Jerusalem and Solomon's bed. The Song plays out the entanglements of this biblical "love triangle," with Solomon being the eventual loser. No matter the number of male leads suggested in this drama (either one or two), both dramatic views are motivated by the presence of a perceived plot or narrative that undergirds the entire Song.[42]

Stoop-van Paridon believes in a unified love song that recognizes the voices of the female protagonist, her beloved shepherd, and King Solomon. However, she parts company with the three-character dramatic view by recognizing another main voice. This extra voice is the attendant of the female protagonist who is with her in the harem of the king. She also believes these four principal speakers are joined by the female chorus, brothers of the female lover, and the guards of the city.

---

41. Representative examples of this view are Dillow, *Solomon on Sex*; Fruchtenbaum, *Biblical Lovemaking*; Glickman, *Solomon's Song of Love*; Goulder, *Song of Fourteen Songs*. Holmyard ("Solomon's Perfect One," 169) thinks Solomon and the Shulammite are the main characters; however, the Shulammite maiden is only one wife among his already "sixty queens."

42. While Phillips (*Exploring the Love Song*) does read the book typologically, he also holds to a shepherd hypothesis. See also Mazor ("Song of Songs," 5), who states, "The plot's characters involve three prominent projectionists and two appendant characters who are of collective features. The three prominent protagonists are the Shulammite (the young woman, the bride), her rustic lover and her royal lover, King Solomon. . . . The two appendant, satellite characters, are the daughters of Jerusalem (the young women in King Solomon's harem) and the Shulammite's brothers."

All of these characters, according to Stoop-van Paridon, have speaking parts in the SoS.[43]

Literal-Didactic View

The literal-didactic view interprets the Song literally but at the same time recognizes that the author is also communicating a lesson. Tanner suggests, "While the Song should be taken literally with its expressions of romantic and sexual bliss in marriage, at the same time this poem seems to communicate a lesson on marital love that goes even deeper. Hence it is didactic as well as literal."[44] Although there are variations to the lessons that the Song is purported to teach, the literal-didactic interpretation follows the two-main-character view. The Song is the development of a relationship between Solomon, the king of Israel, and the Shulammite. Tanner outlines it along these lines: prewedding phase (1:2—3:5), wedding day (3:6—5:1), postwedding complications (5:2—8:4), and conclusion (8:5–14), which "holds the key to the message of the book."[45] He believes the overall structure of the book "corresponds to the chronological development of the relationship."[46]

Love Song Views: Anthology and Unity

In this love song view (or anthology view) the SoS is composed of not one song but a number of different poems or songs. In this interpretive scheme the Song is a collection of loosely connected but thematically related poems.[47] These poems extol the sexual love between a man and woman. Longman suggests, "The Song is an anthology of love poems, a kind of erotic psalter."[48] He offers the theory that the anthology is composed of twenty-three individual love poems.[49] One of the main reasons

---

43. Stoop-van Paridon, *Song of Songs*, 471. By her own admission, she (469) realizes that she is outside the main stream of Song scholarship: "In numerous places I have felt obligated to adopt a standpoint which is different from many, and sometimes all, the other commentators."

44. Tanner, "History of Interpretation," 44.

45. Tanner, "Message of the Song of Songs," 157.

46. Ibid.

47. Dillard and Longman, "Song of Songs," 259.

48. Longman, *Song of Songs*, 43.

49. Ibid., 44. Exum (*Song of Songs*, 33) surveys this position and finds that there is no consensus concerning the number of individual poems in the SoS (and this inconsis-

the anthology view has been put forth is because of the weakness of the dramatic view to demonstrate a unified narrative. Dillard and Longman observe the "dramatic approach fails most obviously because it is unable to demonstrate an obvious plot structure."[50] It is apparent that the controlling element to either accept or reject the dramatic view is based on one's ability to recognize a sequential chronology in the book, and this affects how one views the characters in the SoS. Longman believes "human beings have a strong narrative impulse. We tend to make stories out of the most disparate elements. It is my contention that it is this impulse rather than anything in the Song that leads to a dramatic approach."[51] Since Longman does not see unity of the Song based on a plot or narrative, he opts to view the book as a collection of love poems.

While Longman rejects the unity of the SoS, he does maintain that "the Song speaks through its characters."[52] He believes there is no narrator, but there are the woman, the man, the women of Jerusalem, and the woman's brothers. These are the main characters.[53] However, for Longman, these people are not historical personages. The man is not the historical Solomon and the Shulammite likewise is not linked with a historical female. They are fictitious. For Longman, the characters of the SoS are an "artistic creation" of the author.[54] Fox concurs and parallels such use of fictitious characters with Egyptian love poetry: "The speakers in the Egyptian love songs and the Song of Songs are, as a rule, *personae*, created characters through whom the poet speaks but who are not to be identified with them."[55]

In opposition to the anthology position, another love song view recognizes this love song not as a number of individual love songs but as a single, unified poem. Like the anthology view, this poem celebrates the full orb of the passion of human sexuality within the confines of a

---

tency exposes its weakness). For example, she lists Gordis as having twenty-nine; Falk, thirty-one; and Keel, forty-two.

50. Dillard and Longman, "Song of Songs," 259.

51. Longman, *Song of Songs*, 43. Gunn and Fewell (*Narrative in the Hebrew Bible*, 3) understand this human tendency. They state, "Readers seem to have a powerful urge to make sense."

52. Ibid., 15.

53. Ibid., 15–16.

54. Ibid., 48. Also see Bergant, *Song of Songs*; Alter, *Art of Biblical Poetry*.

55. Fox, *Egyptian Love Songs*, 253.

heterosexual marriage. Following the anthology view, the unified love song view rejects the dramatic approach because, as in Carr's opinion, it does not show "any sort of plot development as one would expect in a story."[56] On the other hand it parts company with the anthology view because, as Carr notes, it demonstrates "the inner cohesion around its central theme of the lovers' mutual longing and surrender."[57] This cohesion is not built on a unifying chronological storyline. It is based on the various Hebrew poetic features such as repetition, metaphors, similes, key words, and other rhetorical devices that develop a singular theme of human love. Because of this poetic unity, Carr argues the Song is not an anthology of individual poems but a single, unified whole. Carr believes that "the Song is not to be taken as a series of sequential events, rather, it is constructed in a chiastic form with the individual units arranged symmetrically around a central pivot."[58] While one may argue concerning what provides the overall structure of the Song, there are a number of scholars who advocate such a perspective.

Exum, who supports such a notion, suggests that the main protagonists of the SoS "are archetypal lovers—composite figures, types of lovers rather than any specific lovers."[59] She observes three principal characters in the poem: the male and female lovers and the daughters of Jerusalem. Exum does not believe the brothers who are mentioned in 1:6, or may be alluded to in 8:8, are actually speakers in the Song and thus are not considered main characters in the Song.[60]

Wisdom Literature View

As representative of this view, Brevard Childs states categorically that the "Song is to be understood as wisdom literature."[61] Childs' statement is important. For if the Song is wisdom literature, he believes "other alternative contexts for interpreting it are ruled out."[62] Thus he rejects any

---

56. G. L. Carr, *Song of Songs*, 44.

57. Ibid.

58. Ibid., 46. While one may disagree with Carr's chiastic structuring of the Song, he is correct to reject unity based on supposed sequential events.

59. Exum, *Song of Songs*, 8.

60. Ibid., 248.

61. Childs, *Old Testament as Scripture*, 574.

62. Ibid. Some scholars such as Dillard and Longman ("Song of Songs," 263) as well as Bergant (*Song of Songs*, 4) also label the Song as wisdom literature. The labeling of

secular, allegorical, or mythical interpretation. He states that the "Song is wisdom's reflection on the joyful and mysterious nature of love between a man and a woman within the institution of marriage."[63]

Since Childs classifies the Song as wisdom literature, he views the structure as a "unity of composition" where "one topic of sexual love is dealt with from a variety of perspectives, particularly the longing before union and the satisfaction of mutual surrender."[64] Because "there does not seem to be any clear movement and certainly no plot,"[65] Childs rejects the dramatic theory. Instead, he believes the references to Solomon provide poetic imagery and anchor the SoS in the genre of wisdom literature.[66] The literal king of Israel is not a character in the wisdom view. There are only the two voices of the unidentified lovers and the collective utterances of the daughters of Jerusalem.

Conclusion

Since the allegorical (both ancient and modern), typological, and dream views each reject a literal reading, these interpretative schemes are not exegetically viable and thus will not be analyzed for their character use. The dramatic views, while maintaining a literal reading of the Song, are equally exegetically suspect since they are built on the presumption that there is an overarching storyline or narrative that bears the unity of the entire Song. Unfortunately, such is not the case. As has already been stated, Dillard and Longman observe the "dramatic approach fails most obviously because it is unable to demonstrate an obvious plot structure."[67] As Exum rightly explains, "To turn it (the Song) into a drama, too much has to be read between the lines.... The dramatic theory has a few adherents today, but readers find it surprisingly hard to resist looking for some kind of story 'behind' the Song's lyrics."[68] The characters of the Song in the dramatic view do lend themselves to a "reading between the lines" and subsequent narrative analysis. However, beginning on such a path

---

the Song according to this genre does not necessarily eliminate further categorizing of this love poem.

63. Childs, *Old Testament as Scripture*, 575.
64. Ibid., 576.
65. Ibid.
66. Ibid., 577, 579.
67. Dillard and Longman, "Song of Songs," 259.
68. Exum, *Song of Songs*, 78.

will not provide an accurate investigation into the rhetorical use of these characters by the biblical author since he did not intend the SoS to be read (or acted) as a narrative drama.[69]

While there is little consensus concerning the overall structure of this love poem or how the various, individual sections relate to one another, these observations do not need to argue against the unity of the Song. Exum astutely proposes,

> Unity is created by an artistic vision—in this case, a distinct and consistent attitude toward love—and by continuity of character portrayal, which leads us to posit the same protagonists throughout and see everything that happens in the poem as happening to them. In a unified literary creation, the meaning of the whole is more than the sum of its parts. Some scholars therefore affirm the unity of the Song without proposing a detailed structural or schematic design.[70]

If Exum is correct, there is no necessity to accept the notion that the Song is simply an anthology of individual love songs because of scholars' inability to articulate the structure of the SoS and its internal relationships among its constituent parts. Roberts, in his massive structural work on the Song, gives evidence of this position when he summarizes his thoughts concerning its structure: "It is not surprising, therefore, that this study does not reach a final conclusion regarding the overall structure of the Song."[71] However, in the next paragraph he states dogmatically: "As far as unity is concerned, if repetition is any indicator of cohesion, then the Song is a cohesive and unified work. The extent of repetitions . . . is simply staggering."[72] Based on Roberts' conclusions concerning the relationship between structure and unity and Exum's observations

---

69. According to Gunn and Fewell (*Narrative in the Hebrew Bible*, 2), a narrative has three defining characteristics: characters (usually three or more), plot, and wordplay. While the SoS does have characters (although scholars will differ on the number), exhibits wordplay (repetition of key elements), it does not evidence a plot. According to these authors, "Plot is a sequence of actions, often explicitly connected in terms of cause and effect, leading from an initial situation, through complication, to some sense of resolution." While those who hold to a literal drama interpretation would disagree, there is no discernable plot that carries through the entire SoS. Again, according to Gunn and Fewell, this concept of "time is crucial for narrative" (ibid.). There is no chronological relationship in the SoS; thus, it is not a narrative.

70. Exum, *Song of Songs*, 34.

71. Roberts, *Let Me See Your Form*, 755.

72. Ibid., 756.

concerning the thematic unity and the recognition of the present shape of the Song in the canon as a unified composition, it is best to deal with the piece as a single, unified whole. Thus, the view that the SoS is an anthology of love songs is not sustainable.[73] Based on the exegetical evidence, it is best to view the Song of Songs as a single, unified wisdom composition.[74] It is from this vantage point that a character analysis of the SoS will proceed.[75]

IDENTIFICATION OF VOICES AND CHARACTERS

This section will seek to cover four topics. First, it will attempt to answer the question, "How does the biblical author of SoS reveal his characters?" Second, it will establish the type of characters and/or voices that are present in this poem. Third, it will attempt to identify all the characters according to their type in the context of the Song. Finally, it will identify the characters according to narrative characterizations (flat, full, and

---

73. If the SoS is an anthology, a character analysis would look much different than if the Song is a unified work. In an anthology one would expect the possibility of different characters in each individual love song. Fox (*Egyptian Love Songs*) makes this point in his study. He notes the boy in "The Crossing" is different from the boy in "Seven Wishes" (205). He explains the different characters are part of different literary works, which are part of an anthology. Since the SoS will be approached as a unified composition, the female protagonist who is introduced in chapter one is the same female protagonist at the conclusion in chapter eight.

74. Childs' (*Old Testament as Scripture*, 574) classification of the SoS as part of the wisdom literature genre sounds similar to the unified love song view. Childs' classification of the Song as wisdom literature does not make it different than this view. His wisdom literature designation simply classifies it into a larger corpus of biblical literature (albeit his position does exclude the other positions mentioned, namely, allegorical, secular and mystical) Those who maintain that the Song is both a unified love song and part of wisdom literature may differ concerning the characters and their role in the composition.

75. While Moore ("Song of Songs," 332n10) has badly misread history's correction to the allegorical interpretation of the Song, he does recognize the connection between the unity of the Song and its characters. Speaking of the female lover, he states, "The more the Song is presumed to be a unified composition (as opposed to a mere compilation), the more its female protagonist emerges as a coherently delineated character." What is true of the female character is true for the other main characters as well. If the Song is simply an anthology of separate love poems, the characters in each poem do not necessarily need to be the same characters throughout. If they are not, a characterization may not be possible.

agent).⁷⁶ This fourfold identification process is needed to determine how the biblical author uses the characters and the voices rhetorically.⁷⁷

How Does the Biblical Author Reveal His Characters?

To identify the character or the voices of the Song, the question that should be posed and answered is, "How do the characters of this biblical piece of poetic literature allow the reader to know them?" Since the characters rarely tell the story, even their own, "How does the narrator reveal the characters to the reader?" Or to inquire in the most specific manner (since characters are in the hands of their author to reveal them as he wills), "What sources does the author have at his disposal to allow the reader to know the characters?" While studying biblical narrative, Alter suggests the readers come to know the character as he (or she) is

> revealed through the report of actions; through appearances, gestures, postures, costume; through one character's comments on another; through direct speech by the character; through inward speech either summarized or quoted as interior monologue; or through statements by the narrator about the attitudes and intentions of the personages which may come as flat assertions or motivated explanations.⁷⁸

If Alter's observation may be summarized and applied to the SoS, its characters are revealed by direct speech, inward speech, and their comments concerning one another. To a lesser degree in the SoS, the characters' actions and the statements of the narrator also reveal the characters. In summary, the readers come to know the persons of the SoS through two major sources: either from the inside (the characters themselves) or the outside (statements by the narrator or author).⁷⁹

---

76. Berlin, *Poetics and Interpretation*, 23–33. Berlin sees three categories rather than two (flat and round). She names her three: full-fledged character, type, and agent. She renames them "to avoid confusion" (23). However, to avoid further confusion by using the term "type," the term "flat" will continue to be used to identify a character who is one-dimensional. The other terms will be defined in their appropriate section.

77. This is an important pursuit especially in relationship to Solomon. Although I disagree with Campbell's allegorical conclusions concerning the king of Israel, he does recognize the current trend of Song scholarship is "to suggest that Solomon has little significance to do with meaning and import" ("Song of David's Son," 19). This analysis will suggest Solomon's (and the other characters') proper role in the SoS.

78. Alter, *Art of Biblical Narrative*, 116–17.

79. While Alter's study shows insight for a character's speech within biblical narrative, Jacobson ("*Many are Saying*," 18) makes the observation and suggestion that the

In the SoS the major source of character information comes from the reader "eavesdropping" on the dialogue of the two lovers.[80] For instance, the entire first chapter (minus verse 1 as the superscription) is a dialogue initiated by the female beloved to either the daughters of Jerusalem or her male lover. All that the reader learns about these characters is gleaned from their conversations. Whether it is the Song or the rest of the OT, the reader learns much about the people in the Bible by hearing them in their own words. Jacobson remarks, "Often the main way that Old Testament authors characterize the men and women of their stories is by letting those characters speak."[81] Gunn and Fewell concur and expand that dynamic of dialogue: "What characters say and how they say it may tell us much about the kind of people they are.... Since biblical characters seldom appear alone, we can compare and contrast characters and take note of how they speak to each other, and in the end, see how one person can help define another."[82]

A second source of character information is revealed by the comments various characters make about one another. The brothers of the female beloved, בְּנֵי אִמִּי, which are spoken of in 1:6, do not share anything. They neither speak nor respond to the one speaking. The audience only knows them by the comments the female beloved shares. The same is true of the guardsmen, הַשֹּׁמְרִים הַסֹּבְבִים בָּעִיר (5:6). All that is known of them is from the lips of the female lover.

While much can be gleaned from the character of the male beloved from his own direct speech, there is one instance where the female lover reveals his desire in her own words. Beginning in 2:10 the female protagonist quotes her lover's words עָנָה דוֹדִי וְאָמַר לִי. In this instance the character information concerning the male is indirect speech. The male lover comments on the "daughters" בָּנוֹת, "queens" מְלָכוֹת, "and concubines" וּפִילַגְשִׁים in 6:8–9. These characters reveal nothing of themselves

---

same dynamic can be applied to biblical poetry as well. While his investigation centers on the Psalms, his comments hold validity for the biblical poetry of the Song. He states, "While many biblical exegetes have fruitfully applied the above insights (direct speech of characters) to the interpretation of biblical narrative, the potential that the insight holds for the interpretation of biblical poetry has been left untapped. In the Psalter, as in biblical narrative, direct discourse also functions to portray the character of those whose speech is quoted."

80. Except for 5:1e, f, it could be argued that the entire SoS is a dialogue.
81. Jacobson, *"Many are Saying,"* 17.
82. Gunn and Fewell, *Narrative in the Hebrew Bible*, 63.

from their own lips. All that is known comes from the quotation of the male beloved.

The third source of information is inward speech. In the SoS there is no inward speech of the main male character. The audience learns nothing of the male from his own verbally expressed thoughts. However, the report of two dreams of chapters 3 and 5 do contain dialogue that may be considered inward speech on the part of the female. Since these are dreams, one could argue that these speeches are taking place in the female lover's mind and are not directed to any other characters in the Song. The audience is simply overhearing her private thoughts.[83]

The fourth source of character information is arrived at by studying the actions of the characters. In the SoS this supply of knowledge is limited since the book is mainly dialogue. For instance, while couched in a conversation, the woman does share the actions of her beloved (2:8–9):

הִנֵּה־זֶה בָּא
מְדַלֵּג עַל־הֶהָרִים
מְקַפֵּץ עַל־הַגְּבָעוֹת
דּוֹמֶה דוֹדִי לִצְבִי אוֹ לְעֹפֶר הָאַיָּלִים
הִנֵּה־זֶה עוֹמֵד אַחַר כָּתְלֵנוּ
מַשְׁגִּיחַ מִן־הַחֲלֹּנוֹת
מֵצִיץ מִן־הַחֲרַכִּים

Behold, he is coming,
Climbing on the mountains,
Leaping on the hills!
My beloved is like a gazelle or a young stag.
Behold, he is standing behind our wall,
He is looking through the windows,
He is peering through the lattice.

These actions do tell the audience much about his character: he is determined (because of his insatiable desire) to be with his beloved and to be with her quickly despite any obstacle. In 5:1 the audience hears more of the male's activities (in his own voice). However, his actions do not

---

83. It could be argued, though, that these dreams sections are only reports of her dreams (albeit in the first person) and thus may be true dialogue. The female lover may be repeating her dream thoughts to the daughters of Jerusalem.

seem to be as much about his activity as they are a brief and fast moving dialogue that reports his amorous dalliance with his lover.

If 3:1 and 5:2 signal dream sequences (or dream reporting), then the woman is revealing her action of dreaming, which may or may not reveal anything about her character. However, again it could be argued that the information about the woman is not gained by her action (dreaming) but by her dialogue about the dream.

The final source in which the listener gains knowledge about the character(s) is from the comments shared by the narrator. In the SoS there is only one instance of a narrator's comment (5:1e, f). This is directly after the male lover exclaims that he has indeed accepted the invitation of his lover (4:16) and he enters her garden. While enjoying physical intimacy, an unknown voice enters their intimacies:

אִכְלוּ רֵעִים
שְׁתוּ וְשִׁכְרוּ דּוֹדִים

Eat, friends;
Drink and imbibe deeply, O lovers.

While there is disagreement concerning the speaker of these metaphorical commands to enjoy sexual intimacy, that the speaker is the narrator and that he is commenting positively on the sexual activity of this couple cannot be dismissed lightly.[84]

In summary, the audience learns about the characters of the Song mainly through their dialogue with one another. Comparatively little quantitative information is gained about the characters from outside sources such as statements by the narrator or secondhand reports from other characters concerning their actions.[85]

Types and Identification of Characters

The characters in the SoS may be classified into two broad categories. They may be either verbal or nonverbal (that is speaking or nonspeaking characters). They may be further classified because they are either actual

---

84. There is a slight possibility that the speaker of 3:6–11 is the narrator as well. If this is true, then the author injects himself as the narrator into two separate segments. This seems doubtful. This concept concerning the narrator as speaker will be further developed in the following sections.

85. The term "little" is not to be confused with unimportant. It only denotes quantity. The narrator's statement (5:1) is extremely important to the theology of the Song.

characters of ancient history or characters that are the literary creation of the biblical author.[86]

Sixty Queens and Eighty Concubines

The "sixty queens and eighty concubines, And maidens without number," שִׁשִּׁים הֵמָּה מְלָכוֹת וּשְׁמֹנִים פִּילַגְשִׁים וַעֲלָמוֹת אֵין מִסְפָּר, are nonverbal characters (6:8; see also 6:9). While these women are reported as having praised the beauty of the female lover, their words are not direct quotations. Their introduction and subsequent praise of 6:9–10 are the recorded words of the male lover.[87] It is possible that these women are figments of the imagination of the male lover (or a literary creation of the biblical writer). Since the Song is not a drama, it leaves open the possibility that the women of this group are not actual personages stating these praises. The man invents these women as a way to convince his

---

86. This is an important endeavor as a correction to the allegorical, typological, and drama views. It is also imperative to identify the characters accurately through the exegetical process so as to avoid the erroneous position which views the man and woman of the Song as god or goddess themselves. See Bullis, "Biblical Tantra," 104.

Since Brenner (*Song of Songs*) holds that the Song is a collection of poems, she sees a number of different male and female voices. She opines that more than one couple is implied because "there is too much diversity in the portrayal of the lovers to assume that only one loving pair is depicted" (29). Therefore, she thinks that there is plurality of main female voices and there are a number of male speakers "who assume the persona of a lover" (ibid., 28). Brenner (ibid., 29) believes there are "several loving couples, linked by the common theme." Harding ("I Sought Him," 54) does not believe that the male and female lovers have separate identities: "this merging of their identities also limits the possibility of the characters taking on separate identities as individuals." While Harding is correct to note the similar similes and metaphors used to describe each lover, she goes too far to assert that the woman resists such a merger of identities and endeavors to reassert her own.

87. Stoop-van Paridon (*Song of Songs*, 337) believes the speaker of 6:10 is the attendant of the female lover, who is also in the harem of the king. By her own admission she realizes that most commentators do not share her opinion. Hess (*Song of Songs*, 204) leaves the word of praise in the mouth of the "queens and consorts." Longman (*Song of Songs*, 182) notes the uncertainty of the speaker in this verse. Exum (*Song of Songs*, 220) is correct to see the man as the speaker of these verses. While she does not support her position, the exegetical evidence does. The man is the undisputed speaker of 6:6–9 as commentators agree. Since there are no closing structural markers or syntactical markers for a change of speakers, there is no reason to suppose a new speaker. Even though Roberts hears 6:10 as emanating from the group of royal women, he states, "Opening in this strophe is well-marked by the interrogative phrase מִי זֹאת, which phrase occurs two other times in the Song (3:6a and 8:51), and always in an opening function. Here, however, it is only opening for the strophe to which it belongs" (*Let Me See Your Form*, 456). This fact would argue for 6:10 being structurally part of the whole of 6:8–10 and not opening a new section or designating a new speaker.

female lover of her uniqueness. While some may argue that these "sixty queens and eighty concubines, and maidens without number" represent the beginning of Solomon's harem (cf. 1 Kgs 11:1–3), it may be wiser to see the numbering as Watson does, that is, as a poetic device.[88] If Watson is correct, then these royal women are nonverbal characters as well as nonhistorical.

Mother

The term, "mother" אֵם, appears seven times in the Song (1:6; 3:4, 11; 6:9; 8:1, 2, 5). However, she is not the same character in each instance. In 3:11 she is the mother to King Solomon. In 8:5, the mother that is spoken about is the mother of the central male character. In the rest of the verses (1:6; 3:4; 6:9; 8:1, 2), she is the mother of the female protagonist. At no time does either mother speak, and no mother is ever spoken to. Mothers are simply referred to because of the familial relationship that giving birth created with a character in the Song.

In 1:6 the female character's mother is a reference that establishes the relationship between the female lover and her brothers who are not called "my brothers" but "my mother's sons, בְּנֵי אִמִּי. In 3:4 the character functions adjectivally: "to my mother's house" אֶל־בֵּית אִמִּי. Here the reference (coupled with the next line, 3:4e) suggests that the female lover wants to enjoy physical intimacy in the same room that her mother did, resulting in her being born. Exum observes that this place "reminds us that the mother has also known the passion that the woman experiences."[89] The use of her mother in 6:9, "She is her mother's only *daughter*; She is the pure *child* of the one who bore her," אַחַת הִיא לְאִמָּהּ בָּרָה הִיא לְיוֹלַדְתָּהּ establishes the female lover as unique in every way and for her entire life. Exum opines, "She enjoys a special status with her lover . . . , a status

---

88. Watson, *Classical Hebrew Poetry*, 147. He refers to this device as numerical parallelism. The reason for their "invention" by the male lover will be pursued under the rhetorical section of this chapter. The "maidens" or "daughters" of 2:2 are used in the same way. This group of daughters is a literary construct.

Even Hess (*Song of Songs*, 203), who understands the Song to be a drama, suggests, "Comparisons to King Solomon's harem (1 Kings 11:3) are not likely intended with such different and unrelated numbers"

89. Exum, *Song of Songs*, 137. Stoop-van Paridon (*Song of Songs*, 151) cross references this passage with Ruth 1:8. However, the situation of the admonition for Ruth to return to her mother's house and the female lover's use of her mother's inner room do not seem congruent.

he pictures having since birth in the eyes of her mother."⁹⁰ Hess believes this citation "implies a sense of the special nature of the female, already chosen from all others by her mother. Surely, it would not be surprising for a mother to choose her daughter above all others. The male may have this sense in mind."⁹¹

The reference to her mother in 8:1 once again establishes the familial relationship with her mother at the center. However, in this instance the relationship that she would like to see created is a physical brother-sister bond. While this is an impossibility, such a domestic relationship would allow the female lover to express her affection for her lover publicly without having to endure the ridicule such a demonstration would surely cause.

מִי יִתֶּנְךָ כְּאָח לִי
יוֹנֵק שְׁדֵי אִמִּי
אֶמְצָאֲךָ בַחוּץ אֶשָּׁקְךָ גַּם
לֹא־יָבוּזוּ לִי

    Oh that you were like a brother to me
    Who nursed at my mother's breasts.
    If I found you outdoors, I would kiss you;
    No one would despise me, either.

Hess suggests, "The brother is a fantasy, for the female only dreams of her lover as a brother."⁹² It might be better to only say that the woman "fantasizes" about her lover being in a family relationship instead of "dreams." Using the term "dreaming" could cause confusion with chapters 3 and 5 where the woman is reporting her actual dreams. Here her mother serves only to create the imaginary relationship that would allow her to fulfill her desire for kisses whenever and wherever she found her lover in public (cf. 1:2).

While she would not mind having the opportunity to display some physical affection for her lover publicly without cultural constraint, there are some intimacies that should be shared in equally intimate and private places—thus once again the reference to her mother's house (8:2; cf. 3:4):

    90. Ibid., 221.
    91. Hess, *Song of Songs*, 203.
    92. Ibid., 228.

אֶנְהָגֲךָ אֲבִיאֲךָ
אֶל־בֵּית אִמִּי תְּלַמְּדֵנִי
אַשְׁקְךָ מִיַּיִן הָרֶקַח מֵעֲסִיס רִמֹּנִי

> I would lead you *and* bring you
> Into the house of my mother, who used to instruct me;
> I would give you spiced wine to drink from the juice of my pomegranates.

Stoop-van Paridon sees the phrase, "to the house of my mother" אֶל־בֵּית אִמִּי, as "hidden language for the womb of the woman."[93] It is probably best to understand this phrase in contrast with the public display of 8:1. While it is culturally acceptable to kiss a brother in the public square, it is not in keeping with public decency to put on display the rest of her desire that she craves in 8:2–3. Exum is correct to note that her explicit yearning is for lovemaking: "Beginning with the second half of v. 2, she imagines lovemaking with her lover, who is not 'like a brother' in this respect."[94]

In each of these five instances, the mother of the female lover is a nonverbal character who neither speaks nor is spoken to. She is only spoken about. While this mother is easily identified as the one who bore the female lover, is she a real, historical person? Even if one held to a drama view, the text does not give enough evidence to identify her historically. In actuality her historicity is tied with the identity of the female lover. If the female lover is not a historical character, then it would make sense to conclude that her mother is simply a literary creation of the biblical author. While the female lover will be discussed subsequently (and that reflection will shed light on her mother as well), it suffices to conclude here that the mother is not a historical person but a literary persona.

While there is discussion concerning the speaker of 8:5, according to Hess, "Recent commentators follow the MT in understanding the woman as speaking here."[95] Since the woman is the speaker, then the reference to "your mother" אִמֶּךָ refers to that of the male lover. This is the only reference to the male character's mother. However, the reference to his mother birthing him under a fruit tree is obscure. Whereas the fe-

---

93. Stoop-van Paridon, *Song of Songs*, 418.
94. Exum, *Song of Songs*, 247.
95. Hess, *Song of Songs*, 236.

male lover remarks that her conception was in a room (3:4), in this verse the male lover's mother goes through labor outdoors. While there are obvious sexual overtones (with her arousal of him, עוֹרַרְתִּ֔יךָ, 8:5a; cf. 2:7; 3:5; 4:16; 5:2; 8:4), the connection with his mother at this place eludes a satisfactory answer. Unfortunately, Murphy is still correct, "The allusions remain obscure. Why is the arousal of love now associated with the place where the mother had once conceived or given birth?"[96] Even without a satisfactory explanation, there is still enough evidence to determine that the male's mother is a nonverbal character. Like her counterpart (i.e., the female lover's mother), her historicity is tied with the historicity of her son. While his historicity will be pursued in the discussion concerning him as a character, it suffices to conclude here that his mother is not a historical person but a literary creation.

In 3:11 there is a specific reference to the mother of King Solomon:

צְאֶ֧ינָה ׀ וּרְאֶ֛ינָה בְּנ֥וֹת צִיּ֖וֹן
בַּמֶּ֣לֶךְ שְׁלֹמֹ֑ה בָּעֲטָרָ֗ה
שֶׁעִטְּרָה־לּ֤וֹ אִמּוֹ֙
בְּי֣וֹם חֲתֻנָּת֔וֹ
וּבְי֖וֹם שִׂמְחַ֥ת לִבּֽוֹ

Go forth, O daughters of Zion,
And gaze on King Solomon with the crown
With which his mother has crowned him
On the day of his wedding,
And on the day of his gladness of heart.

While there is no OT narrative evidence of Bathsheba crowning her son Solomon at his coronation or wedding day, the reference is straightforward. This mother is not the same as the mothers of the two main characters of the Song. Based on 1 Kings, this is clearly King Solomon's

---

96. Murphy, *Song of Songs*, 191. The female lover does refer to him as an "apple tree" in 2:3. Exum (*Song of Songs*, 249) suggests, "An erotic understanding of the arousal of love to which she refers is encouraged by the fact that it was also in just such a setting that the man's mother enjoyed sexual intimacy." While this may be an example of illocution, personal experience (and modern anecdotal evidence) suggests that the labor process is one of the least erotic activities in which a couple may engage. In fact this author has heard of some women who rue the day (or night) they gave into their erotic impulse that would produce such pain.

mother (1 Kgs 1:11). What is equally clear is that while active in the crowning of her son, she neither speaks nor is spoken to nor is she identified specifically in the SoS.

Unlike the mothers of the two lovers, this mother (while unnamed in the text) is a historical personage (2 Sam 11; 12; 1 Kgs 1; 2). It is Bathsheba. However, while those who hold to a drama (or typological) view see her as a historical character, the reference here is probably literary. Murphy suggests, "Neither can one eliminate the possibility that this detail (Solomon's wedding festivities) may only be a poetic flourish.... In the context of the Song the king fiction should be recognized here."[97] While Murphy makes an excellent point, it should be noted that this "fiction" or "poetic flourish" does have its root in a historical event that the audience may be able to recall or imagine. Nevertheless, Solomon's unnamed mother is functioning as a literary allusion to a historical character.[98]

The Watchmen

The watchmen or the guards, those who "make the rounds in the city" הַשֹּׁמְרִים הַסֹּבְבִים בָּעִיר, receive mention in 3:3 and 5:7. In both cases they are nonverbal characters. The text gives no evidence of either direct or indirect speech by the city guards. While Stoop-van Paridon conjectures that these guards are the speakers of the RQs in 3:6 and 8:5, she is in the minority and her reasoning is unconvincing. She also views these "gatekeepers and guards" as historical figures in King Solomon's time who were "appointed for the city of Jerusalem and for the (royal) residence there together with their inhabitants."[99] While these "characters" have their roots in the historicity of the time of the writing of this composition (cf. 1 Sam 22:17; 2 Kings 11; Neh 7:3), they are nonverbal and literary allusions.[100] While they do not speak and seem to be indifferent to the woman's plight (3:3), they do act against the woman later (5:7).

---

97. Murphy, *Song of Songs*, 152.

98. Stoop-van Paridon (*Song of Songs*, 171) believes a double entendre in 3:11 is "very plausible." She suggests the "crown" refers to "the protruding posterior border of the penis" which "is called *atara* . . . meaning crown or corona." Her unique explanation seems to raise more questions than it answers.

99. Ibid., 149.

100. Exum (*Song of Songs*, 137) suggests, "The encounter with the watchmen seems to be a blind motif here . . . a potential story, inviting the reader to fill in the gaps." This seems to be the very dynamic that leads to a dramatic reading of the Song, which

The Brothers

The brothers of the Song are said to appear in two instances. In 1:6 the main female character refers to them as "my mother's sons" בְּנֵי אִמִּי. In this verse there is no evidence that they speak or are spoken to. They are only the subject of the woman's explanation. They are spoken about pejoratively as the reason the female protagonist is שְׁחַרְחֹרֶת. For some unknown reason they are angry with their sister and force her to work in the vineyard under the hot sun.

The next instance of the brothers' presence, which is accepted by a number of scholars, is 8:8–9. Their presence, however, is only assumed because there is no specific mention of the woman's siblings by name, allusion, by other characters, or by the narrator. Here they are neither spoken to nor about. The only exegetical evidence for their presence at this point in the SoS is built on the assumption that the "little sister" is the younger female protagonist of the poem. If this is a true assumption, then the "we" of verse 8 are her brothers. This is the majority view held by commentators at present.[101]

However, there may be another explanation for the speaker(s) of this verse and the relationship of the "little sister" with the speaker. If the speakers are the brothers of 1:6, then the author has allowed a nonverbal character who has not been previously introduced to find a voice later in the Song. This literary dynamic may work in a biblical narrative but not in the Song.[102] It does not work in the Song because the main characters

---

Exum argues against. It may be possible that 3:3 serves as a literary introduction (or a foreshadowing) of future interaction (5:7) between the guards and the woman.

101. That the brothers are the characters at this juncture is predictable for those who hold to a drama interpretation. For a recent commentary (2005) that holds to this position, see Hess, *Song of Songs*, 242. Interestingly, he does allow for the possibility that the brothers are being quoted by the female lover (ibid.; see also LaCocque, *Romance She Wrote*, 180). This is the common view even for those who do not hold to a dramatic reading of the text. For instance, Longman (*Song of Songs*, 215), who sees the Song as an anthology of twenty-three individual songs, still recognizes the brothers as verbal characters in 8:8–9 (cf. Bergant, *Song of Songs*, 100). Even Stoop-van Paridon (*Song of Songs*, 447–50), who, while not necessarily reading against the grain of the Song, is not shy about holding a minority position, remarks that 8:8–9 refer to the female protagonist's brothers. Fox (*Egyptian Love Songs*, 171) believes the speakers are "probably the brothers, mentioned in 1:6." However, he does mention that "it is unlikely, though not impossible, the girls of Jerusalem speak here."

102. For example, in the Genesis narrative, Rebekah is introduced by name in relationship to her father, Bethuel (Gen 22:23). This fact is repeated in 24:15. She is given a voice by the narrator in subsequent verses.

(or, better, the three main voices) are introduced either by their own voice or by being spoken to by another character in the poem within the first chapter. For example, the female protagonist is introduced by her own words in 1:2. The daughters of Jerusalem are introduced by their own plural voices in 1:4 and are quickly addressed by the woman in 1:5. The male lover is presented to the reader by being spoken about in 1:2a but quickly spoken to in 1:2–4b and then questioned by the woman in 1:7. He is further introduced by his own voice in his response to her inquiry in 1:8. No other characters in the Song find a voice nor are they spoken to from this point forward.[103] While other characters appear in the Song, they are never given a voice. It appears that all the voices of the Song are introduced by the author within the first eight verses.[104] After this point, no nonverbal character is ever heard by the audience. Thus, it would be out of character to have this literary pattern broken at this point and at this point only. Davidson, while not dogmatic, concurs when he states that it is far from certain that the brothers ever speak.[105]

On the negative side of the argument, to say that the "we" of 8:8 must mean the brothers is begging the question. Is it not possible that the "we" may be another plural group in the Song? Could it not as easily be the "guards" (3:3; 5:7) or the daughters of Jerusalem who have a "little sister"? In the same vein, is it possible that the young female is related to someone else in the Song, or maybe any "little sister" of Israel? Maybe she is a literary creation of the author for a specific rhetorical effect and not a sibling of a character in the Song at all?

While some may disagree with Garrett's interpretation of the Song as a musical composition with a tenor, soprano, and female chorus, he does argue for the possibility that the brothers do not have a voice: "Interpreters often assert that Song 8:8–9 belongs to the brothers. Nowhere else in the Song, however, does one find any indication that there is a male chorus functioning as 'brothers.' This is the result of

---

103. The only exception is the voice given to the unidentified character of 5:1e, f. This will be further explored in the section under the narrator as a character in SoS.

104. By limiting the main speaking characters to three (the male lover, the female lover, and the daughters of Jerusalem), could this be one of the ancient author's ways of signaling to the reader that this song is indeed not a narrative? According to Gunn and Fewell (*Narrative in the Hebrew Bible*, 2), narrative is composed of "generally three or more characters in a story." The Song only evidences three principal voices.

105. Davidson, *Flame of Yahweh*, 575.

thinking of Song of Songs as a drama rather than as a Song."[106] Exum strongly agrees:

> Since it would be surprising to hear the brothers speak directly now, for the first time in the poem, many suppose that the woman is quoting words her brothers spoke in the past.... The problem with this view is that it appeals to a 'story' that lies outside the poem in order to account for what is being said: it invents a plot where none exists. The woman's brothers appear in one verse of the Song. Not only do they never speak, they are never spoken to. To assign to them a speaking part, even in the form of a quoted speech, is to give them an important role in the Song that the text does not warrant.[107]

Based on the evidence, it is best to suggest that the brothers are nonverbal characters of the Song.

The historicity of the brothers is tied with the identity of the female lover. If the female lover is not a historical character, then it would make sense to conclude that her brothers are not either. The female lover will be discussed subsequently (and that reflection will shed light on her brothers as well). The conclusion remains that the brothers are not historical persons but are manufactured from the imagination of the author for some rhetorical effect.

"Our" Little Sister

אָחוֹת לָנוּ קְטַנָּה וְשָׁדַיִם אֵין לָהּ

We have a little sister and she has no breasts (8:8)

As has been stated previously, this clause does not necessarily infer that the "we" are the brothers. Therefore, the identity of the "little sister" and the speaker of this verse are open to investigation.

LaCocque recognizes the difficulty in identifying the speaker: "It is not easy to decide who is speaking in verses 8–10."[108] He suggests, "One could imagine that the Shulammite is speaking about a younger sister of hers."[109] He quickly rejects this option though and instead opts for the

---

106. Garrett, "Song of Songs," 259.
107. Exum, *Song of Songs*, 256.
108. LaCocque, *Romance She Wrote*, 180.
109. Ibid.

traditional view that the brothers are the speakers and the Shulammite is their sister. Falk as well notes the obscurity when she writes, "This dialogue is one of the more perplexing poems in the collection.... It is difficult to say who is speaking to whom. It sounds like a chorus of older brothers but grammatically it could be either men or women speaking."[110] Stoop-van Paridon summarizes the options as to the voice (or voices) that speak of "our little sister":

> The brothers of the female protagonist; the daughters of Jerusalem; in 8.8 the brothers of the female protagonists and in 8.9 her lovers; the shepherd loved by the female protagonist; the female protagonist who is relating an earlier conversation with her brothers; (or) the sister of the female protagonist.[111]

Since the shepherd is part of the three-character drama, he can be rejected as a candidate for speaking since there are not two male voices in the Song as has been previously stated. Also, arguing against any solitary voice is the author's use of the first person common plural personal pronoun to identify the speakers of this verse. At no other time does a singular character use the first person plural except for the two main characters. Their usage always concerns them as a couple and is always addressed to each other. Based on this evidence, the only viable candidate for the speakers of this verse is the daughters of Jerusalem. They are the only plural company that has spoken at all (cf. 1:11; 7:1).[112]

---

110. Falk, *Love Lyrics*, 132.

111. Stoop-van Paridon, *Song of Songs*, 444. Also see Exum (*Song of Songs*, 256–57) for another summary of possibilities.

112. The NASB lists the "chorus," their designation for the daughters of Jerusalem, as the speakers of verses 8 and 9.

There is a possibility that the "we" in this verse is actually the couple themselves. They are the only ones outside the daughters of Jerusalem who have spoken as a "we." Exum (*Song of Songs*, 254) believes the couple is the speaker of 8:8–9 and is speaking about the female beloved. However, in the next breath, she states that the woman is the voice: "She is the narrator of this vignette" (ibid., 255). Again she suggests that the couple is speaking: "Theirs could be the voice we hear here" (ibid., 257). Garrett ("Song of Songs," 259) also recognizes the possibility that the couple may be the speaker. However, whenever the couple has spoken in this manner, it has always been to each other. In this verse the audience is unspecified. In addition, if the sister is not the female beloved, it would be unusual for the couple to be responsible for the sexual purity of their sister, who would presumably (because of her physical immaturity) be under her own mother's and father's authority.

Behind the scant argument for the brothers being the speakers seems to be the notion that the Song is a drama. Since it is not, there is no compelling (or exegetical)

Although not convinced the daughters of Jerusalem are the speakers, Fox does note the possibility: "It is unlikely, though not impossible, that the girls of Jerusalem speak here."[113] Garrett is much more certain that the daughters are the speakers: "the plural forms in Song 8:8–9 are fairly clear indicators that these lyrics belong to the chorus and not to the soprano or the tenor" (i.e., the female or male voices).[114] While not taking that position, Falk does recognize that grammatically the language of the verse can sustain the argument that the speaker(s) are a group of women.[115]

If the speakers are not the brothers, then the "little sister" is not related to them. Therefore, she is not the female protagonist. Like the other nonverbal characters of the SoS, the little sister is a literary creation of the biblical writer who creates her for a rhetorical purpose. Garrett categorically states, "There is no need to ask about the relationship between the little girl of 8:8–9 and the chorus, as though these were actual characters in a drama or history."[116] Exum thinks, "If vv. 8–9 are attributed to the women of Jerusalem, there is no reason to assume that they are talking about the woman. They could be speaking hypothetically as it were, about a girl who has not reached sexual maturity, referring to her as their 'little sister.'"[117] In this way the daughters of Jerusalem take the responsibility for both the protection of those girls who have not yet reached the sexual maturity for marriage as well as the adornment of

---

reason to tie the sister of 8:8 with the brothers of 1:6. See a fuller discussion under "the brothers."

113. Fox, *Egyptian Love Songs*, 171.

114. Garrett, "Song of Songs," 259. While Garrett recognizes the couple could be the collective speaker of 8:8–9, he suggests, "In the absence of clear evidence to the contrary, it is best to go with the simplest solution, that the first person plural forms imply that the chorus is singing" (ibid.). Exum (*Song of Songs*, 257) argues that the daughters should not be understood as the speakers at this point because "it seems curious, and wholly unanticipated . . . for them to be holding with the woman at this point in the poem." Simply to discount them as speakers because they are "unanticipated" is to disregard the exegetical evidence and make the reader the standard of what to expect or not to expect in Hebrew poetry. While Exum's work is to be admired, her argument is unconvincing at this point.

115. Falk, *Love Lyrics*, 132.

116. Garrett, "Song of Songs," 259.

117. Exum, *Song of Songs*, 257. Goulder (*Song of Fourteen Songs*, 66) believes the girl is hypothetical and is used simply by the woman to advance her argument against a "wealthy but foolish suitor."

those girls who have their marriage day in sight.[118] Thus, the little sister is a nonverbal character, and she is also a literary creation of the author.

THE DAUGHTERS OF JERUSALEM

The daughters of Jerusalem are referenced by name seven times (1:5; 2:7; 3:5, 10; 5:8, 16; 8:4). In every instance they are only spoken to by the female lover. No one else in the SoS ever addresses the daughters of Jerusalem or Zion (3:11).[119] Besides the female and male lovers, the daughters are the only other voice(s) that the reader ever hears throughout the entire SoS. Exum notes well, "The Song is dialogue between a man and a woman (and occasionally the women of Jerusalem)."[120] While scholars may argue on what occasions they raise their voices, there is no doubt that they do speak along with the main male and female voices.[121] Outside the female lover speaking for the couple (e.g., 1:17; 2:15), the daughters are the only group to have the first person plural personal pronouns applied to them.

Keel feels the daughters of Jerusalem (or simply daughters) "are residents of Jerusalem.... The women of Jerusalem are probably used in

---

118. This is not in contradiction to the rest of the OT that sets the responsibility for and the oversight of daughters squarely on the shoulders of the family. As will be seen under the discussion of the identity of the daughters of Jerusalem and their function in the SoS, they take the place of the audience to whom the book is written (thus fathers and mothers, sisters and brothers). That the daughters are entrusted with the care of the younger females is not unusual in the Song since the poem seems to function without reference to patriarchal responsibility at all. Instead, it highlights the role of females. This is further evidenced by the adjuration refrains that are addressed exclusively to the daughters of Jerusalem. However, theologically the responsibility not to arouse such a powerful emotion as love, which is the theme of the refrains, is applicable to all readers.

119. Exum (*Song of Songs*, 150) says of the term "daughters of Zion" that it "is used synonymously with the 'daughter of Jerusalem.'" Similarly, Hess (*Song of Songs*, 122) believes, "The term 'daughters of Jerusalem'... is likely a poetic variant of 'daughter of Jerusalem.'" The term "daughters of Zion" is also used in Isa 3:16, 17; 4:4. Here the "daughters" are divinely disciplined for their pride and later healed. There is no evidence in the Song that the negative characteristics of the "daughters" in Isaiah are true of the same named company of this love song.

120. Exum, *Song of Songs*, 4.

121. While there is discussion concerning the possibility of ever hearing the voices of the brothers, guardsmen, or the "sixty queens and eighty concubines," there is no scholarly disagreement that the daughters do indeed articulate their thoughts at some points in the Song. Without a doubt the daughters speak in 5:9 and 6:1. Other instances such as 1:5, 11 and 8:8 are open to debate.

the Song as the stereotypical public . . . because these spoiled, idle, and curious women of the capital city were said to be especially versed in matters of beauty and love."[122] While Keel is correct that the daughters represent the "stereotypical public" (i.e., the reader), he goes beyond the textual evidence when he characterizes them so pejoratively. From the SoS itself precious little is known about the character of the daughters. In the same manner, Munro reads too much into the daughters' response when she considers them "rather stupid" in 6:1 because they offer to help the female lover find her beloved after the fact.[123] Mitchell observes that the daughters denote "actual women of the city," although he does not characterize them any further.[124]

Stoop-van Paridon feels the queens and concubines of 6:8 form a distinct group. This collection of women is King Solomon's harem. She also believes it is "plausible" that the daughters of Jerusalem (themselves a distinct group) are also residents of the harem as well.[125] While the reference of 6:8 may be a comparison to the king's harem, there is nothing exegetically that ties the daughters to this group. Stoop-van Paridon's presumption that the SoS is a drama seemingly drives her (and others) to such a conclusion.

The preceding pejorative arguments are unconvincing concerning the historical identities of the daughters of Jerusalem. However, the exegetical evidence indicates the daughters are verbal characters in the SoS. Exum summarizes the voices she hears in the SoS: "There are only three clearly distinguishable speaking voices in the poem . . . the woman, the man and the women of Jerusalem."[126] Even though this female company is associated with the literal city of Jerusalem, the daughters are not a historical group. They are a literary creation of the biblical author. Longman cautions against regarding this group as actual women: "The women are a literary device and the question is not so much who are they as what

---

122. Keel, *Song of Songs*, 49. G. L. Carr (*Song of Solomon*, 78) suggests that since the daughters are associated with Jerusalem then they would "display the characteristics of the city girls."

123. Munro, *Spikenard and Saffron*, 43.

124. Mitchell, *Song of Songs*, 594.

125. Stoop-van Paridon, *Song of Songs*, 40. Mazor ("Song of Songs," 5), who follows a three-character dramatic view, thinks that the daughters are the young women of Solomon's harem as well. See also Tanner, "Message of the Song of Songs," 152; Goulder, *Song of Fourteen Songs*, 12.

126. Exum, *Song of Songs*, 182.

is their function within the poems."¹²⁷ Nevertheless, Longman believes they have a distinct character: "They are city girls, young and naïve, inexperienced in matters of love."¹²⁸ However, if they are the speakers of 5:1 (as Longman indicates), they are more sexually experienced than Longman believes, having access to this most intimate moment between the couple.¹²⁹ It is best to follow Exum: "'Daughters of Jerusalem' are the women inhabitants of Jerusalem. . . . There is no compelling reason to think of them as a more select group, such as young unmarried women."¹³⁰ In conclusion, the daughters of Jerusalem are verbal characters in the Song, but they are not historical. They are literary characters.

The Male Lover

The male lover divulges little about his own identity. While his conversation with his lover demonstrates that he enjoys a passionate, amorous, and even erotic relationship with the female protagonist (albeit not without some difficulty, i.e., 2:15), nothing he says reveals his identity. When the female beloved talks about him to others, nothing is shared that identifies him specifically. The male lover is never characterized any more specifically than by the female lover's terms of endearment (or by his desire for her). She calls him "whom my soul loves" שֶׁאָהֲבָה נַפְשִׁי (3:1, 2, 3, 4, etc.), "my beloved" דּוֹדִי (2:3, 8, 9, 10, etc). Although not by the exact term, the female protagonist alludes to him as a shepherd in 1:7–8. In 1:4 and 12 she talks about him in the third person as "he who is the king" שֶׁהַמֶּלֶךְ. The male lover refers to a king in 7:5. In this instance the article is absent, מֶלֶךְ אָסוּר בָּרְהָטִים. It is from these two epithets, king and shepherd, that the scholarly discussion arises concerning the identity of her male beloved.

---

127. Longman, *Song of Songs*, 16.

128. Ibid. There are some scholars who read the woman's response to the daughters in 1:5–6 as a way to correct their caustic gaze, which looks down their collective city nose at the woman's sunburnt beauty (for example, D. M. Carr, *Erotic Word*, 117). However, it may be that the woman is simply self-conscious, self-deprecating (cf. 2:1; 7:1) and cannot understand why anyone would want to look so intently at her. At this point the female lover has probably misread the gaze of the other women. There is no evidence in the rest of the SoS of any animosity between the woman and the daughters. It seems forced to posit such a conflict here.

129. Ibid., 16, 159.

130. Exum, *Song of Songs*, 102–3.

From the conversation between the woman and her lover in 1:7–8, some scholars have seen the male as a simple shepherd. However, since these self-same scholars also recognize Solomon as a character in the SoS, this makes for two main male characters. This has given rise to the dramatic three-character view or the shepherd hypothesis. As has been stated previously, this interpretative scheme may be rejected since there is no overarching plot or narrative and no love triangle between an unknown shepherd, King Solomon, and the Shulammite.[131]

The woman's reference to her lover as king (and the few internal references to Solomon) has caused scholars to speculate that the male lover is none other than King Solomon himself. This has been the predominate characterization of the male lover in the two-character dramatic view. However tempting to see the male lover as Solomon, the exegetical evidence does not support such an identification.[132] This evidence will be further developed under the discussion of Solomon as a character in the SoS. Like the other characters, the male lover is a literary creation of the author. It is best to see the shepherd and king references as figurative language "wherein the woman endows the man with metaphorical roles to express her respect and desire for him."[133] The male beloved is a verbal character who is poetic creation.[134] He is not to be identified with any historical figure.[135]

The Female Lover

By far the most dominant character in the SoS is the female lover, evidenced by the amount of text she monopolizes. By Brenner's account-

---

131. The reason for the poet's reference to the male lover as a shepherd will be developed under the discussion of the rhetorical use of the various characters.

132. This interpretation is built upon the shaky foundation that the SoS is a tightly knit narrative. Since such a narrative foundation is not well-supported, neither is the structure which is built upon it.

133. Longman, *Song of Songs*, 16.

134. In his comparative study with India's love poetry, Mariaselvam (*Song of Songs*, 168) observes that the same dynamic is true of Tamil poetry: "The lovers are idealized types."

135. The author of an unsigned article ("Song of Songs and the Sister-Wife Motif," 13) believes that the shepherd of the SoS is Hezekiah "who courts the faithful remnant (Shulammite) of the northern kingdom.... The shepherd's disappearance and the nightmares (cf. Isa 29:7) of the disconsolate maiden correspond to the horrific period of Assyrian invasion." The unidentified author feels he is following a tradition-historic approach but it "does not preclude other exegetic techniques."

ing, the woman delivers sixty-one and a half verses or 53 percent of the text.[136] The male lover only accounts for 34 percent. Even when she is not speaking, she overshadows the male protagonist's voice by being the sole object of his conversation. Although she speaks the most often and is the object of the other main voice, precious little is known of her identity.

While the male lover makes her the object of his dialogue (1:9–10; 2:2, 10–14; 4:1–15, etc.), he shares nothing of her identity. All he reveals is a description of her physical beauty (but even this is limited). He calls her רַעְיָתִי most often (1:9, 15; 2:2, 10, 13; 4:1, 7; 5:2; 6:4). She is also his אֲחֹתִי כַלָּה (4:9, 12; 5:1; only כַלָּה in 4:8). He also calls her יוֹנָתִי, which is surely a term of endearment since she is a person and not a bird (2:14; 5:2; 6:9). He refers to her figuratively as a prince's daughter, בַּת־נָדִיב, as he addresses her in 7:2.

In 7:1 (and only here) the daughters of Jerusalem call the female lover "the Shulammite." Numerous commentators choose to identify the female voice as the Shulammite, הַשּׁוּלַמִּית.[137] The daughters ask her to return so they can gaze at her beauty. The female lover mirrors their imperative by voicing a question using the same term to identify herself. However, this term is not necessarily a term of personal identity but possibly a title or descriptive term whose exact meaning escapes Song scholars. Exum, while noting the various suggestions concerning the definition of the term does state, "This is not a personal name, since it appears with the definite article."[138] Stoop-van Paridon argues: "The definite article here has a generic meaning and it excludes the possibility that שׁשׁ can be taken as a proper name."[139] Exum writes, "If the man in the Song is Solomon or a type of Solomon, then the woman could be his feminine counterpart. Most likely Shulammite is a derivative of *šlm* (from which both the name Solomon and the word *shalom* are derived),

---

136. Brenner, *Israelite Woman*, 47, 49. There is some discrepancy between the accounting of some scholars concerning the number of verses assigned to each speaker. For example, Weems ("The Song of Songs," 364) numbers fifty-six (or more) for the female lover and thirty-six for the male.

137. Except Stoop-van Paridon, *Song of Songs*, 354. She believes that this term refers to all the young women in Solomon's harem who, when they are presented to Solomon, become the Shulammite.

138. Exum, *Song of Songs*, 226.

139. Stoop-van Paridon, *Song of Songs*, 355.

meaning 'the perfect one.'"[140] Since the term is not a personal name, it does little to aid the reader in specifically identifying the female lover.

While the exact identity of the female lover cannot be ascertained with any degree of certainty, it may be easier to say who she is not. Holmyard sees the female lover as the Shulammite who is "a humble country girl."[141] This vague identification is normal for those who view the Song as having a coherent, narrative plot. Unfortunately, the Song does not exhibit an overarching narrative and, thus, her identity is lost. Sasson theorizes that the female lover is Pharaoh's daughter.[142] However, based on the textual evidence in the Song, this is not the daughter of an Egyptian king. While it is true that Solomon took the Egyptian princess in a marriage alliance (1 Kgs 3:1), there is no evidence that she is the Shulammite. Sasson's argument that the allusion to Pharaoh's mare (1:9) is a forceful and most direct one is not as strong as he thinks. The culturally conditioned metaphor could as easily fit non-Egyptian women since it is based on the power of the woman to create havoc among men by her beauty. Also, since shepherds are loathsome to Egyptians (Gen 46:34), it is likely out of place for the female lover to use a shepherd metaphor throughout the Song to describe her male lover. Maccoby suggests "very tentatively" that the female protagonist is the Queen of Sheba (1 Kgs 10).[143] However, there is no scriptural evidence that Solomon ever had a dalliance with her or married this queen.

The reason the female lover's exact identity alludes scholars is because she is a literary creation. Exum states, "The Song as we now have it is a written text, an artistic creation, and the man and the woman who appear in it are literary creation."[144] She is a character created from the imagination of the biblical author. While Clines recognizes that the woman "is not a real woman" but rather "is a figment of the poet's imagination," his view that the female protagonist is a fantasy woman is unten-

---

140. Exum, *Song of Songs*, 227.
141. Holmyard, "Solomon's Perfect One," 164.
142. Sasson, "King Solomon," 407. See also Davidson, *Flame of Yahweh*, 567–68.
143. Maccoby, "Sex According to the Song of Songs," 58.
144. Exum, *Song of Songs*, 4.

able.¹⁴⁵ She is neither a "strange woman," nor is she a "wish-fulfillment."¹⁴⁶ Clines changes the meaning of *'ishshah zarah* as he applies it to the woman of the Song since she is completely monogamous. There is also no scriptural evidence that she is the literary equivalent of the modern centerfold.¹⁴⁷ On the contrary, the primary focus is on the couple of the Song longing to be together.¹⁴⁸

In summary, the woman of the Song is not an historical character but a literary one created by the biblical author to advance his purpose.¹⁴⁹ "The Shulammite" is also the dominant voice throughout the Song.

SOLOMON AS A CHARACTER

The term "Solomon" שְׁלֹמֹה appears seven times in this love song (1:1, 5; 3:7, 9, 11; 8:11, 12). There is no disagreement that the Solomon referred to in each of these cases is none other than the famous king of Israel himself. Past this point, however, consensus is lost concerning what Solomon is doing in the Song of Songs.

---

145. Clines, "Why Is There a Song of Songs," 13. Clines believes the woman of the Song "is a strange one ... she is literarily, a strange woman, an *'ishshah zarah*—and that is because she does not exist. She is not a real woman, she is a figment of the poet's imagination. What's more, she is his wish-fulfillment dream. He dreams her up precisely because she does not exist. What we have we do not wish for. He is a certain kind of man, who wants a certain kind of woman, a type that is not generally available in his culture. He fantasizes such a woman, he writes his dream, he finds an audience of like-minded men, his poem becomes a best seller." By his own admission, Clines is allowing his Freudian (and psychological) tendencies to drive his assumptions: "I stick by Freud's dictum, '[A] happy person never phantasies, only an unsatisfied one.'"

146. Ibid. Clines is changing the meaning of *'ishshah zarah* from its use in Prov 2:16.

147. Clines (ibid., 8) believes, "The material cause for the Song of Songs is, then, the need for public erotic literature.... The economic context is the existence of a market, with a choice of consumer, and a publishing industry with copying facilities, a promotion department that bills the text ... and sales outlets. And the social context is the one that approves the existence and distribution of erotic literature that verges on soft pornography."

148. While I disagree with his purpose for the Song, Clines is correct to see a specific purpose for this poem. It is meant to motivate the readers not to want a woman like the female lover but to desire a relationship like the one enjoyed by the lovers in the Song. Thus, the Song may be a fantasy, but it is one that may be realized by all married, heterosexual couples this side of the fall.

149. This is contrary to Mariaselvam (*Song of Songs*, 170), who states, "The designation Shulamite by the girl herself is a mere repetition of what the onlookers said, and hence it has no particular significance." It seems presumptuous to deny the significance of a term that is so little understood.

This "Song of Songs" שִׁיר הַשִּׁירִים is associated in some way with Solomon (see אֲשֶׁר לִשְׁלֹמֹה, 1:1). In 1:5 and 3:7 the term "Solomon" is used adjectivally to describe the black color of some specific curtains associated with the king, כִּירִיעוֹת שְׁלֹמֹה, or his couch, מִטָּתוֹ שֶׁלִּשְׁלֹמֹה. This "couch" is further described as a "sedan chair" which Solomon made, אַפִּרְיוֹן עָשָׂה לוֹ הַמֶּלֶךְ שְׁלֹמֹה (3:9). Solomon, as the king on his wedding day, is referred to as the object of the intent gaze of the daughters of Jerusalem, צְאֶינָה וּרְאֶינָה בְּנוֹת צִיּוֹן בַּמֶּלֶךְ שְׁלֹמֹה בָּעֲטָרָה שֶׁעִטְּרָה־לּוֹ אִמּוֹ בְּיוֹם חֲתֻנָּתוֹ וּבְיוֹם שִׂמְחַת לִבּוֹ (3:11). In 8:11 Solomon is depicted as the wealthy landlord who rents out his vineyard at Baal-hamon to others, כֶּרֶם הָיָה לִשְׁלֹמֹה בְּבַעַל הָמוֹן נָתַן אֶת־הַכֶּרֶם לַנֹּטְרִים אִישׁ יָבִא בְּפִרְיוֹ אֶלֶף כָּסֶף. In the following verse (8:12) the female lover addresses Solomon and cryptically tells him: "My very own vineyard is at my disposal; The thousand *shekels* are for you, Solomon, And two hundred are for those who take care of its fruit" כַּרְמִי שֶׁלִּי לְפָנָי הָאֶלֶף לְךָ שְׁלֹמֹה וּמָאתַיִם לְנֹטְרִים אֶת־פִּרְיוֹ. Each of these occurrences characterizes Solomon as a literal, historical figure. Unlike all the other characters of the Song, he is not a literary creation of the artist but a factual person with whom the reader is expected to associate various items with him in some way.

While Falk makes the point that "Solomon is neither a speaker nor a principal character in the Song," she may go too far when she observes, "It is unlikely that the historical person King Solomon is a persona in any of the poems."[150] It is also unlikely that Solomon is, according to Mariaselvam, a poetic fiction who has become a type or archetype of any male lover.[151] Based on the specific references to Solomon (1:5; 3:7, 9, 11; 8:11) and the female lover's actual address to him (8:12), it is best to see him as an historical character that the poet uses rhetorically in a few different ways throughout the SoS.[152] Thus, Solomon is the only character in the entire SoS who is a historical person.

Since Solomon is an historical figure, he cannot be identified as the male lover since the male protagonist is the poet's literary creation. Stoop-van Paridon is correct when she observes, "The male protagonist of the Song is never identified with Solomon, either directly or by sub-

---

150. Falk, *Love Lyrics*, 108.

151. Mariaselvam, *Song of Songs*, 179–80.

152. This point will be further developed in the section concerning the rhetorical use of the characters in the SoS.

stantive allusion."[153] While it is true that Solomon is indeed a factual, historical person, he does not have a voice in the Song.[154] Nowhere does the reader hear his voice as a character and in only one instance is he addressed, although he appears to be absent (8:12). While it is true that the character Solomon has no voice, in actuality, as the author, all the voices and the characters are his own literary creation (except the references to himself).

Solomon as the Author

While the scholarly consensus is moving to accept the unity of the Song, very few are willing to go the next step and advance Solomon as the author as well as a character (or at least an historical reference) in the SoS.[155] However, Exum comes close. While she is arguing against the later work of a compiler or redactor, she argues convincingly for a single author:

> If the Song exhibits cohesiveness, homogeneity, consistency of character portrayal, and a distinctive vision of love—and I believe that it does—is there any need to posit an editor at all? Perhaps the Song was composed by a single author, working within a poetic tradition, and was only lightly edited in the process of transmission.[156]

Although Exum is reluctant to suggest an identity (or even gender) for this author, it does not seem a stretch to suggest that Solomon is indeed the author. Though Garrett is right to remark about the ambiguity of the prepositional phrase לִשְׁלֹמֹה, he may go too far to label it as ambiguous in its context. While there may be a range of meaning for this prepositional phrase, in context no exegetical principle is violated if it is taken

---

153. Stoop-van Paridon, *Song of Songs*, 20.

154. This observation negates the view of three main characters populating the Song: a woman, a shepherd and Solomon. Since Solomon does not speak, it is difficult to imagine him as a verbal character in a poem that is mainly dialogue. Bennett ("Love Over Gold," 31) is one that would hold such a view.

155. Of the most recent commentaries, Exum (2005) is the most current scholar to hold to the unity of the Song. Hess (2005), Stoop-van Paridon (2005) and Estes (2005) hold to a unified composition; however, they see the Song as a dramatic presentation. Davidson (2007), who presents a theology of sexuality in the OT in his *Flame of Yahweh*, believes the SoS is a unified composition. Longman (2001) and Falk (1982) exemplify those who maintain an anthology view and thus would suggest different authors.

156. Exum, *Song of Songs*, 35.

as a reference to Solomonic authorship (1:1).[157] On the contrary, it is the simplest explanation.[158] The reference in 1 Kgs 4:32 concerning the massive number of songs written by Solomon also argues for his authorship of this song as being his best (1:1). The literary argument put forth by Exum, the OT reference to his 1,005 songs, and the evidence of 1:1 points to Solomon as the author of the Song of Songs. At present, this is a minority position. Mitchell demonstrates that few recent scholarly works affirm Solomonic authorship.[159]

While there are a number of scholarly objections to Solomonic authorship, it is important to interact with one such objection by Longman (who will be used as a representative of those who hold his view as well).[160] This is an important objection to respond to since it is Solomon's involvement with multiple wives and concubines that lays the foundation for the author's rhetorical use of Solomon. Among other reasons, Longman argues against Solomonic authorship based on his sordid lifestyle:

> We might question an essential Solomonic role in the Song due to Solomon's dubious reputation in the area of love. Song extols an exclusive, committed relationship.... Yet historical tradition concerning Solomon does not focus on one woman but many wives and concubines.[161]

---

157. The same prepositional phrase is used in relationship to David as the author of a number of psalms (לְדָוִד, Ps 3:1; 4:1; 5:1; 6:1; 7:1; 8:1; 9:1; 11:1; 12:1; 13:1; 14:1; 15:1; 16:1; 17:1; 18:1, 51; 19:1; 20:1; 21:1; 22:1; 23:1; 24:1; 25:1; 26:1; 27:1; 28:1; 29:1; 30:1; 31:1; 32:1; 34:1; 35:1; 36:1; 37:1; 38:1; 39:1; 40:1; 41:1; 51:1; 52:1; 53:1; 54:1; 55:1; 56:1; 57:1; 58:1; 59:1; 60:1; 61:1; 62:1; 63:1; 64:1; 65:1; 68:1; 69:1; 70:1; 86:1; 89:4, 36, 50; 101:1; 103:1; 108:1; 109:1; 110:1; 122:1; 124:1; 131:1; 132:1, 11, 17; 133:1; 138:1; 139:1; 140:1; 141:1; 142:1; 143:1; 144:1; 145:1). Falk (*Love Lyrics*, 108) notes well that at least in Psalms this pointed preposition with David's name indicated that these poems were written by him.

158. Even Longman states, "It seems natural on the basis of this evidence to conclude that the superscription is making the claim that Solomon wrote the Song in its entirety" (4). Nevertheless, he questions Solomonic authorship based on its seemingly late language (4), "Solomon's dubious reputation in the area of love" (5), his minimal role in the Song (6), and his authorship of other books (*Song of Songs*, 6–7).

159. Mitchell, *Song of Songs*, 99. Although it is important to recognize Solomonic authorship, its denial does not change the rhetorical usage of the historical Solomon by the biblical author. It is unlikely another author (even a woman) could have used the historical Solomon as a character for each of the rhetorical purposes in the SoS.

160. See also Lucas, *Exploring the Old Testament*, 177.

161. Longman, *Song of Songs*, 5.

1 Kings 11:1-4 seems to bolster Longman's case:

> Now King Solomon loved many foreign women along with the daughter of Pharaoh: Moabite, Ammonite, Edomite, Sidonian, and Hittite women, from the nations concerning which the LORD had said to the sons of Israel, "You shall not associate with them, neither shall they associate with you, *for* they will surely turn your heart away after their gods." Solomon held fast to these in love. And he had seven hundred wives, princesses, and three hundred concubines, and his wives turned his heart away. For it came about when Solomon was old, his wives turned his heart away after other gods; and his heart was not wholly devoted to the LORD his God, as the heart of David his father *had been*.

Solomon's multiple dalliances certainly make it difficult to harmonize the passionate monogamy present in the SoS with his thousand amorous partners. To synchronize the theme of the Song and Solomon's many romantic relationships, some scholars argue that the Song is a product of Solomon's youth with one wife. However, it is best to realize that no matter the date of composition during Solomon's life, readers would still automatically reference it to Solomon's entire life.[162] It is unsatisfactory to posit it to a time that encompasses his youthful and innocent first marriage. Although it may seem a contradiction, it is best to recognize that Solomon simply wrote better than he lived.[163]

While Longman is correct that the reference to Solomon paints the king with a negative brush in 8:11-12, his conclusion does not necessarily have to follow logically. He says, "Finally, 8:11-12 paints a negative picture of Solomon as one who tries to buy love but is ridiculed for the attempt. It is doubtful that Solomon would characterize himself this way."[164] However, is it not possible that the wisest of all men actually

---

162. Anderson (*Song of Solomon*, 73) suggests, "The Song of Songs was probably written before all of that (1 Kings 11:3), before Solomon dissipated his potential by surrendering his principles. The Song deals only with the relationship between the king and his first bride, the Shulamith." See also Mitchell, *Song of Songs*, 99; Dillow, *Solomon on Sex*, 7, 10. However, Solomon is not known for his supposed first relationship. Centuries after Solomon's life at the time of the writing of Nehemiah, the wise king is still recognized for his many foreign wives which turned his heart (Neh 13:26). He is never referenced as a paragon of monogamy. Time did not help Solomon's reputation.

163. This observation only concerns the reference to Solomon in 8:12. The rest of the references seem to be positive.

164. Longman, *Song of Songs*, 6. While doubtful, it is not impossible and the author's rhetorical use of himself makes it probable. This will be demonstrated in the rhetorical

wrote better than he lived? That he is considered the wisest of all men of his time is without a doubt:

> God gave Solomon wisdom and very great discernment and breadth of mind, like the sand that is on the seashore. And Solomon's wisdom surpassed the wisdom of all the sons of the east and all the wisdom of Egypt. For he was wiser than all men, than Ethan the Ezrahite, Heman, Calcol and Darda, the sons of Mahol; and his fame was *known* in all the surrounding nations. He also spoke 3,000 proverbs, and his songs were 1,005. And he spoke of trees, from the cedar that is in Lebanon even to the hyssop that grows on the wall; he spoke also of animals and birds and creeping things and fish. And men came from all peoples to hear the wisdom of Solomon, from all the kings of the earth who had heard of his wisdom. (1 Kgs 4:29–34)

> So King Solomon became greater than all the kings of the earth in riches and in wisdom. And all the earth was seeking the presence of Solomon, to hear his wisdom which God had put in his heart. (1 Kgs 10:23–24)

Wisdom, however, does not equal sinlessness. It seems that an unfair limiting factor is applied to Solomon. Scholars want Solomon wise and sinless before they consider the possibility that he is capable of writing better than he lived. Although Scripture is silent, is it not possible that Solomon became angry even though he wrote against anger in Proverbs?[165] Scripture is clear that Solomon wrote about the fear of the Lord (e.g., Prov 2:1–5), but it is equally clear that he forsook the fear of God by going after foreign gods (1 Kgs 11:4–11). Although the wisest of the wise, the author of this portion of holy writ still sinned in his wisdom. Dillow cautions that practice does not negate authorship: "The fact that Solomon may have been a hypocrite doesn't necessarily disqualify him from writing about how he *should* behave."[166]

---

use of the characters in the Song. Garrett ("Song of Songs," 24) argues against Longman's notion of moral unfitness by observing, "One should realize that an enormous amount of great literature on love . . . was written by people whose personal lives did not fully reflect the high ideals that their words expressed. Virtuous lives and virtuous words do not always go hand in hand."

165. Cf. Prov 14:29, 35; 15:18; 16:32, etc.

166. Dillow, *Solomon on Sex*, 10. Italics are original. Although I disagree with Dillow's reason for his harmonization of Solomon's life and writing, he does make an excellent point. Dillow believes Solomon wrote the Song as a young man before he accumulated his large harem. Although Kaiser ("True Marital Love," 113) does not identify the author of the Song, his conclusion concerning the writer points to Solomon based on 8:7: "He

Solomon wisely knew that his many marriage entanglements did not allow him to enjoy the passionate desire of one of which the Song speaks. On the contrary, he recognizes that he is the example of just the opposite, and he ridicules his own life to make a profound point (8:11–12). Again Dillow postulates,

> If Solomon wrote this book while practicing polygamy, it would be a powerful argument against the fruitlessness and emptiness of having many wives. It would be a poem emphasizing the beauty of ideal love written by one who had experienced the opposite. He could write from experience that polygamy is not fulfilling as the way to find a maximum marriage.[167]

While Conway does not recognize the unity of the SoS, he does capture well this dynamic between lifestyle and authorship: "And indeed Solomon must have been superlatively wise to have written poems in which his greatness is slightly ridiculed. That of course would be by no means incredible in a man of genuine wisdom—on the contrary would be characteristic."[168]

Solomon is both a historical character in the Song who is referenced but never speaks as a character (although he is addressed). He is also the author of the Song who wrote better than he lived and uses his own well-known amorous relationships rhetorically.[169]

The Narrator

Since all of the characters of the Song are not historical (with the exception of Solomon and he never speaks), then it is a logical conclusion that the speech of the verbal characters is not their own but the words of the poet. When the poet puts his words in the characters' mouths, the reader does not hear the sound of the poet but the words of the characters themselves. Thus, in the SoS the majority of what the reader hears is from the mouth of the speakers and not the poet directly. However,

---

(the author) discovered that the object of one's desire cannot be intimidated, bought, or bullied into a loving relationship."

167. Dillow, *Solomon on Sex*, 10.
168. Conway, *Solomon and Solomonic Literature*, 89.
169. This position argues against Brueggemann (*Solomon*, 214), who sees Solomon's connection to the Song as merely secondary. However, Brueggemann does recognize the poetic use of Solomon throughout the poem.

when the poet enters his own poetry, he becomes a narrator.[170] While the SoS is not a narrative, Exum is correct to recognize that

> Every text has a narrator; it's just that in the Song there is no narrative description.... Canticles consists entirely of speeches. ... Voices that seem to reach us unmediated lend the illusion of immediacy to what is actually reported speech, a written text whose author and narrator are brilliantly effaced.[171]

However, she may be too quick to discount the fact that "the narrator doesn't intrude" in the SoS.[172] For in the last bicolon of 5:1 an unidentified voice speaks who may indeed be the narrator of the Song: "Eat, friends; Drink and imbibe deeply, O lovers," אִכְלוּ רֵעִים שְׁתוּ וְשִׁכְרוּ דּוֹדִים.

While Bergant leaves this commanding voice unidentified, other scholars have thought, according to Stoop-van Paridon, that the words come from a variety of potential speakers: "the man; both lovers in ecstasy; bystanders or outsiders; the chorus of wedding guests; attendants assisting the bride; the daughters of Jerusalem; the woman herself; the poet himself."[173] Stoop-van Paridon adds Solomon to the list as well.[174] Since the male and female lovers are the ones addressed, they cannot be the speaker either individually or as a couple. Since the only other speakers are the daughters of Jerusalem, all others may be eliminated. Stoop-van Paridon's suggestion that Solomon, as a character, is the speaker is conjecture without any exegetical warrant. The only other option is to choose between the daughters of Jerusalem or the voice of the narrator.

That the daughters of Jerusalem are the speakers here is unlikely for a number of reasons. First, nowhere else in the Song do they ever command the couple either jointly or individually, and it is unlikely at this crucial juncture for them to do so. Second, the daughters never take the

---

170. While Gunn and Fewell (*Narrative in the Hebrew Bible*, 53) are writing concerning biblical narrative, their suggestion is helpful concerning the relationship between the narrator and character: "It might be helpful sometimes to think of the narrator as a character, distinct from the other characters. The narrator is a character who tells the story while the others characters enact it." While the Song is not a narrative, it is helpful to recognize the narrator as a character to identify the speaker of the last bicolon of 5:1. Berlin (*Poetics and Interpretation*, 58) disagrees: "The narrator is never a character in the story." See also Longman (*Song of Songs*, 15).

171. Exum, "Ten Things Every Feminist Should Know," 27.

172. Ibid.

173. Stoop-van Paridon, *Song of Songs*, 246.

174. Ibid.

initiative to speak and here they break into the conversation between the lovers. It is clear that the speaker of this sentence is an uninvited guest who takes the initiative to comment on the action and dialogue of the couple. Third, if it is true that the couple is consummating their love (or engaging in foreplay), the presence of the daughters at such an intimate, private scene is unexplainable.[175] Thus, the daughters of Jerusalem do not seem to be viable candidates for the voice of this command to the lovers.

It is best to see the speaker of this sentiment as the voice of the poet who doffs his invisibility as author, dons the character of the narrator, and breaks into the couple's lovemaking. Although she is writing concerning interpretation of biblical narrative, Berlin makes an interesting point that may apply:

> Direct speech ... is the most dramatic way of conveying the characters' internal psychological and ideological point of view....
> It often happens that direct discourse and its related narration share verbal similarities. This may mean that the narrator is confirming the words of the characters.[176]

In the last clause of 5:1, the narrator uses the same verbs that the male lover has just expressed, "eat" אָכַל and "drink" שָׁתָה. In addition, the female lover uses one of the verbs as well ("eat" אָכַל in 4:16). In light of Berlin's observation concerning the verbal similarities, the narrator is not simply confirming the words and the actions of the couple but encouraging them to enjoy the sexual relationship, as expressed in the "eating" and "drinking" metaphor, to its fullest with his double imperatives. This recognition of the narrator as a character is an important step in the interpretative process. In this case the narrator affirms by his commands that he approves of the intimate play of the couple.[177]

---

175. Even if the daughters are viewed as literary creations (and thus are not real), their comment confirms their presence at an inappropriate occasion. If the woman was constrained by the societal regulations to signs of public affection such as kissing (8:1), would society ever condone in its literature such voyeurism?

176. Berlin, *Poetics and Interpretation*, 64.

177. It should be noted that the narrator, according to Sternberg (*Poetics of Biblical Narrative*, 51), is always truthful in his assessments: "The Bible always tells the truth in that its narrator is absolutely and straightforward reliable." While Sternberg is concerned with biblical narratives, his observations seem to hold true for the poetry of the Song as well. Jacobson (*"Many are Saying,"* 19) does not believe that the same principle holds true for the narrator of the Psalms. Fox recognizes that the unidentified speaker

Another reason to see the speaker of the commands as the narrator is because of the omniscient sense one has about the setting. It is obvious that the couple is in a sexual situation that the reader overhears but is not privy to see. The speaker, on the other hand, gives the sense that he is closer to the action than the reader and is actually seeing and hearing the delight of the couple unfold before him. This omniscient point of view must be the narrator. Jacobson remarks, "In biblical narrative the narrator is assumed to be omniscient."[178] What is true in narrative seems to hold true in this instance of biblical poetry. This speaker in his dual role as character (narrator) and author is the only truly omniscient player on the scene.

Conclusion

While not a narrative, the Song evidences the use of certain characters. These characters may be verbal or nonverbal, historical or literary inventions. Only four characters are given voice in the SoS: the female and male protagonists, the daughters of Jerusalem, and the narrator of 5:1.[179] All other characters are assigned nonspeaking parts by the biblical poet. Only two characters are actual historical personages: Solomon as a character (by description and address) and Solomon as the unidentified narrator. All the other characters, while they may resemble historical individuals, are actually literary creations of the biblical author, who is Solomon.

Character Analysis: Flat, Full, or Agent?

Linafelt makes the point that although the Song is lyric poetry, there is "a certain amount of characterization."[180] Longman reflects that while the Song is not a narrative, "the characters whom we hear in the Song have a consistency of persona."[181] Based on these observations, it is both

---

in some Egyptian love songs such as "The Orchard" is "the authorial voice." This voice gives "authoritative advice" to the other characters in the poem (Fox, *Egyptian Love Songs*, 255). However, he does not see such a narrator's voice in the Song (ibid.).

178. Jacobson, *"Many are Saying,"* 19.

179. If one discounts the narrator as a character, then the number of main characters in the Song is three. There are also three characters in a number of the lament psalms: the psalmist, an enemy (or enemies), and God (e.g., Ps 3; 5; 6; 13).

180. Linafelt, "Arithmetic of Eros," 252.

181. Longman, *Song of Songs*, 15. Fox (*Egyptian Love Songs*, 217) concurs and adds, "We do not need to follow them [proponents of the dramatic theory] in assuming an

possible and profitable for the characters of the Song to be analyzed.[182] Since the characters are literary creations, this is an important factor to consider for interpretation. Fox astutely observes, "If the speakers are personae we must ask not only what the lovers are like, but also how the poets view them and present them to us."[183] Such an analysis enables the reader to know how the poet is presenting the characters and to recognize the relative importance of each character in the Song. The characters being presented as full, flat, or agent determines their importance in the composition. Once the characters are analyzed according to these categories, this becomes a safeguard for assigning too much importance to a character who is an agent and not assigning enough importance to a character who is full.[184] Another purpose of this analysis is to understand what type of person each character is and how the reader is to relate to him or her. Berlin writes, "The purpose of character description in the Bible is not to enable the reader to visualize the character, but to enable him to situate the character in terms of his place in society, his own particular situation, and his outstanding traits—in other words, to tell what kind of person he is."[185]

According to Berlin, in a narrative composition the reader comes to understand a character through description of his inner life, speech, action, and contrast with another character.[186] While there is limited character action in the Song, the main manner of understanding its characters is through their speech with one another and/or about one another.

---

ongoing narrative continuity in order to recognize consistency in character portrayal." In addition, D. M. Carr (*The Erotic Word*, 115) states, "The characters seem to stay the same.... Nevertheless, there is no clear plot or logical sequence."

182. This analysis will build upon the characterization analysis of Gunn and Fewell, *Narrative in the Hebrew Bible*; Berlin, *Poetics and Interpretation*; and Sternberg, *Poetics of Biblical Narrative*.

183. Fox, *Egyptian Love Songs*, 253.

184. There are times, however, when God himself is a flat character because only one or a few divine traits are exhibited. It does not necessarily follow that as a "flat character" he is unimportant. For instance in Ps 13, God may be considered a flat character because he is viewed simply as silent from the perspective of David. In that psalm, God is not an unimportant character. On the other hand, in Ruth 1 Elimelech and his two sons, Mahlon and Chilion, are flat characters whose only characterization is that they die.

185. Berlin, *Poetics and Interpretation*, 36.

186. Ibid., 34–40.

Definitions

Kaiser proposes a threefold categorization concerning character analysis: "round (or full-fledged), flat and as an agent."[187] Gunn and Fewell define a flat character as one who "possesses few qualities or personality traits (perhaps only one)."[188] Berlin notes that flat characters "do not stand out as individuals."[189] Kaiser observes that a round or full-fledged character possesses "many traits, is more complex, and therefore less predictable."[190] He also defines an agent as one who "has no personality at all, but simply functions to move the story along."[191]

Sixty Queens and Eighty Concubines

The sixty queens, eighty concubines, and maidens without number are flat characters. Whether they are real (i.e., part of Solomon's harem) or not (the presence of unlimited maidens would argue against Solomon's harem) is not the issue. What is the issue is how the poet presents these royal ladies to the reader. In this case these women represent the women of the royal court. Keel thinks the three different groups of women is a "courtly pyramid of rank."[192] Keel may be accurate since these same women respond indirectly (through the voice of the male lover, 6:10) and place the female protagonist well above themselves into the heavenly realm. While they may have rank themselves as queens or concubines, the female lover is well above them in beauty, uniqueness, and social rank. Thus, the male lover uses these ladies of court, their numbers, their ranks, and even their words to praise his female beloved. Outside of their

---

187. Kaiser, "Narrative," 74. While Berlin's work on characterization should be appreciated, her changing the terminology of the "flat" character to "type" may create more confusion than it solves. Berlin is correct, however, in recognizing the threefold categorization instead of using only the two categories of flat or round (Berlin, *Poetics and Interpretation*, 23).

188. Gunn and Fewell, *Narrative in the Hebrew Bible*, 75.

189. Berlin, *Poetics and Interpretation*, 23.

190. Kaiser, "Narrative," 74.

191. Ibid. The agent functions to move the narrative forward. However, based on this analysis none of the characters are ever presented to the reader as simple agents. Each displays at least one characteristic that raises them to the level of a flat character. It may be that since the Song is not a narrative that an agent (or agents) is unnecessary since this poem does not follow a plot line which needs to be moved along to its resolution.

192. Keel, *Song of Songs*, 217.

courtly description, which assumes great beauty (Esth 1:11; 2:2), the poet shares nothing else about these women. They are flat characters.

MOTHER

Whether the character is the female lover's mother (3:4; 8:2), the male protagonist's mother (8:5), or even Solomon's mother (3:11), they are all flat characters. They are flat because the only trait that is revealed is the relationship that is established at birth with the other characters of the Song. To infer that the female's mother is not in favor of her relationship is simply reading too much into the poem.[193] The poet is revealing nothing more about these characters except their relationship with the one they brought into this world. Even when the mother of Solomon (3:11) could have been identified by name as Bathsheba and verified (2 Sam 12:24), the poet does not. Instead he chose to hide her behind her son's identity. If he had named her specifically, that would have allowed her to be a fuller character since it is assumed that the reader would have been familiar with Solomon's famous mother and would have added other details to her character in 3:11. However, by not naming her, the poet controls (to some degree) what other information the reader would bring to this character. He simply desires the audience's focus to be on the royal pageantry of her son's wedding.

THE WATCHMEN

Although all the characters of the Song are artistic creations (except Solomon), the watchmen are doubly fictitious, since they are a creation of the poet and of the female lover's imagination while in her two dreams (3:3; 5:7). The description of these characters by the author in both instances, הַשֹּׁמְרִים הַסֹּבְבִים בָּעִיר, indicates that they are flat characters. In 3:3 the guards, presumably on their security circuit around the city at night, are accosted by the frantic female searching for her lost lover. Although she finds and questions the individuals who should know the coming and going of people at night in the city, their response is not given. Whether they are helpful or not is unimportant to the poet. He simply presents them to the reader without any evaluation or informa-

---

193. Pope, *Song of Songs*, 421. If this analysis is correct, it may tame some fanciful interpretations as to the part mother plays in this poem. Stoop-van Paridon, *Song of Songs*, 150.

tion that would even allow the reader to draw a firm conclusion. They are simply there as those who patrol the city.

In 5:7 the same phrase appears to describe the watchmen. In this case they also do not speak. However, they are the ones who discover the woman and they take seemingly violent action against her. But even in this, they are presumably acting in concert with their character. It would not be unusual for city watchmen to discover and meet out the proper discipline.[194] Since the woman makes no complaint against their actions and there are no other comments by other characters or the narrator, the reader is left to assume that their actions are justified, albeit unsettling to modern sensibilities. In any case the guards act simply as guards. Their actions are usual and predictable for their function. They are one-dimensional or flat characters.

The Brothers

The female lover's brothers are referenced only one time (1:6). In this instance they are not even called "brothers" but a seemingly less complimentary term, בְּנֵי אִמִּי. This phrase functions to distance the woman from them but while still maintaining (rather begrudgingly) the familial relationship of brother and sister. The brothers are flat characters. They never speak nor act in the reader's presence. Their disposition towards their sister is self-reported. Beside their family relationship, the only other information that can be gleaned about them is their anger toward the female protagonist for some unknown reason and their authority to make her a keeper of the vineyard, שָׂמֻנִי נֹטֵרָה אֶת־הַכְּרָמִים. In each of these cases, the brothers are acting congruently with their relationship with their sister, that is, as brothers.[195] Their presence only justifies the lover's explanation of her darkened skin. While it is tempting to read between the lines of their anger and look for motive, the author leaves no poetic room for such speculation. These characters are presented as the female lover's brothers who at one point allow their anger to dictate an action against their sister that results in her skin being exposed to the searing rays of the sun. The poet shares nothing else about the brothers nor is the brothers' collective character ever developed past this seeming

---

194. Guards are noted at various times in the OT (e.g., 2 Kgs 11:6, 11, 19; Neh 7:3). In Eccl 12:3 the watchmen of the house are used figuratively, שֹׁמְרֵי הַבַּיִת.

195. 2 Samuel 13:20 gives evidence of a brother having some sway over his sister. Genesis 37–50 provides ample scriptural proof for evidence of brotherly anger.

sibling rivalry. The reader perceives the brothers as flat characters. Since the author simply pictures these male siblings as angry at this one point and does not develop them any further, is it not futile speculation to endeavor to ascertain the exact cause of the brothers' anger when the poet decides not to?

The Little Sister

Like the mother and brothers in the SoS, the "little sister" in 8:8 (אָחוֹת לָנוּ קְטַנָּה וְשָׁדַיִם אֵין לָהּ) is a flat character. While she has a definite function in the Song, her character is built on a sibling relationship. The reader knows she is sexually immature because her siblings (through the voice of the daughters of Jerusalem) mention that she has no breasts. The readers also hear that her siblings desire to adorn and protect her for her future marriage day. At no time does the "little sister" ever develop into a fuller character. The audience always observes this character as the "little sister." The poet adds nothing to her that allows the reader to perceive her differently than sexually immature.

The Daughters of Jerusalem

Munro feels that the daughters of Jerusalem "appear to be not only sceptical (5.9) but also rather stupid (6.1), offering to respond to her [the female lover's] request for help only when her lover has already been found (6.2)."[196] A poetically sensitive closer reading reveals that they are neither stupid nor skeptical; they are simply flat characters. She is right to conclude, however, that "very little information is given about them."[197] This is a clue that they are flat characters.

The daughters are addressed by the female protagonist by name seven times (1:5; 2:7; 3:5, 10; 5:8, 16; 8:4). Each time they act as an audience to the woman except in 3:10. Here they are recognized for their exquisite fitting of Solomon's sedan chair or litter, אַפִּרְיוֹן. They initiate conversations with the woman in 5:9; 6:1; 7:1; 8:5, 8. However, their brief conversations (which never exceed two verses and are rhetorical questions) seem to be an excuse to allow the woman to share her thoughts and feelings. Through these conversations nothing is revealed about the daughters themselves. In fact their conversations seem to divulge more

---

196. Munro, *Spikenard and Saffron*, 43.
197. Ibid.

about the female lover than themselves. Their dialogue adds very little to their own character development.

Little is gained about the daughters through their speech, and their association with Jerusalem only slightly deepens their character. As mentioned earlier, Keel suggests that the daughters are the "spoiled, idle, and curious women of the capital city . . . especially versed in matters of beauty and love."[198] While it is tempting to accept Keel's description and round out the daughters' character, the text does not put them in that pejorative light. Keel is correct to look for an added description of the daughters based on their association with the capital city of Israel. However, the scriptural evidence is too scant to say with certainty how the cosmopolitan association helps the modern reader understand the character of the daughters.[199] It is possible that the original reader understood exactly what their association with the royal city meant and that that meaning has been lost to the contemporary audience.[200]

The Male Lover

At first glance the male lover may be misconstrued as a one-dimensional, flat character. All the audience knows about him is in relationship to his female paramour. He expresses no self-image and never speaks about himself. All his thoughts are voiced as dialogue and only to his friend. He never engages the daughters of Jerusalem and they never speak with him. He cares for nothing other than his own beloved. The reader has the feeling that if the female lover is absent, the male lover would be utterly silent. Nevertheless, he is a round or full-fledged character.

Kaiser defines a round character as someone who "has many traits, is more complex, and therefore less predicable, but more real."[201] The male lover is definitely less than predictable in his first response to his

---

198. Keel, *Song of Songs*, 49.

199. It is true the daughters of Zion are synonymous with the daughters of Jerusalem (3:10; cf. 3:11) however, it may be too much to link the daughters of the Song with the daughters of Isa 3:16–24. There the prophet clearly sees the daughters deserving divine judgment because of their sinful attitude. However, to suggest the daughters always act this way wherever they are found in Scripture is reading too much into the Song.

200. It is possible the daughters are actually round or full-fledged characters because of their association with Jerusalem. It may have been the author's intention to use the city's name to conjure images of this group by having them connected with that specific city but without actually stating what those connections are. However, based only on their portrayal in the SoS, they do not seem to be round characters.

201. Kaiser, "Narrative," 74.

lover in 1:8. After she has spoken about him and to him and shared her desire to enjoy his lovemaking once again (1:2), she inquires as to where he will be resting at noon (1:7). His enigmatic response in the form of a rhetorical question is quite unexpected (1:8). The reader may expect an emphatic reply as to his exact location so he could enjoy an afternoon tryst. But he teases her and prolongs their passion and desire.

The male lover is one who is sensitive to the self-perceived image of his friend. In 2:1 she expresses her feeling metaphorically that she is simply one female among many others. He, however, uses the same horticultural image and exalts her well above the other women by agreeing that she is indeed a flower but the others are mere thorns, חוֹחִים. He is also communicative. He is free with his compliments of her beauty (1:9) and initiates conversation (2:10–14; 4:1–15; 6:4–10; 7:2–10). He is knowledgeable of horticulture (4:12–15), architecture (6:4), animal husbandry (1:8), foreign horses (1:9), military matters (1:9; 6:4), zoology (2:8; 4:8) and geography (4:8). While it might be an understatement, he desires her as much as she wants him. Figuratively, he is a gazelle that is able to climb mountains and leap over hills to get to his beloved (2:9). Nothing will stand in his way to be with her. Once with her, his desire is only satisfied as he completely consumes and possesses her (5:1). Then and only then, is he able to sleep (7:10).

From her lips the reader discovers that physically he is beyond compare (5:10–16), totally desirable (or as BDB phrases it, "All of him is delightfulness"), וְכֻלּוֹ מַחֲמַדִּים (5:16).[202] He is simply יָפֶה. To her he is metaphorically both her shepherd (1:7; 6:2) and her king (1:4, 12). She believes his skill in lovemaking is more intoxicating than wine.[203] While he does enjoy her sexually, she considers him both a lover and friend, זֶה דוֹדִי וְזֶה רֵעִי.

The author of the Song displays his male lover in a rather narrow characterization. Unlike other biblical characters, the male lover of the Song exposes no fears, failures, or personal faults.[204] Nevertheless, he

---

202. BDB 326.

203. Bloch and Bloch (*Song of Songs*, 137) remark, "Your *dodim* ... is a comprehensive term for lovemaking, that is kissing and caresses as well as intercourse."

204. Some may evaluate his nocturnal visit in chapter 5 as "his fault." However, since it is her dream, he never actually approaches her. She only dreams that he did. Therefore, he is not guilty as charged. There are, however, some issues threatening the relationship in 2:15, but the reader is uncertain if the "foxes" are external pressures on the relationship or interpersonal shortcomings of the couple individually.

is a round character since his relationship with his beloved is so fully developed and unpredictable. This limited characterization should be expected since the theme of the poem is love and he is not the dominant voice.

The Female Lover

There is no disagreement among scholars that the dominant character and voice is the female lover. Through her own voice and the voice of her companion, the poet draws her round character on the pages of this song. While the male protagonist reveals nothing about himself, the female lover demonstrates that she has a self-awareness about herself but it is sometimes contradictory. In her opening dialogue with the daughters of Jerusalem (1:5–6), she verbally deflects their gaze by explaining that the dark color of her skin is not of her own choosing but is the result of her brothers' anger. Having been made the keeper of a vineyard (1:6), she is unable to care for her own body, resulting in her less than flattering tan. However, in her self-consciousness, there is also the seemingly contradictory realization that she is lovely, נָאוָה (1:5). This realization does not last long. In a dialogue with her lover, her self-consciousness turns to self-deprecation. In an initial statement she observes that she is simply one common flower among a valley full of women (2:1). When the daughters ask her to return so they can gaze at her, she responds with a query concerning their motivation for desiring to look so intently at her (6:13).

While the male lover exposes no fears or faults, the female protagonist reveals both. The woman's greatest fear expressed in the SoS is her inability to find her lover. As she rehearses her nocturnal experiences to the daughters of Jerusalem, her fear of not being able to find him is a reoccurring nightmare, עַל־מִשְׁכָּבִי בַּלֵּילוֹת בִּקַּשְׁתִּי אֵת שֶׁאָהֲבָה נַפְשִׁי בִּקַּשְׁתִּיו וְלֹא מְצָאתִיו. Through the repetition of the dreams ("nightly") and the double use of the verb, בָּקַשׁ, it is readily apparent that her fear is a reoccurring one. The depth of her trepidation is evidenced by her going out alone at night in the middle of a city to search desperately for him (3:3). While she is found, he is not. Her fright is also demonstrated by the manner in which she holds him and would not let go once she finds him, אֲחַזְתִּיו וְלֹא אַרְפֶּנּוּ (3:4).

While there is scholarly debate concerning the exact meaning of the second dream sequence (5:2—6:3), it is possible that this nighttime episode exposes a fault.²⁰⁵ Whatever the motivation, it is clear the woman denies (or at least delays) access to her bedroom by her lover. The consequences of her action follow quickly. Her reoccurring dread is realized when finally opening the door to find that he is gone.²⁰⁶ Since her lover did not answer her pleas at the opened door, she again initiates a seemingly frantic midnight search. This time, however, the silent city guards find her and deal with her harshly. They strike her, bruise her, and take her veil, הִכּוּנִי פְצָעוּנִי נָשְׂאוּ אֶת־רְדִידִי (5:7). Their dealings are indeed harsh (and illogical) especially in light of the fact that the female lover commits no transgression that would engender such legal action. However, if their actions are connected to her refusal (which they are exegetically) and the guards are part of this dream sequence (which they are), then the reader is aware that their treatment of the woman is disciplinary. Since the woman (as well as the author) says nothing about their behavior towards her, the reader is correct to assume that it is justified.²⁰⁷

The biblical author reveals more of the female lover's character through her attitude. It is clear that she believes in monogamy. Her lover is the same throughout and is always the one whom her soul loves, שֶׁאָהֲבָה נַפְשִׁי (1:7; 3:1, 2, 3, 4). This same lover is her beloved and friend, זֶה דוֹדִי וְזֶה רֵעִי (5:16). She realizes that her exclusivity is returned by him, לְדוֹדִי וְעָלַי תְּשׁוּקָתוֹ אָנִי (7:10). She also understands the enormous power

---

205. Since this is a dream, it is possible that it does not expose a fault but a fear. The dream may encompass what she fears are the negative consequences *if* she does not allow her lover's nocturnal (or at least ill-timed) access to lovemaking. This episode also exposes her unpredictability. Based on her actions and attitude thus far, the reader would not expect her to refuse any advances by her lover.

206. The connection between the two dreams sequences is strengthened by her response to his absence each time: "I searched for him, but I did not find him; I called him, but he did not answer me" (5:6). "I must arise now and go about the city; In the streets and in the squares I must seek him whom my soul loves. I sought him but did not find him" (3:2).

207. Again, it should be remembered that this is a dream of the woman. Her nighttime consciousness runs her through the potential consequences of refusal. There is nothing real about his possibly ill-timed request, her refusal, and the guards' harsh treatment of her. What are true, however, are the feelings that linger after such a dream. In reality, when she awakes from this nightmarish vision, she realizes he is right beside her and he is totally hers (6:2–3). This is the only position that makes sense exegetically. If the Song is a drama and Solomon is a character, would Solomon (or even the male lover) put up with such treatment against his lover? Solomon executed Shimei, who simply cursed his father, David (1 Kgs 2:8–9). Guards who mistreat his love would not escape his wrath.

of love (8:6–7). In light of love's vast power, she is keenly concerned that others not arouse this emotion until the proper time (2:7; 3:5; 8:4). Her attitude is also one that embraces sexual desire (1:2; 2:6; 8:3) and does not deny sexual feeling or arousal (5:4–5). She does not deny that without the presence of her lover, she is hopelessly lovesick, שְׁחוֹלַת אַהֲבָה אָנִי (2:5; 5:8). The only "cure" is to be cradled in his arms and enjoying his intimate caresses (2:6).

Through her actions the reader learns that she is not shy sexually. Rather abruptly (from the reader's point of view) the Song begins in the middle of her desire. In the opening verse she tells of her desire for sexual intimacies that she has already experienced and thoroughly enjoyed more than wine (1:2). She is free to invite her lover into her (4:16) and allows herself to be possessed and consumed completely by her lover. Her "garden" (4:12) becomes his "garden" (5:1). She is comfortable initiating sexual adventures (7:13) and is a creative lover (7:14).

This lover is one who accepts her faults (5:2—6:1), is verbally playful (1:7–8), and who is also sensitive to the threats to her relationship with her lover (2:15). She is also sensitive to cultural mores. Although desire drives her to want to brazenly kiss her lover in public, convention stops her (8:1). Although she exhibits various sensitivities, she is also forceful. She is the one who vigorously exhorts King Solomon that mutually exclusive love cannot be bought with wealth or royal status (8:11–12).

From her lover's mouth the reader learns that the female protagonist is physically attractive (1:8, 15; 2:10, 13; 4:1, 7; 6:4, 10; 7:7). Not only is she a simple beauty, she is a unique beauty above all other women (5:9; 6:1). Her lovemaking is also beautiful as well, מַה־יָּפוּ דֹדַיִךְ (4:10). She is entrancing (6:5). She is also powerful; a king could be held captive by her hair (7:6). Metaphorically, she is a luscious garden to enjoy (4:10–15) and a fruitful tree to climb (7:7).

The female lover is indeed a round figure. The author reveals through her own words and the language of her lover a somewhat complete female personality. A number of her strengths and weaknesses, desires and fears are readily apparent. Although she is unnamed and specifically unidentified, she is definitely the most developed character in the Song.

Solomon

While scholars disagree as to Solomon's authorship of the Song, none disagrees that he (or his name) plays some part in it. This analysis would like to suggest that Solomon is a fully developed, full-fledged character in SoS.[208] A reason for this suggestion is that since the author is in control of what the reader hears and how he hears it, then it logically follows that when he mentions Solomon, he desires his audience to make associations or connections with the famous king of Israel.[209] While Dell does not articulate specifically how Solomon "pervades" the Song, she does suggest, "The character of Solomon seems to pervade the Song in a more profound way than is often assumed."[210] By contrast, however, one reason the author may not have further identified the male and female lovers by proper names (or as historical personages) is because he desires to control completely how the reader perceives them. By allowing the reader to learn about these characters only through the information present in the Song, the author strictly controls how the reader relates to them.[211]

On the other hand, once the author introduces a character of whom his readers are historically well aware, the readers bring their accumulated information about that character to their reading of the text. For example, if the Song's author specifically introduces the female lover as Pharaoh's daughter, the audience may approach her part in the Song with a preconceived perception of her character. The same may be true if the poet names the mother of 3:11 as Bathsheba instead of letting this character stay in the background as simply "his mother." If Bathsheba is purposely named, the reader's focus may be turned from the splendor of Solomon's wedding to the presence of his well-known (albeit adulter-

---

208. This is contrary to Childs and others who believe Solomon is simply mentioned as a way to tie the book to wisdom literature. Childs (*Old Testament as Scripture*, 579) writes, "The historical references to Solomon serve primarily to classify the material within its genre" (i.e., wisdom literature). Although this may be true, it does not tell the whole story of Solomon's placement in the Song, who is himself the author. However, Childs (578) suggests that Solomon may serve as a foil in chapter 8.

209. This is a fairly common practice in modern English literature as well. If a writer mentions, "It was the best of times, it was the worst of times," the reader knows he is referencing Charles Dickens' novel, *A Tale of Two Cities*.

210. Dell, "Does the Song of Songs Have Any Connections to Wisdom?" 24.

211. The importance of this dynamic is demonstrated in the next section, "Rhetorical Use of the Characters."

ous?) mother instead. While the author could have specifically identified her, he chooses not to in order to suit his literary purpose. Also, once the reader is historically familiar with a character outside the composition in which he or she plays a part, the author is not necessarily in complete control of how his character's part in the present composition is received or how the reader will relate to that character.[212] In Solomon's case, this is the author's exact literary design. In this manner he need not develop Solomon as a character in the Song because he is already so well developed in Israel's national history. All the author needs to do is simply identify him as such. Once the character is identified as "Solomon," the author allows the reader to bring all the historical and biblical information he or she has to the character.[213]

This dynamic is clearly seen in 1:5. In this verse, the author uses two similes that the woman employs to describe her skin's blackness. One concerns the curtains of Solomon, כִּירִיעוֹת שְׁלֹמֹה. There is no disagreement that the historical Solomon is a reference for these יְרִיעָה. According to Exum, every scholar (except Pope) views the reference to Solomon.[214] Exum believes the linkage to Solomon is "poetically suggestive of royal splendor; it links this verse to Solomon's name in the title and to the king and courtly setting."[215] Keel states, "Whether the black יריעות are tapestries, curtains or wall hangings, since they are connected to Solomon one should understand them as artistic and precious palace furnishings."[216] Bloch and Bloch remark, "'Solomon's curtains' . . . may well belong to the accoutrements of his royal splendor, a memory of which has been preserved in folklore."[217] Each of these scholars demonstrates that they are linking the concept of royalty by association with Solomon's name, although the concept of royalty is never mentioned in the text. Solomon

---

212. If Bathsheba is mentioned, one can imagine the audience being transported back to the adulterous affair between David and Bathsheba and the subsequent grievous consequences. Bringing such a history to the Song could ruin the celebratory tone the author is trying to set.

213. Nehemiah uses the biblical record to remind the postexilic Jews in Israel of the dangers of foreign women (Neh 13:26).

214. Exum, *Song of Songs*, 104.

215. Ibid.

216. Keel, *Song of Songs*, 47.

217. Bloch and Bloch, *Song of Songs*, 140. Writing about the need for Solomonic association, Bergant (*Song of Songs*, 14) states, "The extravagance associated with the court of Solomon is an important theme."

Poetic Characters

is so well known as king that the "royal" association is natural and expected. It is apparent the author desires the audience to make the comparison between the color of the woman and the curtains of Solomon, of which they must have been aware, for some rhetorical purpose. If the reader is not able to make the connection, the comparison would be missed; the simile would be lifeless and the rhetorical purpose lost.

The second mention of Solomon concerns an item that has been made by the king himself and lovingly outfitted (3:7, 9). The exact identity of מִטָּה, or Solomon's אַפִּרְיוֹן, is unimportant for the discussion. What is important, however, is what image it conjures up in the reader's mind. Exum notes:

> Whatever the precise meaning of the various terms used to describe it, it is clear that the palanquin is lavish in craft and ornamentation. It is made from not just any wood but wood imported from Lebanon (cedar wood would be fitting for Solomon) and adorned with silver and gold and coveted purple cloth. Purple dye from the murex shellfish was expensive and thus a symbol of royalty.[218]

Longman further notes that it suggests "Solomon's wealth and grandeur." This is the point of association between the object and his name.[219] Keel observes the "imported Lebanese wood is a regular feature of the splendor that the tradition associates with the name of Solomon."[220] Keel is quite right to recognize the rich cedar wood itself summons the tradition of Solomon. It is this picture of grand, royal wealth, combined with luxurious, extravagant pageantry that the poet successfully identifies with Solomon.[221] As the *Dictionary of Biblical Imagery* states, "Historically, Solomon was widely recognized for his fabulous wealth."[222]

The first three references to Solomon are adjectival. The author uses Solomon to describe more specifically the "curtains" and "the traveling couch." It is only in this next reference that King Solomon himself is called to be the subject of the gaze of the daughters of Jerusalem (3:9).

---

218. Exum, *Song of Songs*, 149.

219. For God-given wealth and riches, see 1 Kgs 3:13. For Solomon's lavish house, see 1 Kgs 6. For more on his wealth, see 1 Kgs 9:28—10:29.

220. Keel, *Song of Songs*, 131.

221. The purpose of which will be discussed in the section concerning the rhetorical use of the characters.

222. "Solomon," *Dictionary of Biblical Imagery*, 804.

The rich description in the previous verses of the wedding procession (of which the traveling couch is part) is clearer when one considers that there is no extant record of the day of Solomon's wedding. Any reader not privy to the festivities of that day itself would be at a loss mentally to recreate such a scene. However, the luxurious setting of the previously described procession gives a significant clue that his wedding is a royal affair sparing no cost. Based on the wealth and luxury that is on display, any subsequent reader is able to imagine what a royal wedding would be like because of its association with Solomon.

Thus far, the references to the king have been portrayed positively, if not extravagantly. However, in the next instances a cryptic darkness regarding the king's character begins to emerge. In the fourth reference the reader is informed that Solomon had a vineyard at Baal-hamon (8:11). While the geographical place is unidentified, the title means "possessor of abundance," which would fit Solomon's magnificent wealth.[223] However, the term, "vineyard," is a metaphorically loaded word in the Song. For instance, in 7:12 literal vineyards are the rendezvous for the couple's lovemaking. In 1:6 the reader realizes the vineyard that the woman is unable to tend is actually her own body. As Exum rightly surmises, "We suspect that Solomon's vineyard is something more than a collection of grapevines in a place called Baal-hamon."[224] The imagery of the vineyard as the female body and the association of Solomon's vineyard at Baal-hamon, the "possessor of abundance," leads the reader to conclude that what may be actually referred to is the multitude of wives and concubines Solomon possessed as king. Based on 1 Kgs 11:3–4, when Solomon was old he had indeed accumulated a vast "vineyard" of loves: "seven hundred wives, princesses, and three hundred concubines."[225] This pejorative reference to Solomon may be an historical illustration, "If a man were to give all the riches of his house for love, it would be utterly despised" (8:7). Although Solomon is a man of great wealth (1 Kgs 10:23), he can-

---

223. BDB 128.

224. Exum, *Song of Songs*, 260.

225. Keel (*Song of Songs*, 281) remarks that the vineyard is Solomon's harem. There may be a possibility that SoS 6:8 is a reference to Solomon's harem at the time of his writing this song. If so, rhetorically it may set the stage, suggesting that the next references to the king will not be as positive as the preceding ones. Up to this instance all the references have been positive. With the mention of so many queens and concubines (of one man), there may be a subtle shift. Keel sees this connection between these references.

not buy an unquenchable love like the one experienced by the couple of the Song.[226] As the writer, Solomon knows this dynamic because this love is built on exclusivity between two people, not between a husband and a thousand different "wives." This uncomplimentary reference to Solomon's inability to purchase love sets up the female protagonist's direct address to the king in the next verse.

The last reference to Solomon (8:12) is a direct address to him: כַּרְמִי שֶׁלִּי לְפָנָי הָאֶלֶף לְךָ שְׁלֹמֹה וּמָאתַיִם לְנֹטְרִים אֶת־פִּרְיוֹ, literally "my vineyard, which is mine, before me, the thousand are for you, Solomon and two hundred to the ones who keep its fruit."[227] Solomon's vineyard (which was entrusted to others) is fundamentally different from this one under the domain of the female and is protected by herself (8:10). This woman's own vineyard, the woman assures the king, who thinks love can be bought, is her own body (which is the place of love) and is under her own control. According to the female lover, it "is mine to give" (NIV).[228] It cannot be bought for any price (8:7). Thus, King Solomon is being lampooned.[229] While Solomon's harem may be extensive and expensive ("the

---

226. That this is a timeless concept is illustrated by the British music group, The Beatles. They popularized this concept with their 1964 hit, "Can't Buy Me Love." Written by Paul McCartney, released 1964 in the USA by Capitol Records.

227. There is discussion concerning the speaker of this verse. For instance, Exum (*Song of Songs*, 260), Stoop-van Paridon (*Song of Songs*, 459), and Keel (*Song of Songs*, 282) believe the male is the one who addresses Solomon directly. Hess (*Song of Songs*, 246–47), Goulder (*Song of Fourteen Songs*, 69), and Garrett ("Song of Songs," 263) suggest it is the woman. The woman has been the main voice in the Song, and it seems strange to put such a climactic statement into the mouth of the supporting voice (i.e., the man). This has not been the practice of the author thus far. In addition, the first person personal pronoun use suggests the woman. The man never uses a string of personal pronouns as in 8:12 (see appendix 1 for examples) and he never uses the term "my vineyard" to refer to his lover. He uses גַּנִּי (5:1) but never כַּרְמִי. Lastly, with the absence of any exegetical evidence, there is no reason to see a change of speaker from verse 10, which is clearly the woman, to verse 12 (men do not have שָׁדַי כַּמִּגְדָּלוֹת!). Nevertheless, as Longman astutely notes, "The speaker, whether the man or the woman, makes a contrast by picking up on the *vineyard* image of the previous verse.... The speaker seems to be saying in effect that Solomon can keep his harem. However, the speaker's vineyard is his or hers alone" (Longman, *Song of Songs*, 220; italics are original). The identity of the speaker does not change Solomon's part in this section of the Song or the contrast the author is exposing.

228. NASB: "my very own vineyard is at my disposal."

229. Exum (*Song of Songs*, 261) wrestles with this concept: "If Solomon is the butt of a joke or the object of criticism, then we would have here a very different treatment of Solomon and royalty from what we find elsewhere in the Song, where King Solomon

thousand"), it cannot compare to the one vineyard the couple enjoys. Longman notes, "This poem ... may be read as supportive of exclusive, devoted sexual love and against polygamy and promiscuity."[230] Writing about the love of the couple in contrast to the relationship Solomon has with his many "wives," Hess remarks, "The committed relationship here attains a joy and human delight that multiple sexual encounters (whether polygamous or promiscuous) can never achieve."[231] From Solomon's perspective, Garrett writes, "But he had no experience of love as the singer. ... Solomon was the *Baal Hamon*, the lord of the mob. He owned a great many things and people but knew them only from a distance."[232]

The reference to Solomon in 1:1 does not identify Solomon as a character in the Song but as its probable author. This ascription to Solomon anchors the book to the wisest of wise (1 Kgs 10:23), and it firmly grounds the poem in the genre of wisdom literature of the ancient Hebrews. Thus, in this genre one would expect the presentation of negative examples to motivate one to follow the path of wisdom.[233] Solomon and his own many intimate relationships is the foil to the couple's relationship in the Song. While it may seem unlikely, according to Longman, for Solomon to take such a part, it is not impossible nor improbable. The reader realizes that, as the author, Solomon wrote better than he lived (as least as it relates to an exclusive love relationship).[234]

In summary of his character analysis, Solomon is a round, full-fledged literary character. Unlike the other characters of the Song, he is a historical person as well. Thus Solomon is a full-fledged, historical character. By using Solomon as a round character, the poet (Solomon, himself) brings to the Song well-known allusions to his royalty and

---

is portrayed positively (3:6–11)." Exum may not be giving enough credit to her readers to discern between allusions to royalty and a king's lifestyle. Surely, one can aspire to be president of the United States without following the immorality of certain chief executives. This concept will be further developed under the rhetorical use of Solomon.

230. Longman, *Song of Songs*, 220.

231. Hess, *Song of Songs*, 246.

232. Garrett, "Song of Songs," 263.

233. For instance, Prov 5:7–14 gives the example of a man who would engage in illicit sex. This is to motivate the son (or reader) not to follow that same path.

234. It is not that Solomon does not belong in the Song because of his lifestyle but it is because of his lifestyle that he is there! This dynamic of "writing better than he lived" may ease the discomfort of conservative scholars who have a difficult time harmonizing Solomon's authorship, his place in the book, and his sordid love life.

his own numerous amorous relationships. The reader recognizes that Solomon, the King of Israel, known for his royalty and wisdom (1 Kgs 10) is a character in the Song. That is how Solomon desires himself to be viewed, as a character in the Song, full of wisdom and of failure, a truly full-fledged (albeit) tragic character.

Narrator

The last character to be analyzed is the narrator.[235] His voice is heard in the couple's most intimate sexual moment in 5:1: "Eat, friends; Drink and imbibe deeply, O lovers," אִכְלוּ רֵעִים שְׁתוּ וְשִׁכְרוּ דּוֹדִים. This voice is different from any other in the Song. The reader finds this voice in an erotic environment where no character save the amorous couple is expected. It cannot be the daughters of Jerusalem. They never command the couple nor do they ever address the couple. They only dialogue with the woman, and they certainly would not command her since she is the dominant voice in the Song.

This speech has a commanding presence to it. The voice speaks but five words, continuing the eating and drinking metaphor that the couple began early in the chapter. Based on the information provided in three imperative verbs and two plural nouns, the narrator is a flat character. The only two qualities that his speech exposes are his ability to command the couple to enjoy thoroughly and completely their passion. It also reveals his presence at this most intimate of scenes in which he knows what this couple is saying and doing to one another. During this time, he offers his approval by way of a twofold command to the lovers to continue doing what he is observing.

Conclusion

The majority of the characters in the Song are flat characters. They are one-dimensional. The full-fledged or round characters are generally not developed outside of their relationship with one another. Only Solomon and the female protagonist display any faults or fears. It is with this cast of characters that the author of the Song builds his rhetorical message to persuade his readers to his point of view.

---

235. The term "narrator" may not be the best to use since this voice does not tell a story (as in a biblical narrative) nor is he heard any other time. However, at present, it is useful to distinguish this voice of 5:1 from the rest of the voices of the SoS and from the author.

Rhetorical Use of the Characters

While Weems is incorrect in her statement of the purpose of the Song, she is right to recognize that "poets, like ancient and modern speakers, design their messages with a specific audience in mind: to instruct, build upon, defend, challenge, or correct prevailing assumptions."[236] The author of the Song uses a number of rhetorical devices to communicate that message to his audience. These devices are necessary because the audience may not be initially predisposed to the author's position and may even be hostile to his message. Sternberg believes that various rhetorical devices demonstrate the biblical poet did not write or speak to a "like-minded reader" but he faced "uphill work for consensus."[237] While the inclination of the original audience to the author or his work is unknown to the modern exegete, there was a need to persuade (or encourage) the reader to the biblical author's point of view. To persuade the audience, the poet uses certain rhetorical devices that match his message. In the Song one of those rhetorical devices is his use of the characters, which are used in various ways to move a potentially hostile or indifferent reader to God's point of view.

It is important to recognize the characters as rhetorical devices because persuasion in the SoS does not come from appeal to law or religious practice. There is no call to obedience based on the covenant. As Alter observes, "It is only in the Song of Songs that there is no hierophant, no memorializer of national experience, but instead two voices of two lovers, praising each other, yearning for each other, proffering invitations to enjoy."[238] Thus, it is the two main participants that move the reader to want to experience the same pleasure as the Song's couple.[239]

236. Weems, "The Song of Songs," 167.
237. Sternberg, *Poetics of Biblical Narrative*, 444.
238. Alter, *Art of Biblical Poetry*, 186.
239. It is their words, mainly to each other, that create such a garden of pleasure that the reader is motivated to enter. While it would take another work to track the ramifications, speech act theory with its emphasis on the reader's involvement with performative speech acts may contribute to how the character's speech creates and invites the reader to enjoy such an environment for themselves. Botha (*Jesus and the Samaritan Woman*, 73), although writing concerning speech-act in biblical narrative, observes, "The story or narrative is then related with the aim of inducing the audience to react in the intended way and to adopt the intended viewpoint and subsequently to participate with vigor in the whole experience represented and (re)created in the literary work." Although Briggs ("Uses of Speech-Act Theory," 263) does not mention the Song specifically (or biblical poetry), his suggestion is interesting as one contemplates

The reason this persuasion works is the reader is able to relate to characters that are like him. Once that relationship is created between reader and character, the character can help shape the reader's response to the author's message. Jacobson notes well, "Poetry does create voices. These voices do evoke responses in readers and readers will tend to resonate more strongly to those voices that are like them."[240] While Jacobson is writing regarding the Psalms, his words hold true for the poetry of the Song as well.

Rhetorical Use of the Sixty Queens

Whether "the sixty queens and eighty concubines and maidens without number" (6:8) are a literary creation or a veiled reference to Solomon's harem, their rhetorical purpose is the same. As a means of comparison, the author employs this upper echelon of women expressed in a royal hierarchy to express the utter beauty of the female. In this instance, the male lover does not put down other women to exalt his lover as he had done previously (2:2). Here the male creates an image of a female royal court, which would presumably exhibit a vast amount of the most beautiful women (Esth 1:11; 2:3). He then raises his lover by comparison well above all of them into the heavens (6:9–10). Bergant remarks, "By tracing a sequence of increasing numbers—sixty, eighty, countless—the man is underscoring the limitless superiority of the woman he loves, another way of illustrating her uniqueness."[241] She also believes this courtly reference reintroduces "the royal fiction," which may be true since the woman sees herself over her people (6:12). Rhetorically, the sixty queens and their entourage is used by the author to create a unique comparison not with just any women but with the

---

the form and function of the Song: "Speech-act theory is relevant to several different aspects of interpreting the Bible: to speech acts within the biblical narrative as well as to attempts to articulate theological and hermeneutical proposals for reading and being acted upon by the text."

240. Jacobson, *"Many are Saying,"* 144. This dynamic is seen clearly where any man or woman can relate to the passion, desire, and pleasure of this couple.

Even though all the characters (except Solomon) are the author's literary creation, this does not keep the reader from identifying with them. Reflecting that the lovers are "images of the poet," Landy (*Paradoxes of Paradise*, 62) notes, "Their affairs, vagaries, emotions, reflect a psychic process, common to all of us."

241. Bergant, *Song of Songs*, 78. See Watson, *Classical Hebrew Poetry*, 147. He refers to this device as numerical parallelism.

Rhetorical Use of Mother

The rhetorical use of the three mothers in the SoS (his, hers, and Solomon's) is directly tied to the familial relationship established by the use of this term. It is assumed in each instance that the character "mother" plays the same rhetorical role since the character is defined by that same term. For instance, Solomon's mother crowning him on his wedding (3:11), the female lover's mother (3:4), and the male lover's mother (8:5) are all used rhetorically to establish and reveal a special familial relationship. Rhetorically, however, there is disagreement on the exact usage. Keel suggests the reference in 3:4 is used "to call attention to the fact that her mother, her model and her confidant . . . has also known passion that now controls the daughter. The young woman now assumes her mother's role."[242] Longman simply states, "The mother is mentioned in contexts that have to do with sexuality."[243] Writing on the mother's house reference (3:4), Hess surmises based on Ruth 1:8 that "the primary association of a young woman is with the house of her mother rather than father."[244] Murphy summarizes the current discussion of the role of the mother: "It is a strange fact that the mother is so frequently referred to in the work. . . . The mother is mentioned also in Egyptian love poetry, but it is not clear why her role is so prominent."[245] Davidson suggests, "The motif of wholism in sexuality also entails solidarity with the larger units of family and friends."[246] Thus, the mothers give their approval to the passionate relationship of the couple. While this suggestion is inviting, the mothers never speak their approval. Also, the character reference is to their mother's house three times (3:4; 8:2, 5), to another relationship one time (1:6), and three times to the actual mother-child relationship established at birth (3:4; 6:9; 8:1). Only in 3:11 does the reader see any seemingly approving action by the mother. Exum believes the use of the mother demonstrates public approval of the couple's union at least in

---

242. Keel, *Song of Songs*, 124.
243. Longman, *Song of Songs*, 17.
244. Hess, *Song of Songs*, 105.
245. Murphy, *Song of Songs*, 146.
246. Davidson, *Flame of Yahweh*, 586.

3:11 and 8:2.[247] There is a reference in Genesis to Isaac taking Rebekah into his mother's tent (24:67). However, this sheds little additional light on the significance of sexual activity in the mother's house (or tent) in the Song.

It could be the references to "mother" rhetorically associate the passion of the couple with the past sexual experiences of their respective mothers (3:4; 8:5). This would demonstrate that this couple's sexual desire is not a new emotion for their generation. It may also be that some of the maternal references link the passion of the couple to procreation (3:4; 6:9; 8:5). While procreation and children are not the focus or the goal of the sexual pleasure of the couple, they are a distinct possibility. This could be a veiled rhetorical reminder of that fact.

Rhetorical Use of the Watchmen

The watchmen appear twice in the Song and their two appearances could not be any more different. In their first appearance, they find the female lover roaming the streets at night. Here they are completely indifferent to the woman's search. In their second appearance, they again find her roaming the streets at night searching for her lost love. This time, however, their treatment of her is anything but indifferent. On this night they treat her harshly. Exum feels the watchmen serve as a blind motif— "a potential story, inviting the readers to fill in the gaps."[248] This is unlikely since "filling in the gaps" has led a number of scholars to see the Song as a narrative and that has not helped interpretation. It is doubtful that gap-filling here would be any more successful. Exum also believes the watchmen "strike a discordant note."[249] This could only be true if their unresponsiveness is seen in a negative light because there is no other information that leads one to such a conclusion. It could just as easily be, as Hess points out, that their nonresponsiveness is an apt reaction since they do not know where the female's lover has gone.[250] It may be there is some ambiguity in the watchmen's inaction on the part of the female lover which serves simply to introduce the watchmen.

Rhetorically however, it might be best to seek another solution. All the nonverbal characters (except Solomon) are only in the Song as they

---

247. Exum, *Song of Songs*, 150.
248. Exum, *Song of Songs*, 137.
249. Ibid.
250. Hess, *Song of Songs*, 105.

relate to the female main character. There are no agents (who are basic characters who do not relate deeply to the main characters) because no character is needed to move the Song along because it is not a narrative, which needs to be moved along to its next literary point. Thus, all the characters relate only to the woman, even the watchmen.[251] Therefore, the reason for the watchmen's indifference (3:3) is because the woman has done nothing wrong to cause them to act (unlike their actions in chapter 5). Some may suggest that part of the job of a night watchman in the city is to help a frantically distraught woman search for her lover. However, since this is her dream, her unconsciousness does not need their help searching for him. For whatever reason, her nighttime vision is playing at this specific scenario.

Once the female protagonist begins her second frantic nocturnal search, the watchmen take immediate and harsh action against her (5:7). They appear omniscient, knowing without outside information that the woman deserves their unsympathetic treatment (as does the reader). Feminist scholars should not assault this interpretation since it is the woman's dream and she is in complete control of it.[252] Also, the female lover never complains about their discipline (which, if true, would be reason to complain). Rhetorically, the watchmen are used by the author to communicate the inappropriateness of the female lover's response. Their inaction in chapter 3 demonstrates she has done nothing wrong to be missing her lover even in her dream. Their quick and sure actions against her in chapter 5 show the reader that her imaginary reluctance is met with equally imaginary discipline. It is reading too much into their character to see their gender as the reason for their rhetorical use.[253]

---

251. Linafelt ("Arithmetic of Eros," 252–53) views the watchmen as "a third point in the triangle set up with the two lovers," who "serve to keep the lovers apart" and "function in poetry to intensify erotic desire by protracting the absence." While this approach is novel, it has no support in the text. The watchmen never interact remotely with the male lover and are never seen as causing separation between them.

252. In reality the author is in control of the dream. Since the woman is a literary creation, so is her dream.

253. Exum (*Song of Songs*, 198) states, "One cannot ignore the fact that it is a woman whom the poet represents as abused by men in a role of authority." While this fact should not be ignored, neither does it have to carry the rhetorical purpose that Exum supposes.

Rhetorical Use of the Brothers

Mazor suggests the brothers' rhetorical purpose is to yield "a sense of roundness, of completely circularity, which endows *The Song* with a sense of completeness."[254] The difficulty with this suggestion is that for this to be true, the brothers need to appear at the beginning and end of this love poem. It has been demonstrated that they do not need to be the speakers of 8:8–9. Thus, the brothers are limited to one, nonspeaking reference (1:6), and their structural or rhetorical purpose cannot be to provide a sense of closure to the book.

It is better to see the brothers (or better, "my mother's sons") as the cause of the woman's sunburnt skin color. While it may be true that brothers had responsibility for their sisters in the ANE, it is reading too much into this verse to surmise anything more than that their anger caused her to neglect caring for her own body. Rhetorically, the results of this sibling rivalry point out that there is a problem, even a self-perceived one, in this couple's love relationship: the self-perception of the female lover. Although the Song has the feeling of a garden of paradise, some problems remind the reader that the garden is marred. It is not perfect. Not only must the couple struggle to be together and enjoy each other's presence, there are times that certain problems need to be overcome as well. The woman's self-perception that she is less than beautiful is one of those times. Other problems seem to appear in 1:6; 2:1; 3:1; 4:8; 5:6, 7; 8:1.

Rhetorical Use of the Little Sister

Garrett recognizes that

> There is no need to ask about the relationship between the little girl of 8:8–9 and the chorus, as though these were actual characters in a drama or history. The whole point behind introducing the little girl is to provide a vehicle that allows the Song to elaborate on the transformation from virgin to wife.[255]

The "little sister" is a literary creation, but it is not to show the female lover's transformation from virgin to wife, as Garrett assumes. The poet uses this little girl rhetorically to provide a contrast between the little

---

254. Mazor, "Song of Songs," 23. It is better to see this "circularity" not based on the brothers but based on the woman's unquenchable desire for her lover (1:2; 8:14).

255. Garrett, "Song of Songs," 259.

girl and the female lover. Clearly, the little girl cannot be the main object of discussion since the female lover always occupies the poem's center stage as either the speaker or object of the other characters. Therefore, the little girl helps the reader understand something about the female protagonist. The author desires his audience to understand the contrast between these two females. The contrast centers on their breasts, which marks girls as either sexually mature or immature. The little girl is physically childlike, שָׁדַיִם אֵין לָהּ. By contrast, the female lover has שָׁדַי כַּמִּגְדָּלוֹת. Because of her sexual immaturity, the little girl needs protection to guard her purity and adornment to draw the right husband (8:9). Since the female lover is well fortified with כַּמִּגְדָּלוֹת שָׁדַי she does not need the same embellishment. Exum remarks, "In contrast to the aforementioned little sister, she requires neither reinforcement to protect her from suitors nor ornamentation to attract one. She possesses her own enhancement, an erotic one, her breasts."[256] In contrast to the little sister who needs protection against unwanted male intruders, the female lover has no such need. She has already been "conquered" (2:4; cf. 6:4). Her lover scales her prominent "walls" and takes complete possession of her once she surrenders herself to him (2:4). With her self-capitulation comes peace (8:9).

Rhetorical Use of the Daughters of Jerusalem

There is a wealth of suggestions as to the rhetorical use of the daughters of Jerusalem. Although Linafelt's arithmetic needs correcting, he believes, "The voice of the daughters of Jerusalem . . . serve a . . . rhetorical function of evoking or even provoking the passionate response of the lovers."[257] Longman feels the daughters are a literary device whose function is more important than their identity. He states, "They are city girls, young and naïve, inexperienced in matters of love. It is here they find their function as a sounding board, a contrast, and students of the woman."[258] Murphy states, "The Daughters function primarily as a foil for the woman's own reflections. . . . They neither describe themselves nor reveal their own feelings and values; they are present solely to pro-

---

256. Exum, *Song of Songs*, 258.

257. Linafelt, "Arithmetic of Eros," 250. By Linafelt's math, the characters in the Song create a triangle with the two lovers which creates a geometric space. It is in this space that the vision of eros is articulated.

258. Longman, *Song of Songs*, 16.

mote what the woman wishes to say."²⁵⁹ Similarly Munro suggests that they are "a literary device which enables the woman to explore her feelings more fully. If they are silent and unresponsive, revealing none of their feelings or values, it is only so that she can better articulate her own."²⁶⁰ Goulder believes the daughters act as a chorus and "bridge the gap between one scene and the next."²⁶¹ Bloch and Bloch observe, "The daughters of Jerusalem act as a kind of chorus, a foil to the Shulamite and an audience.... The daughters of Jerusalem represent the social milieu in which the lovers move, answering their needs for public testimony and public validation."²⁶² Alter also sees the daughters as "representatives of the social realm" noting that that realm "is a world of conventions, divisions, restrictions and collective expectations."²⁶³ However, these daughters, according to Alter, "can have no real understanding of or access to the inner sanctum where the lovers hold each other close."²⁶⁴ Keel remarks, "The daughters of Jerusalem are probably used in the Song as the stereotypical public."²⁶⁵

While each position may have merit and may add to one's understanding of the daughters' function, Exum recognizes and articulates their rhetorical function the best: "The women of Jerusalem are the audience within the poem whose presence—because it makes the relationship between the lovers less private, less closed—facilitates the reader's entry into the poem's world of erotic intimacy."²⁶⁶ To summarize Exum's position, the daughters are the rhetorical stand-in for the reader. For instance, there is no need to make the daughters swear not to arouse or awaken love—they are a literary creation—they are not real and thus there is no danger for them. However, the danger does exist for the reader. They need to heed the warning and swear not to arouse love until the proper time (2:7; 3:5; 8:4).

259. Murphy, *Song of Songs*, 84–85.
260. Munro, *Spikenard and Saffron*, 43–44.
261. Goulder, *Song of Fourteen Songs*, 13.
262. Bloch and Bloch, *Song of Songs*, 6.
263. Alter, "An Ode to Intimacy," 32. This observation is contrary to the woman's adjuration to the daughters not to arouse love. If they could not experience this love for themselves, the adjuration is pointless.
264. Ibid.
265. Keel, *Song of Songs*, 49.
266. Exum, *Song of Songs*, 101.

The same rhetorical dynamic is in place in the interrogative of 8:5. The daughters pose a question to which they already know the answer. So what is their function? Exum notes well, "By having the women of Jerusalem speak at this point, the poet once again reminds us of the presence of the audience, onlookers who participate in the unfolding of the lover's relationship, and so encourages the reader's involvement."[267] When the female protagonist interacts with the daughters, she is rhetorically interacting with the reader. According to LaCocque, "The reader is eminently active."[268] This draws the reader into the poem and persuades him or her to accept her position on love.

The use of the masculine plural pronominal suffix -כֶם in reference to the female daughters of Jerusalem (2:7; 3:5; 8:4) may also grammatically strengthen this position. Bascom, writing about the use of the second person masculine plural pronoun, states, "In fact the feminine plural in general is reserved for cases where no man could possibly be included."[269] Since the poet has the daughters stand in for the general audience, which would include males, the pronoun use may suggest that this is the rhetorical strategy of the author. Noticing the use of the second person masculine plural imperatives in 2:5, Exum concurs, "The plural imperatives reveal an awareness of the audience on the part of the poet.... Ultimately the woman's words are addressed to the audience of the poem, its readers."[270]

It may be that the daughters do serve a number of rhetorical functions in the Song as scholars have noted. However, it is probably best to see those functions in connection with the audience or the reader of the poem.

---

267. Ibid., 249.

268. LaCocque, *Romance She Wrote*, 57.

269. Bascom, "Hebrew Poetry," 98. It should be noted that Waltke and O'Connor observe, "The masculine pronoun is often used for a feminine antecedent" (*IBHS*, 302). By Mitchell's (*Song of Songs*, 685) reckoning, the combination of the direct object marker and the second person masculine plural pronoun appears 299 times in the OT and the same combination in the feminine gender "never appears in the OT." This may account for the pronoun use. However, it still leaves open for discussion Exum's observation regarding the masculine imperatives.

270. Exum, *Song of Songs*, 116.

Rhetorical Use of the Female and Male Lovers

These two characters may be discussed together since they are both literary creations of the biblical poet and their rhetorical purpose is similar. There is nothing known about these lovers outside of their interaction with one another. It is as if there is no life without each other. When they are parted from one another, they pine for each other and overcome any hurdle to be together (2:8). Even though each lover describes the other in seemingly great and sometimes erotic detail, there is not enough detail to paint an exact representation of either. For instance, from the description presented in the SoS, the reader does not know if the woman is tall or short. Though the woman is certainly יָפָה, is her beauty Rubenesque full-bodied or bone thin? The same observation may be made of the man as well. The reader feels he or she can genuinely picture these lovers and yet they defy exact representation.[271] It is as though they can depict any lover, and that is the exact rhetorical purpose of the Song's poet.[272] Since they defy exact description, any male or female reader may identify with them.[273] Longman recognizes this rhetorical feature: "The man and woman of the Song are not historical personages but rather poetic types, and as such the poet invites the readers to identify with them."[274] Exum notes more specifically, "By providing access only to the voices of the lovers, to what they say and not who they are, the poet is able to identify them with all lovers. Their love is timeless."[275] In essence, any

---

271. Brenner recognizes this dynamic in the various *wasf* sections concerning each lover. The point of these descriptions is not to paint an exact representation of the beloved but one of desire. Brenner ("Gazing Back at the Shulammite," 296) writes, "Ultimately the emotive content of desire is paramount; no visual image is perhaps intended per se; and the object of desire remains precisely that mysterious entity instead of being transformed into a revealed aesthetic edifice."

272. This is contrary to Clines ("Why Is There a Song of Songs?" 13), who believes the rhetorical purpose of the author is to create an erotic fantasy of a sexually charged woman for the male population of Israel. While it may be that the Song can be loosely termed a fantasy (there are no other concerns outside of each other, such as jobs, wars, cooking, cleaning, etc), clearly the author desires the reader to enter into it and not simply wish to possess such a woman!

273. It appears that this couple is physically flawless, but the reality is probably much different. Although there may be beautiful people in the world, there is no such thing as physically perfect people. However, the Song conveys quite clearly that they are perfect in each other's sight.

274. Longman, *Song of Songs*, 62.

275. Exum, *Song of Songs*, 8. In his study on the similarities between the SoS and Tamil love poetry, Mariaselvam (*Song of Songs*, 168) recognizes the same dynamic in

woman is able to become the female lover and any man the male lover, making this celebration of love their own. Sparks sees the same dynamic in Mesopotamian love poetry of Dumuzi and Inanna: "Dumuzi and Inanna are multivalent figures who stand for any couple," and "it is very sensible to presume that these texts were sometimes used in ordinary marriage ceremonies quite apart from their usual cultic usage."[276]

However, not only does the Song's poet allow the reader the opportunity to become either the male or female character, by its complete rhetorical force it creates a response in the reader to want to identify with a character. By depicting this lush erotic environment of passion, the reader's own desires are stirred.[277] He (or she) yearns to create the same passionate atmosphere in his or her marriage.

This rhetorical purpose may not have been achievable using historical personages as the main voices of the Song. For as Exum realizes, "Real lovers die, but the love that is celebrated here lives on ... because it is love in progress, not a story about famous lovers of the past."[278] There are just enough physical details in the Song for anyone to see themselves as these lovers. However, there are not enough historical particulars that would exclude the reader from relating to a historical character. Thus, all readers are provided an equal opportunity to experience this type of love relationship at the proper time in their own lives.

Rhetorical Use of Solomon

The character of Solomon has a twofold rhetorical purpose.[279] When his name is used adjectivally (1:5), it demonstrates a relationship between some object and ancient royalty. For instance, the curtains of Solomon were presumably dark in color, and thus they become a fitting simile

---

India's ancient love poetry (150 BC–250 AD): "The love-sentiments expressed in the poems live long after the poet or even the characters. For, this love relation has been by now made a paradigm for all love-relations into which anyone sees himself or herself reflected and thus feels at home."

276. Sparks, *Ancient Texts*, 129.

277. Sternberg (*Poetics of Biblical Narrative*, 475) recognizes that the biblical author through various rhetorical devices shapes the reader's response to the characters and events in a narrative. The same shaping dynamic is at play in this poem as well.

278. Exum, *Song of Songs*, 3.

279. Webb (*Five Festal Garments*, 19) believes that Solomon is simply idealized. He reasons that Solomon could not possibly place himself in the book as "the villain." He misses the possibility that this is not an either-or but a both-and situation. Solomon is both "idealized" (1:5; 3:11) and "vilified" (his term).

for the color of the woman's skin. However, more is probably at play than simple color. The simile of color is already established with the tents of Kedar. This line is intensified by its reference to Solomon's curtains.[280] Therefore, the reference is probably not simply to the dark color of the curtains but to their dark, rich color befitting a king. Bergant notes, "The extravagance associated with the court of Solomon is an important theme in these poems."[281] This simile communicates the fact that the female lover is richly beautiful. The couch of Solomon plays the same rhetorical role (3:7, 9). Since it is associated with Solomon, it contains all the trappings of wealth and royalty. Longman suggests the couple's own wedding is associated with the royalty of Solomon to demonstrate "the magnificence of the wedding and, by association, the marriage relationship itself."[282] Exum sees that the reference to Solomon (3:6–11) is "only about Solomon for what he represents, a lover-king par excellence, then vv. 6–11 belong to the realm of poetic fancy in which lovers take on various identities.... That Solomon here is a guise or role in which the woman casts her lover seems to be the most likely sense of these verses."[283] While Exum's suggestion is inviting and may be correct, it is possible that this is not poetic fancy per se, but the wedding event is actually anchored in ancient history. The specific references to Solomon seem to point in that direction since the poet could have left the king unidentified and generic (1:4). If it is a reference to a historical event, it does not necessarily change the rhetorical purpose as stated by Exum; it simply makes the imagery more concrete by referencing the wedding of the most famous and wealthiest king of all Israel. Brueggemann agrees, "The references are rhetorical maneuvers designed to evoke an imagined environment of wealth, joy, beauty, and well-being, with Solomon here regarded as a full embodiment of such situations."[284]

The second rhetorical purpose is Solomon himself as a historical character. While the first rhetorical purpose is positive (1:5; 3:7, 9, 11), this one is negative. These references (8:11, 12) are used to show

---

280. Kugel's (*Idea of Biblical Poetry*, 8) explanation of Hebrew parallelism is "A is so, and *what's more*, B is so." According to Kugel somehow line B is an intensification of the first line.
281. Bergant, *Song of Songs*, 14.
282. Longman, *Song of Songs*, 136.
283. Exum, *Song of Songs*, 141.
284. Brueggemann, *Solomon*, 209.

that Solomon is a negative example of the theme of the SoS. The reader knows historically that Solomon is not the model of exclusive love relationship (1 Kgs 11:3). Whether out of political necessity or simply because he could, Solomon accumulated wives and concubines and is well known for his marital collection. Thus, Solomon uses his own life as a foil to the exclusive relationship between the two lovers of the SoS. Bennett states, "Solomon also functions as a foil for a monogamous relationship. This is achieved more by naming Solomon (the author relies on the reader's prior knowledge of Solomon's harem) than by describing his vast harem."[285] Exum is correct to see Solomon as "a king-lover par excellence."[286] However, he is not a positive example of a lover, as he believes affection can be bought or shared among many. Haverluck writes, "For here it is made most plain that the king and his kind of garden is in fundamental conflict with that of the lovers."[287] While it may seem incongruent, the man who is considered the wisest of the wise uses his own well-known amorous reputation rhetorically as a foil to contrast the celebration of exclusive love of the female lover with Solomon's own "love" of a thousand. In reality, there is no conflict. The reader realizes there is no real option but to choose the woman's position. The choice is plain.[288] In essence, the woman says to the reader (implicitly through

---

285. Bennett, "Love Over Gold," 34. While Rabin ("Song of Songs," 213) believes "Solomon's values are mentioned only to be refuted, perhaps even ridiculed," he goes too far to see that the reference to King Solomon actually represents the "world of men." Brueggemann (*Solomon*, 210), who cautiously follows Hunter, also goes too far viewing the SoS as a "protest" against the idea that "women are commodities and objects that function to support commercial and political interests" and a "protest" against patriarchy. Hunter ("Song of Protests," 124) believes the SoS is a protest against the rest of the OT: "Song of Songs stood in opposition to prevailing public morality as expressed and taught in the rest of the Old Testament."

286. Exum, "Seeing Solomon's Palanquin," 307.

287. Haverluck, "Song of Love," 16.

288. The reason the reader would follow the woman is because the author has created the male and female lovers in such a way so that the reader is able to relate to them and thus take their position. Although Gunn and Fewell (*Narrative in the Hebrew Bible*, 47) recognize this dynamic in narrative, it holds true in this instance of biblical poetry as well: "The power of narrative lies in its ability to imitate life, to evoke a world that is like ours, to reproduce life-like events and situations, to recreate people that we understand and to whom we can relate." While the world of the SoS is idyllic, it is not different than the one readers who are lovers would want to inhabit. In this world the readers relate to the lovers. Because this same relationship is not created between the reader and Solomon (he is only a distant but richly famous historical character), the reader disdains his position of love but embraces the female's.

Solomon's lifestyle), "You could have multiple partners like him, but many (bought by power and wealth) are not better than one. Solomon wrote better than he loved."[289] While Solomon casts a dark cloud, it is but a small one. The poet uses the king as a foil to highlight the exclusiveness of the couple.

Rhetorical Use of the Narrator

The narrator's voice is used in two specific ways in 5:1. The author employs his voice to confirm the words and actions of the lovers and to provide divine approval. While Berlin is writing about OT narrative, her observation is useful in this case as well. She notes that when the narrator and a character "share verbal similarities. . . . the narrator may be confirming the words of the character."[290] This is the case where the narrator's voice echoes the eating and drinking metaphors the female and male lovers have just exchanged (4:16—5:1). The narrator is not simply confirming their words but also their intimate actions as well. This confirmation is important in that the narrator's words tell the truth. Like Berlin, Sternberg is observing the rhetorical role of the narrator in biblical narrative. However, it is worth quoting him at length because he captures so well the author's purpose for the narrator's voice at this crucial juncture in this piece of biblical poetry.

---

289. This observation could help Williams and other scholars who cannot harmonize Solomon as a character in the SoS and Solomon as the author of the SoS. Williams ("Most Excellent of Songs,") muses in a blog, "I have often been puzzled by more conservative scholars who argue for Solomonic authorship of the Song and maintain that it is a celebration of human erotic love within the context of a monogamous marriage relationship. Was not Solomon known for his many wives and concubines (1 Kings 11)? I don't see how he could be held up as a modern paragon of love and faithfulness." This observation may be an answer to Williams' honest question. This explanation of Solomon's life and writing may be a more academically honest harmonization than Davidson proposes. Davidson (*Flame of Yahweh*, 568) suggests, "One must not allow the later dark history of Solomon to detract from the ideal." Simply not allowing Solomon's marital history to intrude on interpretation is not possible. Solomon's cloud over the SoS is too dark and too large and it does not answer the rhetorical use of Solomon as a character.

290. Berlin, *Poetics and Interpretation*, 64. Sternberg (*Poetics of Biblical Narrative*, 476) agrees (albeit more forcefully). He observes that the narrator "judges" the characters by his comments about them or their actions through epithets or loaded language. When the narrator reuses the same metaphors as the lovers, this is likely "loaded language." See also Gunn and Fewell, *Narrative in the Hebrew Bible*, 59–63.

> The Bible always tells the truth in that its narrator is absolutely and straightforwardly reliable. Historians may quarrel with his facts and others call them fiction; but in context his remain accounts of the truth communicated on the highest authority.... Follow the biblical narrator's ever so uncritically, and by no great exertion, you will be making tolerable sense of the world you are in, the action that unfolds, the protagonists on stage and the point of it all.[291]

The point of the narrator's incursion into this couple's private lovemaking is to mark their actions, hidden behind the double entendre of feasting, as deserving of his authoritative endorsement.

The biblical narrator's approval in this erotic scene carries more weight than simply a storyteller's support. As Davidson rightly notes, "The omniscient narrator/poet at this high point in the Song seems to have a ring of divine authority and power—to be able to bestow a blessing and approbation upon the consummation of the marriage of the bride and groom."[292] While Davidson may be reading too much into this picture, he is correct to hear the "ring of divine authority." The voice of the unidentified narrator is God. Dillow observes, "The poet seems to say this is the voice of God Himself. Only the Lord could pronounce such an affirmation. He, of course, was the most intimate observer of all."[293] If the anonymous voice is God's, the poet is using his short twofold command rhetorically to cast his divine favor over the most intimate of human activities between a man and a woman.[294]

The Theology of the Characters

As Osborne rightly notes concerning a metaphor as a figure of speech, "Theology rarely stems from the metaphor itself but rather from the

---

291. Sternberg, *Poetics of Biblical Narrative*, 51.
292. Davidson, *Flame of Yahweh*, 591.
293. Dillow, *Solomon on Sex*, 86.

294. While it is outside the scope of this project to pursue, a legitimate question is the absence of the voice of God. "Why not let God speak for himself in the SoS, instead of 'hiding' his voice behind the unnamed narrator?" It may be that since Israel's neighbors were so heavily engaged in various fertility cults that Solomon may have felt the need to keep a respectable distance between God and the act of sex. As Phipps ("Plight of the Song of Songs," 83) writes, "In Hebrew culture sex had been demythologized; it was considered a proper sphere for man but not for deity."

whole context of which it is part."²⁹⁵ What is true of the metaphor is also true of the author's use of his characters. Only in the context in which they interact does theology flow from the authorial utilization of any person in the SoS.

It is important to articulate the theology arising from these characters because, as Waltke observes, "Biblical authors often intentionally avoid stating their theology in a clear and concise form and, instead, seek to evoke a visceral response from their readers. They employ rhetoric to communicate the message in order to effect behavior."²⁹⁶ In the Song characters or voices have been used rhetorically to make certain points and in the Bible those points are necessarily theological in nature. As Bright observes, "All biblical texts are expressive of theology in that all are animated, if at times indirectly, by some theological concern." Earlier he states, "There are no nontheological texts in the Bible."²⁹⁷ While David Carr does not believe there is any theological significance in the details of love, some of the characters sing a different theological song.²⁹⁸

The Theology of the "Siblings"

The brothers of the female protagonist (1:6) exhibit no theological truths. The "sons of my mother" simply are the instruments that are to blame for the female lover's sunburnt color. While the woman's perception of her darkened complexion has some theological ramifications (i.e., love, even in a garden, is not without problems), the brothers themselves are theologically insignificant. Since they play no other part in the SoS, there is no exegetical evidence to suggest that theologically these brothers are somehow responsible for the purity of their sister. While this dynamic is true in other scriptures (Gen 34:13; 2 Sam 13:22), this theological observation cannot be made from the SoS.

The supposed little sister (8:8–9) also exhibits no theology. The author utilizes her as a literary contrast to the main female character. While these verses may indicate a truth that an immature female needs

---

295. Osborne, *Hermeneutical Spiral*, 188.
296. Waltke, *Old Testament Theology*, 91.
297. Bright, *Authority of the Old Testament*, 170, 143.
298. D. M. Carr, *The Erotic Word*, 129. Since the purpose of this treatise is to surface the theology that flows naturally from specific rhetorical devices, this section will limit itself only to those theological insights that flow from the author's use of the characters themselves in their immediate context.

her family's protection and preparation for marriage, it is a stretch to see this as a weighty theological concern of this Song. On the contrary, it is the theology of the sexually mature female that is center stage and is celebrated within the confines of marriage.

The Theology of the Mothers

There may be no theological significance of the mother of Solomon crowning him on the day of his marriage (3:11). Her use may simply be to add a female of note to the festive, royal scene. This is in keeping with the tenor of the book in which the female gender is highlighted throughout the SoS to the near exclusion of males, except the male lover. (There is no mention of a father or his house).

The theological use of the male and female lover's mothers is enigmatic. It may be the woman's passion provides a generational continuum. Her mother felt and acted the same way. This is why she seeks to bring her lover back to her mother's house to demonstrate a connection with the past generation (3:4; 8:5). It may be the mother and her home represents the place where the female lover learned about sexual pleasure and responsibility (Ruth 3:1–6). There is not enough contextual evidence to support any further theological observations. The theological import of these characters may become clearer as their rhetorical usage is studied further.

The Theology of the Watchmen

In their first appearance, the watchmen are theologically insignificant (3:3). However, their second appearance carries certain theological weight (5:7). The author uses the watchmen to communicate the inappropriateness of the actions of the female lover. Their inaction in chapter 3 reveal she has done nothing wrong to be searching for her lover. Their quick and sure actions against her in chapter 5 prove to the reader that she is culpable for turning her lover away. Her imaginary reluctance is met with equally imaginary discipline.[299] However imaginary, it is discipline nonetheless.

The Theology of the Daughters of Jerusalem

While the daughters of Jerusalem are the only verbal characters in addition to the male and female lovers, it is expected that their collective

---

299. This theological concept is expounded in 1 Cor 7:3–5.

voice would carry significant theological weight. However, it is not what they say (or do not say) that exhibits this insight. In their dialogue with the woman, they function as a sounding board to allow the lover to express her emotions and passions. They never share their own thoughts. Their theological contribution is bound with what they are told not to do by the woman and subsequently whom they represent in the poem.

While the SoS paints an erotic picture of the celebration of desire, it is not love without boundaries. The adjuration refrains communicate that love is not to be aroused or awakened until the proper time. This theological charge is directed to the daughters each time. Since the daughters rhetorically stand in for the reader, the adjuration is aimed ultimately at him or her. Because of the power of love (8:6–7), the reader is to take the charge seriously: do not arouse or awaken love until it pleases. However, at the proper time the reader is free (and encouraged) to give him or herself over to desire and to enter into the same celebration of passionate love.

THE THEOLOGY OF THE MALE AND FEMALE LOVERS

The most obvious theological observation concerning these characters is that one is a *male* lover and the other is a *female* lover.[300] This celebration of marital pleasure is between a man and a woman

The amount of conversation between this couple also exemplifies for the reader that their own marriage should be one of mutual admiration. While there is limited action in the SoS, the couple's relationship is sustained and nurtured by the quantity and quality of dialogue between them. However, it should not be misconstrued that a couple's relationship should be platonic only. On the contrary, this couple reveals for every couple that marriage should contain healthy doses of physically passionate activities that finds satisfaction in sexual release. On a number of occasions, dialogue turns to physical intimacy (5:1; 7:9, 10). All human senses enter the bedroom.

The male and female lovers exhibit a desire for each other that is portrayed as normal, proper, and pleasurable. Yet the text does more than simply show that desire is permissible. Through the two main pro-

---

300. A number of these theological observations have already been cited in chapter 2. The reason for the repetition is because the lovers are represented not only as characters but also in the use of the personal pronouns. To avoid unnecessary redundancy most of the observations will only be listed and not detailed.

tagonists, this composition actually arouses desire in the reader. Writing on the Song, Walsh keenly observes, "It is palpably erotic, startling and exciting the reader, including him or her in the narrated passions.... It will enlist the reader's empathy with feelings of longing and arousal in the text. If all goes well ... then the longings within the reader's heart are stirred awake."[301] Desire is meant to drive the characters of the poem (and its readers) into each other's arms. However, the theology of the Song makes equally plain that desire should not be denied (5:3).

There is an equality in the sexual relationship between the male and the female lovers. While this theological observation is true, there is no evidence to suggest that an equalitarian relationship exists between the couple in SoS. The best one may surmise from the theology of the Song is that the woman is equal with the man in the area of sexual relationship. Nothing is stated implicitly or explicitly concerning how their relationship functions outside the confines of this unique vineyard. In reality one cannot (and should not extrapolate) an egalitarian position from their relationship since this couple is a literary creation. They are not real; hence, they do not have a life outside their own garden paradise to evaluate. Clines is correct when he states, "We cannot help observing that their world is a very narrow one."[302] However, while his concern for this couple is admirable, "And we worry about what will happen to their love when they leave the garden, as they must, for the world of economic and social necessity,"[303] it is misplaced. This couple never leaves the garden because they are not real.

From the female character a theology of female sexuality emerges. Walsh remarks, "A woman's sexuality is developed, sustained and celebrated, not as object, but from a woman's perspective and that of her

---

301. Walsh, *Exquisite Desire*, 42.

302. Clines, "Why is There a Song of Songs," 23.

303. Ibid. Walsh (*Exquisite Desire*, 140) is such an example (see also Hunter, "'Sweet Talk'"). She is reading too much into the dominant use of the voice of the female when she states that there is an "antipatriarchal bent to the Song." However, the female voice is dominant not to correct or to add balance to the OT but because her voice is the voice of the main character in this genre. By G. L. Carr's ("Love Poetry Genre," 310) accounting, the woman speaks the majority of the time in ancient love poetry: "This two-to-one ratio of female to male speeches is consistent across the genre." This accounting observation may also deflate the support for a woman author because of the predominance of feminine voice.

male lover(s)."[304] The woman initiates sex, enjoys sex, and is a creative lover. She is free to describe her lover sexually as well as herself. She is, as Bergant observes, "not intimidated by eroticism."[305] Weems summarizes this theology of female sexuality well: "With the Song, women find in the Bible permission to initiate, enjoy, and long for the erotic."[306]

The Theology of Solomon

Solomon as author sets the Song firmly in the genre of wisdom literature. Childs notes succinctly, "The ascription of the Song of Songs to Solomon ... sets these writings within the context of wisdom literature. ... The Song is to be understood as wisdom literature."[307] In general, wisdom literature instructs God's people how to live life wisely, skillfully, or theologically. Since the Song is part of this genre, House recognizes the Song's contribution to wisdom literature as "wise living exhibited through wise loving."[308] Single people who follow the adjurations not to arouse love before marriage are living wisely. Married couples, who abandon themselves enthusiastically to this sexual passion, live wisely as well. Because of the Song's link to Solomon, Webb believes this linkage "strongly suggests that the Song is intended to have a didactic dimension to it. It is meant to lead us, via its presentation of love of this man and this woman, to reflection on the nature of love itself."[309]

Solomon as an historical character sets himself firmly as the theological example not to follow if one wants to live wisely in this area of sexual relationships. While the Song extols the beauty of monogamy and exclusivity, Solomon pursued a far different and foolish course (1 Kgs 11:1–6).[310] Webb observes that "the more women Solomon has,

---

304. Walsh, "Startling Voice," 133.

305. Bergant, "'My Beloved is Mine,'" 29.

306. Weems, "The Song of Songs," 268. This only applies within the confines of a heterosexual marriage.

307. Childs, *Old Testament as Scripture*, 574.

308. House, *Old Testament Theology*, 463.

309. Webb, *Five Festal Garments*, 24.

310. While there is little concern for modern individuals in the West to collect wives and concubines in Solomonic numbers, the threat of cybersex does allow one potentially to multiply partners. According to a MSNBC survey (http://www.horizonz.com/statistics.htm), twenty-five million Americans visit cybersex sites between one and ten hours per week. This may indicate that some married spouses are seeking partners outside their own marriages.

the less deeply personal and fulfilling can be his relationship with any one of them."[311] The reader would be wise to choose a different path than Solomon.

The Theology of the Narrator

The voice of the unidentified narrator is God himself. With this identification the theology of divine approval is clearly heard. Dillow observes, "Only the Lord could pronounce such an affirmation. He, of course, was the most intimate observer of all. . . . Thus, the Lord pronounces His full approval on everything that has taken place. He encourages them to drink deeply of the gift of sexual love."[312] God is casting his divine favor over the most intimate of human activities between a man and a woman within the confines of a heterosexual marriage.

If 3:6—5:1 is the structural center or thematic pivot as Dorsey and other scholars propose, it could be that this divine sanction does not simply concern this one event but his endorsement covers the entire book as well. If it is not, it is still clear that God is providing not only his support for this incident but his encouragements to couples to enjoy completely the joys of all physical intimacies. This support would be true as well of the entire poem thematically if not structurally.

Conclusion

Little theology is to be constructed from the flat characters of the SoS. They act to expose the theology of the author through his use of full characters. However, theology flows naturally out of the rhetorical use of these characters. Once the persons of the SoS are identified and the rhetorical purpose of the author realized in their use, the theological observations set firmly on a solid foundation. While her theology is suspect with regard to the scriptures, Bekkenkamp does realize the function a theological text may have: "The function of a theology source-text can be described as giving shape, value and direction to human existence."[313]

---

311. Webb, *Five Festal Garments*, 27.

312. Dillow, *Solomon on Sex*, 86.

313. Bekkenkamp, "Into Another Scene of Choices," 59. This exercise in exposing the theological value of the Song may demonstrate to Bekkenkamp that not all pastors seek to theologically "cover-up" the Song. She writes, "Clergymen questioning the theological value of the SoS usually did so out of disapproval of its erotic undertones" (55). On the contrary this exercise seeks to anchor the celebration of the erotic and sensual firmly on theological grounds. Sex should not be judged right simply because it happens to feel good. It should be enjoyed within marriage knowing it carries God's approval.

Vanhoozer reiterates but more personally when he writes, "The canon is not primarily the source of data for a theoretical science. On the contrary, the canon is a covenantal norm, a norm that regulates our life with God and one another."[314] The poet desires that his divinely inspired song theologically shape the practices and values of believers in the area of physical relationships. God desires that married people celebrate sex and single people would not arouse this emotion before marriage.

---

314. Vanhoozer, *The Drama of Doctrine*, 219.

5

Conclusion

Solomon wrote a song celebrating passion and desire between a man and a woman within the confines of marriage. This poem is not a narrative that traces a historical couple through the ups and downs of their love relationship. It is an artistic creation that places the two main literary characters into a lush and near perfect environment. In this garden setting the characters reveal themselves through their conversation. This sometimes erotically charged dialogue paints on the reader's imagination the pleasure of fulfilled desire. For this couple, longing is only satisfied in the presence of the other. When absent from each other, they yearn for one another and their desire drives them over every obstacle to be one. The movement of the book from her first voiced longing to her final wish is achieved by this progression of absence to presence. For this couple presence produces shalom; absence is always to be struggled against. No good comes from absence except a desire to be present with the other.

While there is no appeal to the Law, no divine commands, no mention of priests or the temple, the astute audience understands that the Song calls for a reproduction of its message in the life of each married couple that is wise enough to hear the theological notes of this ancient love song. Linafelt is certainly correct concerning the theology of the SoS: it is a "theology that persuades by seduction rather than by argument."[1]

Webb believes the Song of Songs (as well as the rest of The Five Scrolls) represents a theological frontier.[2] This study has made a foray into that mostly uncharted theological territory. The thrust of this exploration has been a multidisciplinary one. Three separate literary devices were analyzed exegetically, rhetorically, and theologically within their

---

1. Linafelt, "Lyrical Theology," 305.
2. Webb, *Five Festal Garments*, 135.

canonical context. This project catalogued the biblical author's use of first person pronouns, rhetorical questions, and his employment of the various characters who appear among the pastoral setting of this ancient love poem. It proposed an explanation for the rhetorical function of each of these literary features within their own individual context. It not only exposed some of the biblical theology that naturally flows from the author's use of these three elements but also demonstrated how that biblical theology is derived from those devices. The Song of Songs is certainly artistically pleasing, but at the same time (and more importantly) it is theologically enriching. Its theology deserves the church's attention.

TOPICS FOR FUTURE STUDY

Because the focus of this project has been limited to the contributions of but three literary features of the SoS, it has left much territory unexplored. However, it may point to future exploration. For instance, it has been demonstrated that the author's use of the first person personal pronoun plays a significant role rhetorically and theologically. This leads to an obvious question: Does the author's use of the second and/or third person pronouns have a similar role? Likewise, rhetorical questions have a noteworthy impact on the theological message of the Song. What is the significance of other types of interrogatives in this poem specifically and in biblical Hebrew poetry in general?

While this study has contributed to the biblical theology of the Song, there is a need for a full and complete biblical theology on the book itself that does justice to the rest of the rhetorical devices and that is based on the exegetical evidence. For instance, how is geography used in the Song? Since this work has demonstrated the significant contribution a rhetorical analysis provides for the interpretation and theology of specific literary devices, if subjected to the same methodology, how does the biblical author employ geography? Such a rhetorical use of geography and how that usage impacts the Song's theology may prove fruitful for future study.[3] Also, since dialogue is such a major literary device,

---

3. After this project was successfully defended in April 2008, a PhD work by Timothy Martin Sigler became available. Sigler ("Emotional Geography in the Song of Songs: A Literary Study of the Contexts of Love") anticipated such a study by studying the rhetorical force of the geographical images and suggesting what "implications the Song's emotional geography may have upon a biblical theology of the city" (v).

what is the rhetorical function of direct and indirect discourse and its theological importance?[4]

While this study has focused on the parts of the Song, the vexing question concerning its overall structure remains. If the division of the Song into any number of unified segments is accurate, a legitimate question arises as to what it is that unifies each individual cycle into this one unique שִׁיר. Is that connection thematic, structural, syntactical, or something else?

Or asked another way, how does the Song move from start to finish? Once the overall structure reveals itself, then an investigation into its rhetorical effect may be undertaken. Hopefully, this work and the ones that follow will help believers, individually and corporately, better understand and apply the divine wisdom of this most sublime song.

---

4. Jacobson's work in the Psalms (*"Many are Saying"*) may provide the starting point for such a work. Speech-act theory may provide insight in this regard both exegetically and theologically. For as Botha (*Jesus & the Samaritan Woman*, 83) notes concerning characters, their speeches, and its impact on the readers, "One of the presuppositions . . . is that religious texts have some purpose, that is that it has pragmatic implications and thus is not only or chiefly interested in being an illocutionary act, *id est*, having some sort of intention or expressing some sort of intention, but it is chiefly a perlocutionary act, that is, it is meant to achieve some pragmatic aim with regard to its readers."

Appendix 1

A Chart of the Occurrence of the Hebrew First Person in the Song of Songs

Watson recognizes the advantage of charting various poetic devices of biblical poetry. He states, "To achieve objectivity and in the interests of accuracy it is occasionally helpful to draw up tables of repeated words, structural patterns, alliterating consonants, word-pairs, repeated words in parallelism, formulae, vocabulary peculiar to a poem, etc."[1] Although there is little agreement to the divisions of the Song, this chart is divided into seven units or cycles. The cycles are the closest approximation to major sections or units that are recognized at the present time.

Legend:

F	= feminine[2]	M/F	= plural
M	= masculine[3]	X	= 1st person occurs in verse
X#	= 1st person occurs a certain number of times in the same verse	X cf	= concerning the couple from the female
		X cm	= concerning the couple from the male
X d	= voice of daughters of Jerusalem	X p	= "I" as independent pronoun
		X v	= "I" conjugated with a verb

---

1. Watson, *Classical Hebrew Poetry*, 19.
2. BH is not marked for feminine gender in the first person. These instances reflect the author's understanding of the gender of the person speaking.
3. See footnote 2.

Verses correspond to BHS	אֲנִי תִּי "I" (F)	נִי "Me" (F)	יִ "My" (F)	נוּ "Us," "Our" (M/F)	נ "We" (M/F)	תִּי "I" (M)	נִי "Me" (M)	יִ "My" (M)
1:1								
2		X						
3								
4		X2		X cf	X d 3 X cf			
5	X p							
6	X p X v	X5	X2					
7	X v	X	X					
8								
9							X	X2
10								
11					X d			
12		X						
13		X	X2					
14		X	X					
15								X
16			X	X cf				
17				X cf 2				
2:1	X p							
2								X
3	X2 v		X2					
4		X2						
5	X p	X2						
6		X	X					
7	X v							

A Chart of the Occurrence of the Hebrew First Person in the Song of Songs

Verses correspond to BHS	אֲנִי ‎ תִּי ‎ "I" (F)	נִי ‎ "Me" (F)	י ‎ "My" (F)	נוּ ‎ "Us," "Our" (M/F)	נ ‎ "We" (M/F)	תִּי ‎ "I" (M)	נִי ‎ "Me" (M)	י ‎ "My" (M)
2:8			X					
9			X					
10		X	X					X2
11								
12				X cm				
13								X2
14							X2	X
15				X cf 2				
16	X p	X	X					
17			X					

Verses correspond to BHS	אֲנִי ‎ תִּי ‎ "I" (F)	נִי ‎ "Me" (F)	י ‎ "My" (F)	נוּ ‎ "Us," "Our" (M/F)	נ ‎ "We" (M/F)	תִּי ‎ "I" (M)	נִי ‎ "Me" (M)	י ‎ "My" (M)
3:1	X v X v		X2					
2	X v X v X v X v		X					
3		X	X					
4	X v X v X v X v X v X v		X2					
5	X v							

Verses correspond to BHS	אֲנִי תִּי "I" (F)	נִי "Me" (F)	יִ "My" (F)	נוּ "Us," "Our" (M/F)	נ "We" (M/F)	תִּי "I" (M)	נִי "Me" (M)	יִ "My" (M)
3:6								
7								
8								
9								
10								
11								
4:1								X
2								
3								
4								
5								
6						X v	X	
7								X
8							X2	
9						X v X v		X
10								
11								
12								X
13								
14								
15								
16			X2					
5:1						X v X v X v X v		X8

A Chart of the Occurrence of the Hebrew First Person in the Song of Songs

Verses correspond to BHS	אֲנִי ‎ תִּי	נִי	י	נוּ	נ	תִּי	נִי	י
				"Us," "Our" (M/F)	"We" (M/F)			
	"I" (F)	"Me" (F)	"My" (F)			"I" (M)	"Me" (M)	"My" (M)
5:2	X p	X	X2				X	X6
3	X v X v X v X v		X2					
4			X2					
5	X v-p em-phatic		X3					
6	X v-p em-phatic X v X v X v	X	X3					
7		X4	X					
8	X v X p							
9				X d				
10			X					
11								
12								
13								
14								
15								
16			X2					
6:1					X d			
2			X					
3	X p	X	X2					
4								X
5							X2	

(Continued on page 232)

Verses correspond to BHS	אֲנִי תִי "I" (F)	נִי "Me" (F)	י "My" (F)	נוּ "Us," "Our" (M/F)	נ "We" (M/F)	תִי "I" (M)	נִי "Me" (M)	י "My" (M)
6								
7								
8								
9									X2
10								
11	X v							
12	X v	X	X2					
7:1				X cm?				
2								
3								
4								
5								
6								
7								
8								
9						X v X v X v		
10			X					

A Chart of the Occurrence of the Hebrew First Person in the Song of Songs

Verses correspond to BHS	אֲנִי / תִּי "I" (F)	נִי "Me" (F)	ִי "My" (F)	נוּ "Us," "Our" (M/F)	נ "We" (M/F)	תִּי "I" (M)	נִי "Me" (M)	ִי "My" (M)
7:11	X p	X	X					
12			X		X cf 2			
13	X v		X		X cf 2			
14	X v		X	X cf				
8:1	X v X v	X2	X					
2	X v X v X v	X	X2					
3		X	X					
4	X v							
8:5	X v							
6		X						
7								
8				X 2 d				
9				X 2 d				
10	X p X v		X					
11								
12			X3					
13							X	
14			X					

APPENDIX 2

A Suggested Thematic Element Outline

Thematic elements	First Cycle	Second Cycle	Third Cycle	Fourth Cycle	Fifth Cycle	Sixth Cycle	Seventh Cycle
	1:2—2:7	2:8–17	3:1–5	3:6—5:1	5:2—7:10	7:11—8:4	8:5–14
Separation	1:2	2:8–9	3:1	3:6–11	5:2—6:1	8:3	8:13–14
Desire	1:2–4	2:10–14	3:2–3	4:1–7	5:4–16	7:12–13	8:6–7
Obstacle	1:5–6	2:15	3:1–3	4:8	5:3–6	8:1	8:8–12
Union	1:7—2:3a	2:15	3:4	4:9–5:1d	6:2—7:9	7:11—8:2	8:5–7
Transition	2:3b–7	2:16–17	3:5	5:1e-f	7:10	8:4	

Bibliography

Alter, Robert. *The Art of Biblical Narrative*. New York: Basic Books, 1981.
———. *The Art of Biblical Poetry*. New York: Basic Books, 1985.
———. "An Ode to Intimacy." *BRev* 18 (2002) 24–32, 52.
Allender, Dan B., and Tremper Longman III. *Intimate Allies*. Wheaton: Tyndale, 1995.
Anderson, Dan. *Song of Solomon*. Neptune: Loizeaux Brothers, 1987.
Arbel, Daphna V. "'My Vineyard, My Very Own, is for Myself.'" In *The Song of Songs: A Feminist Companion to the Bible*, edited by Athalya Brenner and Carole R. Fontaine, 90–103. Second Series. Sheffield: Sheffield Academic Press, 2000.
Archer, Gleason L. *A Survey of Old Testament Introduction*. Rev. ed. Chicago: Moody, 1994.
Arnold, Bill T., and John H. Choi. *A Guide to Biblical Hebrew Syntax*. Cambridge: Cambridge University Press, 2003.
Barton, John. "On the Canonicity of Canticles." In *Perspectives on the Song of Songs*, edited by Anselm C. Hagedorn, 1–7. Berlin: de Gruyter, 2005.
Bascom, Robert A. "Hebrew Poetry and the Text of the Song of Songs." In *Discourse Perspectives on Hebrew Poetry in the Scriptures*, edited by Ernst R. Wendland, 95–110. New York: United Bible Societies, 1994.
Bekkenkamp, Jonneke. "Into Another Scene of Choices: The Theological Value of the Song of Songs." In *The Song of Songs: A Feminist Companion to the Bible*, edited by Athalya Brenner and Carole R. Fontaine, 55–89. Second Series. Sheffield: Sheffield Academic Press, 2000.
Bell, Rob. *Sex God*. Grand Rapids: Zondervan, 2007.
Bellis, Alice Ogden. *Helpmates, Harlots, and Heroes: Women's Stories in the Hebrew Bible*. Louisville: Westminster/John Knox, 1994.
Bennett, Stephen. "Love over Gold: The Song of Songs for Aotearoa-New Zealand." *IRM* 91 (2002) 31–40.
Bergant, Dianne. "My Beloved is Mine and I am His (Song 2:16): The Song of Songs and Honor and Shame." *Semeia* 68 (1994) 23–40.
———. *The Song of Songs*. Berit Olam: Studies in Hebrew Narrative and Poetry. Collegeville: Liturgical Press, 2001.
Berlin, Adele. *The Dynamic of Biblical Parallelism*. Rev. ed. Grand Rapids: Eerdmans, 2008.
———. "On Reading Biblical Poetry: The Role of Metaphor." In *Congress Volume: Cambridge 1995*, edited by John A. Emerton, 25–36. Supplements to Vetus Testamentum. Leiden: Brill, 1997.
———. *Poetics and Interpretation of Biblical Narrative*. Winona Lake: Eisenbrauns, 1994.
———. "Point of View in Biblical Narrative." In *A Sense of Text: The Art of Language in the Study of Biblical Literature*, 71–113. Winona Lake: Eisenbrauns, 1983.

Bernard of Clairvaux, *Song of Solomon*. Translated and edited by Samuel J. Eales. London: Elliot Stock, 1895. Reprint, Minneapolis: Klock & Klock, 1984.

Bernat, David. "Biblical *Wasfs* beyond Song of Songs." *JSOT* 28 (2004) 327–49.

Black, Fiona C. "Beauty or Beast? The Grotesque Body in the Song of Songs." *BibInt* 8 (2000) 302–23.

Bloch, Ariel, and Chana Bloch. "From in the Garden of Delights." *Judaism* 44 (1995) 36–63.

———. *The Song of Songs: A New Translation*. Berkeley, Calif.: University of California Press, 1995.

Blumenthal, David R. "Where God Is Not: The Book of Esther and Song of Songs." *Judaism* 44 (1995) 80–92.

Boer, Roland. "The Second Coming: Repetition and Insatiable Desire in the Song of Songs." *BibInt* 8 (2000) 276–301.

Botha, Eugene. *Jesus and the Samaritan Woman: A Speech Act Reading of John 4:1–42*. Leiden: Brill, 1991.

Bramer, Stephen J. "The Genre of Amos." *BSac* 156 (1999) 42–60.

Braun, Joachim. *Music in Ancient Israel/Palestine*. Translated by Douglas W. Scott. Grand Rapids: Eerdmans, 2002.

Brenner, Athalya. "The Food of Love: Gendered Food and Food Imagery in the Song of Songs." *Semeia* 86 (1999) 101–12.

———. "Gazing Back at the Shulammite, Yet Again." *BibInt* 11 (2003) 295–300.

———. "Introduction." In *The Song of Songs: A Feminist Companion to the Bible*, edited by Athalya Brenner and Carole R. Fontaine, 17–24. Second Series. Sheffield: Sheffield Academic Press, 2000.

———. *The Israelite Woman*. Sheffield: JSOT, 1985.

———. "'My' Song of Songs." In *The Song of Songs: A Feminist Companion to the Bible*, edited by Athalya Brenner and Carole R. Fontaine, 154–68. Second Series. Sheffield: Sheffield Academic Press, 2000.

———. Review of *Song of Songs*, by Tremper Longman III. *CBQ* 66 (2004) 292–93.

Brenner, Athalya, and Fokkelien van Dijk-Hermmes. *On Gendering Texts: Female and Male Voices in the Hebrew Bible*. Leiden: Brill, 1993.

Brenton, Lancelot Charles Lee. *Septuagint Version of the Old Testament: With an English Translation and with Various Readings and Critical Notes*. Grand Rapids: Zondervan, 1974.

Briggs, Richard S. "The Uses of Speech-Act Theory in Biblical Interpretation." *CR* 9 (2001) 229–76.

Bright, John. *The Authority of the Old Testament*. Grand Rapids: Baker, 1975.

Brown, Francis S. R. Driver, and C. A. Briggs. *Hebrew and English Lexicon of the Old Testament*. Oxford: Clarendon, 1951.

Brueggemann, Walter. "Jeremiah's Use of Rhetorical Questions." *JBL* 92 (1973) 358–74.

———. *Solomon: Israel's Icon of Human Achievement*. Columbia: University of South Carolina Press, 2005.

———. *Theology of the Old Testament*. Minneapolis: Fortress, 1997.

Brug, John F. *Commentary on Song of Songs*. Milwaukee: Northwestern, 1995.

Buechner, Frederick. "The Bible as Literature." In *A Complete Literary Guide to the Bible*, edited by Leland Ryken and Tremper Longman III, 40–48. Grand Rapids, Zondervan, 1993.

Bullinger, E. W. *Figures of Speech Used in the Bible*. London: Eyre and Spottiswoode, 1898. Reprint, Grand Rapids: Baker, 2003.

Bullis, Ronald K. "Biblical Tantra: Lessons in Sacred Sexuality." *T&S* 9 (1998) 101–16.
Burrus, Virginia, and Stephen D. Moore. "Unsafe Sex: Feminism, Pornography, and the Song of Songs." *BibInt* 11 (2003) 24–52.
Butting, Klara. "Go Your Way: Women Rewrite Scriptures (Song of Songs 2.8–14)." In *The Song of Songs: A Feminist Companion to the Bible*, edited by Athalya Brenner and Carole R. Fontaine, 142–53. Second Series. Sheffield: Sheffield Academic Press, 2000.
Cainion, Ivory J. "An Analogy of the Song of Songs and Genesis Chapters Two and Three." *SJOT* 14 (2000) 219–59.
Cainion, Ivory J. "An Analogy of the Song of Songs and Genesis Chapters Two and Three." *SJOT* 14 (2000) 219–59.
Callow, John. "Units and Flow in the Song of Songs 1:2–2:6." In *Biblical Hebrew and Discourse Linguistics*, edited by Robert Bergen, 462–88. Dallas: Summer Institute of Linguistics, 1994.
Campbell, Iain D. "The Song of David's Son: Interpreting the Song of Solomon in the Light of the Davidic Covenant." *WTJ* 62 (2000) 17–32.
Carr, David M. *The Erotic Word*. New York: Oxford University Press, 2003.
———. "Gender and the Shaping of Desire in Song of Songs." *JBL* 119 (2000) 233–48.
Carr, G. Lloyd. "Is the Song of Songs a 'Sacred Marriage Drama'?" *JETS* 22 (1979) 103–14.
———. "The Love Poetry Genre in the Old Testament and the Ancient Near East: Another Look at Inspiration." *JETS* 25 (1982) 489–98.
———. "שלם" In *Theological Wordbook of the Old Testament*, edited by R. Laird Harris, Gleason L. Archer, and Bruce Waltke, 2:930–32. Chicago: Moody, 1980.
———. *The Song of Solomon*. Donwers Grove: IVP, 1984.
———. "Song of Songs." In *A Complete Literary Guide to the Bible*, edited by Leland Ryken and Tremper Longman III, 281–95. Grand Rapids, Zondervan, 1993.
Chafer, Lewis Sperry. *Systematic Theology*, edited by John L. Walvoord et al. 2 vols. Wheaton: Victor Books, 1988.
"Character Types." In *Dictionary of Biblical Imagery*, edited by Leland Ryken, James C. Wilhoit and Tremper Longman III, 137–38 Downers Grove: InterVarsity, 1998.
Chave, Peter. "Towards a Not Too Rosy Picture of the Song of Songs." *Feminist Theology* 18 (1998) 41–53.
Childs, Brevard S. *Biblical Theology of the Old and New Testaments*. Philadelphia: Fortress, 1993.
———. *Introduction to the Old Testament as Scripture*. Philadelphia: Fortress, 1979.
Chisholm, Robert B. Jr. *From Exegesis to Exposition*. Grand Rapids: Baker Books, 1998.
Clarke, Ros. "Song of Songs: A Biblical Theology." Master's thesis, Oak Hill College, London 2005–2006. Online: http://www.beginningwithmoses.org/ articles/ songofsongs.pdf.
Clines, David J. A., ed. *The Dictionary of Classical Hebrew*. Vol. 1. Sheffield: Sheffield Academic Press, 1993.
———. "Reading the Song of Songs as a Classic." Online: www.shef.ac.uk/bibs/ DJCcurres/Classic.html. Dec. 2000.
———. "Why Is There a Song of Songs and What Does It Do to You If You Read It?" In *Interested Parties: The Ideology of Writers and Readers of the Hebrew Bible*, 94–121. JSOTSup 205. Sheffield: Sheffield Academic Press, 1995.
Constable, Thomas L. "Notes on the Song of Solomon." Sonic Light, 2007. Online: http://www.soniclight.com/constable/notes/pdf/song.pdf.

Conway, Moncure Daniel. *Solomon and Solomonic Literature.* Chicago: Open Court, 1899.

Corney, Richard W. "What Does 'Literal Meaning' Mean? Some Commentaries on the Song of Songs." *AThR* 80 (1998) 494–16.

Craigie, Peter C. "Biblical and Tamil Poetry: Some Further Reflections." *SR* 8 (1979) 169–75.

Creason, Stephen. Review of *Biblical Hebrew and Discourse Linguistics*, edited by Robert D. Bergen. *JNES* 58 (1999) 138–40.

Crenshaw, James L. *Old Testament Wisdom: An Introduction.* Atlanta: John Knox, 1981.

Cross, Frank Moore. *From Epic to Canon: History and Literature of Ancient Israel.* Baltimore: John Hopkins University Press, 1998.

Danker, Fredrick William. *A Greek Lexicon of the New Testament and Other Early Christian Literature.* 3rd ed. Chicago: University of Chicago Press, 2000.

Davidson, Richard M. *Flame of Yahweh: Sexuality in the Old Testament.* Peabody: Hendrickson, 2007.

———. "Is God Present in the Song of Songs?" *JATS* 16 (2005) 143–54.

———. "The Literary Structure of the Song of Songs Redivivus." *JATS* 14 (2003) 44–65.

———. "Theology of Sexuality in the Song of Songs: Return to Eden." *AUSS* 27 (1989) 1–19.

De Regt, Lénart J. "Discourse Implications of Rhetorical Questions in Job, Deuteronomy and the Minor Prophets." In *Literary Structure and Rhetorical Strategies in the Hebrew Bible*, edited by L. J. de Regt, J. de Waard and J. P. Fokkelman, 51–78. Netherlands: Van Gorcum, 1996.

———. "Functions and Implications of Rhetorical Questions in the Book of Job." In *Biblical Hebrew and Discourse Linguistics*, edited by Robert Bergen, 361–73. Dallas: Summer Institute of Linguistics, 1994.

De Waard, J. "Hebrew Rhetoric and the Translator," In *Literary Structure and Rhetorical Strategies in the Hebrew Bible*, edited by L. J. de Regt, J. de Waard and J. P. Fokkelman, 242–51. Netherlands: Van Gorcum, 1996.

Deere, Jack S. "Song of Songs." In *Bible Knowledge Commentary*, edited by John F. Walvoord and Roy B. Zuck, 1:1009–23. Wheaton: Victor Books, 1988.

Delitzsch, Franz. "Song of Solomon." In *Commentary on the Old Testament*, edited by C. F. Keil and F. Delitzsch, 6:497–628. Peabody, Mass.: Hendrickson, 1966.

Dell, Katherine J. "Does the Song of Songs Have Any Connections to Wisdom?" In *Perspectives on the Song of Songs*, edited by Anselm C. Hagedorn, 8–26. Berlin: de Gruyter, 2005.

Dijk-Hemmes, Fokkelien van. "The Imagination of Power and the Power of Imagination: an Intertextual Analysis of Two Biblical Love Songs." *JSOT* 44 (1989) 75–88.

Dillard, Raymond B., and Tremper Longman III. "Song of Songs." In *An Introduction to the Old Testament*, 257–60. 2nd ed. Grand Rapids: Zondervan, 2006.

Dillow, Joseph C. *Solomon on Sex.* Nashville: Nelson, 1977.

Dillow, Joseph, Linda Dillow, Peter Pintus, and Lorraine Pintus. *Intimacy Ignited.* Colorado Springs: NavPress, 2004.

Dillow, Linda, and Lorraine Pintus. *Intimate Issues.* Colorado Springs: Waterbrook, 1999.

Dobbs-Allsopp, F. W. "The Delight of Beauty and Song of Songs 4:1–7." *Int* 59 (2005) 260–77.

———. "Late Linguistic Features in the Song of Songs." In *Perspectives on the Song of Songs*, edited by Anselm C. Hagedorn, 27–77. Berlin: de Gruyter, 2005.

Dorsey, David A. *The Literary Structure of the Old Testament: A Commentary on Genesis–Malachi*. Grand Rapids: Baker, 1999.

———. "Literary Structuring in the Song of Songs." *JSOT* 46 (1990) 81–96.

"Dove." In *Dictionary of Biblical Imagery*, edited by Leland Ryken, James C. Wilhoit and Tremper Longman III, 216–17. Downers Grove: InterVarsity, 1998.

Dumbrell, William J. *The Faith of Israel: A Theological Survey of the Old Testament*. Grand Rapids: Baker, 1988.

Eichrodt, Walther. *Theology of the Old Testament*. Translated by J. A. Baker. Philadelphia: Westminster, 1967.

Elliott, Mary Timothea. *The Literary Unity of the Canticle*. Frankfurt: Lang, 1989.

Erickson, Millard J. *Christian Theology*. Grand Rapids: Baker, 1985.

Ernst, Judith. *Song of Songs: Erotic Love Poetry*. Grand Rapids: Eerdmans, 2003.

Estes, Daniel J. "Entering the Garden of Intimacy: A Poetic Reading of Song of Songs 4:8–5:1." Paper presented at the Annual Meeting of the Evangelical Theological Society, Washington, DC. November 15–17, 2006.

———. *Handbook on the Wisdom Books and Psalms*. Grand Rapids: Baker, 2005.

———. "The Hermeneutics of Biblical Lyric Poetry." *BSac* 152 (1995) 413–30.

Exum, J. Cheryl. "How Does the Song Mean? On Reading the Poetry of Desire." *SEÅ* 64 (1999) 47–63.

———. "The Poetic Genius of the Song of Songs." In *Perspectives on the Song of Songs*, edited by Anselm C. Hagedorn, 78–95. Berlin: de Gruyter, 2005.

———. "Seeing Solomon's Palanquin (Song of Songs 3:6–11)." *BibInt* 11 (2003) 301–16.

———. *Song of Songs: A Commentary*. Louisville: Westminster John Knox, 2005.

———. "Ten Things Every Feminist Should Know about the Song of Songs." In *The Song of Songs: A Feminist Companion to the Bible*, edited by Athalya Brenner and Carole R. Fontaine, 24–35. Second Series. Sheffield: Sheffield Academic Press, 2000.

Falk, Marcia. *Love Lyrics from the Bible*. Sheffield: Almond Press, 1982.

Fee, Gordon D., and Douglas Stuart. *How to Read the Bible for All its Worth*. 3rd ed. Grand Rapids: Zondervan, 2003.

Fields, Weston W. "Early and Medieval Jewish Interpretation of the Song of Songs." *GTJ* (1980) 221–31.

Fisch, Harold. *Poetry with a Purpose: Biblical Poetics and Interpretation*. Indiana: Indiana University Press. 1988.

Fokkelman, J. P. *Reading Biblical Poetry: An Introductory Guide*. Translated by Ineke Smit. Louisville: Westminster John Knox, 2001.

Follis, Elaine R. *Directions in Biblical Hebrew Poetry*. Sheffield: Almond Press 1987.

Fontaine, Carole R. "The Voice of the Turtle: Now it's *MY* Song of Songs." In *The Song of Songs: A Feminist Companion to the Bible*, edited by Athalya Brenner and Carole R. Fontaine, 169–85. Second Series. Sheffield: Sheffield Academic Press, 2000.

Foster, John L. *Hymns, Prayers and Songs: An Anthology of Ancient Egyptian Lyric Poetry*. Atlanta: Scholars Press, 1995.

Fox, Michael V. "Scholia to Canticles (i 4b, ii 4, i 4ba, iv 3, v 8, vi. 12)." *VT* 33 (1983) 199–206.

———. *The Song of Songs and the Ancient Egyptian Love Songs*. Madison: University of Wisconsin Press, 1985.

Freehof, Solomon B. "The Song of Songs: A General Suggestion." *JQR* n.s. 39 (1949) 397–402.

Fruchtenbaum, Arnold G. *Biblical Lovemaking: A Study of the Song of Solomon*. San Antonio: Ariel Press, 1983.

Galik, Marian. "The Song of Songs (Šir Hašširim) and the Book of Songs (Shijing): An Attempt in Comparative Analysis." *AAS* 6 (1997) 45–75.

Garrett, Duane. "Song of Songs," In *Song of Songs/Lamentations*, 1–265. Word Biblical Commentary. Nashville: Thomas Nelson, 2004.

Garrett, Duane, and Paul R. House. *Songs of Songs/Lamentations*. Nashville: Nelson, 2004.

Geller, Stephen A. "Through Windows and Mirrors into the Bible, History, Literature and Language and the Study of Text." In *A Sense of Text: The Art of Language in the Study of Biblical Literature*, 3–40. Winona Lake: Eisenbrauns, 1983.

Gerstenberger, Erhard S. *Theologies of the Old Testament*. Minneapolis: Fortress, 2002.

Gesenius, Wilhelm, E. Kautzsch, and A. E. Cowley. *Gesenius' Hebrew Grammar*. 1909. Reprint, Oxford: Oxford University Press, 1970.

Gibson, J. C. L. *Language and Imagery of the Old Testament*. London: SPCK, 1998.

Gledhill, Tom. *The Message of the Song of Songs*. Downers Grove: InterVarsity, 1994.

Glickman, Craig. *Solomon's Song of Love*. West Monroe, Louisiana: Howard, 2004.

Gonzaga, Gian, et al. "Romantic Love and Sexual Desire in Close Relationships." *Emotion* 6 (2006) 163–79.

Gordis, Robert. "A Rhetorical Use of Interrogative Questions in Biblical Hebrew." *AJSL* 49 (1932–1933) 212–17.

———. *The Song of Songs*. New York: Jewish Theological Seminary of New York, 1954.

Goulder, Michael D. *The Song of Fourteen Songs*. Sheffield: JSOT, 1986.

Grab, Ginger. "The Song of Songs and the Erotic." *Living Pulpit* 1 (1992) 24–25.

Greenstein, Edward L. "How Does Parallelism Mean?" In *A Sense of Text: The Art of Language in the Study of Biblical Literature*, 41–70. Winona Lake: Eisenbrauns, 1983.

Grossberg, Daniel. *Centripetal and Centrifugal Structures in Biblical Poetry*. Atlanta: Scholars Press, 1989.

———. "Nature, Humanity, and Love in Song of Songs." *Int* 59 (2005) 229–42.

Grudem, Wayne. *Systematic Theology: An Introduction to Biblical Doctrine*. Grand Rapids: Zondervan, 1994.

Guillaume, Phillippe. "Caution: Rhetorical Questions!" *BN* 103 (2000) 11–16.

Gunn, David M., and Danna Nolan Fewell. *Narrative in the Hebrew Bible*. New York: Oxford University Press, 1993.

Hagedorn, Anselm C. "Of Foxes and Vineyards: Greek Perspectives on the Song of Songs." *VT* 53 (2003) 337–52.

Harding, Kathryn. "'I Sought Him but I Did Not Find Him': The Elusive Lover in the Song of Songs." *BibInt* 16 (2008) 43–59.

Harrison, R. K. *Introduction to the Old Testament*. Grand Rapids: Eerdmans, 1969.

Hart, Archibald D., Catherine Hart Weber, and Debra L. Taylor. *Secrets of Eve: Understanding the Mystery of Female Sexuality*. Nashville: Word, 1998.

Haverluck, Bob. "Song of Love, Song of Revolt: Re-Reading the Song of Songs." *ARTS* 14 (2002) 14–20.

Heimbach, Daniel R. *True Sexual Morality: Recovering Biblical Standards for a Culture in Crisis*. Wheaton: Crossway, 2004.

Held, M. "Rhetorical Questions in Ugaritic and Hebrew." *ErIsr* 9 (1969) 71–79.

Hess, Richard S. *Song of Songs*. Grand Rapids: Baker, 2005.

———. "Song of Songs: Not Just a Dirty Book." *BRev* (2005) 30–40.

Hocking, C. E. *Rise Up My Love*. West Glamorgan, UK: Precious Seed, 1988.

Hodge, Charles. *Index to Systematic Theology.* London: Thomas Nelson, 1876.

———. *Systematic Theology.* 3 vols. 1927. Reprint, Grand Rapids: Eerdmans, 1982.

Horine, Steven C. "An Integrative Literary Approach to the Song of Songs." PhD diss., Westminster Theological Seminary, 1999.

House, Paul R. *Old Testament Theology.* Downers Grove: InterVarsity, 1998.

Howard, David M. "Recent Trends in Psalms Study." In *The Face of Old Testament Studies,* edited by David W. Baker and Bill T. Arnold, 332–44. Grand Rapids: Baker, 1999.

Hubbard, David A. *Ecclesiastes, Song of Songs.* Communicator's Commentary. Dallas: Word, 1991.

Hunter, Richard. "'Sweet Talk': Song of Songs and the Tradition of Greek Poetry." In *Perspectives on the Song of Songs,* edited by Anselm C. Hagedorn, 228–44. Berlin: de Gruyter, 2005.

Jacobson, Rolf A. *"Many are Saying":* The Function of Direct Discourse in the Hebrew Psalter. New York: T. & T. Clark, 2004.

Jenson, Robert W. *Song of Songs.* Interpretation: A Biblical Commentary for Teaching and Preaching. Louisville: John Knox, 2005.

Jerome. "Letter LXVI." In *Nicene and Post-Nicene Church Fathers,* edited by Philip Schaff and Henry Wace, 6:60–65. Peabody: Hendrickson, 1994.

Kaiser, Walter C., Jr. "Narrative," In *Cracking Old Testament Codes,* edited by D. Brent Sandy and Ronald L. Giese Jr., 69–88. Nashville: Broadman & Holman, 1995.

———. *Toward an Exegetical Theology.* Grand Rapids: Baker, 1991.

———. *Toward an Old Testament Theology.* Grand Rapids: Zondervan, 1978.

———. "True Marital Love in Proverbs 5:15–23 and the Interpretation of Song of Songs." In *The Way of Wisdom: Essays in Honor of Bruce K. Waltke,* edited by J. I. Packer and Sven K. Soderlund, 106–16. Grand Rapids: Zondervan, 2000.

Keefer, Kyle, and Tod Linafelt. "The End of Desire: Theologies of Eros in the Song of Songs and *Breaking the Waves.*" *JRF* 2 (1998). No pages. Online: http://www.unomaha.edu/jrf/endofdes.htm.

Keel, Othmar. *The Song of Songs.* Translated by Frederick J. Gaiser. Minneapolis: Fortress, 1994.

Kinlaw, Dennis F. "Song of Songs." In *Expositor's Bible Commentary,* edited by Frank E. Gaebelein, 5:1199–1244. Grand Rapids: Zondervan, 1991.

Klein, William W., Craig L. Blomberg, and Robert L. Hubbard Jr. *Introduction to Biblical Interpretation.* Nashville: Thomas Nelson, 1993.

Knierim, Rolf. "Criticism of Literary Features, Form, Tradition and Redaction," In *Reading the Hebrew Bible for a New Millennium,* edited by Wonil Kim et al., 1–41. Harrisburg: Trinity Press International, 2000.

Knight, G. A. F. "A Theology of Sex." *RTR* 36 (1977) 1–7.

Koops, Robert. "Rhetorical Questions and Implied Meaning in the Book of Job." *BT* 39 (1988) 415–23.

Kravitz, Leonard S., and Kerry M. Olitzky. *Shir Hashirim: A Modern Commentary on the Song of Songs.* New York: URI Press, 2004.

Kugel, James. *The Idea of Biblical Poetry: Parallelism and Its History.* Baltimore: John Hopkins Press, 1981.

Kuntz, J. Kenneth. "Biblical Hebrew Poetry in Recent Research, Part 2." *CR* 7 (1999) 35–79.

———. "Recent Perspectives on Biblical Poetry." *RelSRev* 19 (1998) 321–27.

Labuschagne, C. J. *The Incomparability of Yahweh in the Old Testament.* Leiden: Brill, 1966.

LaCocque, Andre. *Romance She Wrote*. Eugene, OR: Wipf and Stock, 1998.

LaHaye, Tim, and Beverly LaHaye. *The Act of Marriage*. Grand Rapids: Zondervan, 1976.

Laird, Martin. "Under Solomon's Tutelage: The Education of Desire in the Homilies of the Song of Songs. *Modern Theology* 18 (2002) 507–25.

Landy, Francis. *Paradoxes of Paradise: Identity and Difference in the Song of Songs*. Sheffield: Almond Press, 1983.

———. "The Song of Songs." In *The Literary Guide to the Bible*, edited by Robert Alter and Frank Kermode, 305–19. Cambridge: Belknap, 1987.

Lavoie, Jean-Jacques. "Woman in the Song of Songs." In *Women Also Journeyed with Him*, 75–80. Collegeville: Liturgical Press, 2000.

Lasor, William Sanford, David Allan Hubbard, and Frederic William Bush. "The Song of Songs." In *Old Testament Survey*, 510–19. Grand Rapids: Eerdmans, 1996.

Leick, Gwendolyn. *Sex & Eroticism in Mesopotamian Literature*. New York: Routledge, 2003.

Lewis, Gordon R., and Bruce A. Demarest. *Integrative Theology*. Grand Rapids: Zondervan, 1996.

Lichtheim, Miriam. *Ancient Egyptian Literature: A Book of Readings*. Vol. 2, *The New Kingdom*. California: University of California Press, 1976.

Lim, Johnson T. K. "Towards a Final Form Approach to Biblical Interpretation." *STJ* 7 (1999) 1–11.

Linafelt, Tod. "The Arithmetic of Eros." *Int* 59 (2005) 244–58.

———. "Lyrical Theology: The Song of Songs and the Advantage of Poetry." In *Toward a Theology of Eros*, edited by Virginia Burrus and Katherine Keller, 291–305, 440–42. New York: Fordham University Press, 2006.

Long, Gary Alan. "Simile, Metaphor, and the Song of Songs." PhD diss., University of Chicago, 1993.

Longman, Tremper, III. "Biblical Narrative." In *A Complete Literary Guide to the Bible*, edited by Leland Ryken and Tremper Longman III, 69–79. Grand Rapids, Zondervan, 1993.

———. "Biblical Poetry." In *A Complete Literary Guide to the Bible*, edited by Leland Ryken and Tremper Longman III, 80–94. Grand Rapids, Zondervan, 1993.

———. "Introduction." In *A Complete Literary Guide to the Bible*, edited by Leland Ryken and Tremper Longman III, 15–39. Grand Rapids, Zondervan, 1993.

———. "The Literature of the Old Testament." In *A Complete Literary Guide to the Bible*, edited by Leland Ryken and Tremper Longman III, 95–107. Grand Rapids: Zondervan, 1993.

———. *Song of Songs*. New International Commentary on the Old Testament. Grand Rapids: Eerdmans, 2001.

Loprieno, Antonio. "Searching for Common Background: Egyptian Love Poetry and the Biblical Song of Songs. In *Perspectives on the Song of Songs*, edited by Anselm C. Hagedorn, 105–35. Berlin: de Gruyter, 2005.

Lyke, Larry. "The Song of Songs, Proverbs, and the Theology of Love." In *Theological Exegesis: Essays in Honor of Brevard S. Childs*, edited by Christopher Seitz and Kathryn Greene-McCreight, 208–23. Grand Rapids: Eerdmans, 1988.

Maccoby, Hyam. "Sex According to the Song of Songs." *Commentary* (1979) 53–59.

Mahaney, C. J. "Sex, Romance, and the Glory of God: What Every Christian Husband Needs to Know." In *Sex and the Supremacy of Christ*, edited by John Piper and Justin Taylor, 151–82. Wheaton: Crossway, 2005.

Malul, Meir. *Knowledge, Control and Sex: Studies in Biblical Thought, Culture and Worldview*. Israel: Archaeological Center Publication, 2002.

Mariaselvam, Abraham. *The Song of Songs and Ancient Tamil Love Poems*. Rome: Editrice Pontificio Istituto Biblico, 1988.

Marks, Ed. "The Economy of God in the Song of Songs." *A&C* 4 (1999) 24–35.

Martens, Elmer A. "The Flowering and Floundering of Old Testament Theology." In *A Guide to Old Testament Theology and Exegesis*, edited by Willem A. VanGemeren, 169–81. Grand Rapids: Zondervan, 1999.

―――. "Old Testament Theology Since Walter C. Kaiser, Jr." *JETS* 50 (2007) 673–91.

Mazor, Yair. "The Song of Songs or the Story of Stories?" *SJOT* 1 (1990) 1–29.

McCabe, Robert V. "The Message of Ecclesiastes." *DBSJ* 1 (1996) 85–112.

McGinniss, Mark. "'Let Him Kiss Me' An Exploration Of The Use Of The First Person In The Song Of Songs And Its Impact On The Theology Of The Song." ThM thesis, Baptist Bible Seminary, 2006.

Meier, Samuel A. *Speaking of Speaking: Marking Direct Discourse in the Hebrew Bible*. Cologne: Brill, 1992.

Merrill, Eugene H. *Everlasting Dominion: A Theology of the Old Testament*. Nashville: Broadman & Holman, 2006.

―――. "Isaiah 40–55 as Anti-Babylonian Polemic," *GTJ* 8 (1987) 3–18.

Meynet, Roland. *Rhetorical Analysis: An Introduction to Biblical Rhetoric*. Sheffield: JSOT, 1998.

Meyers, Carol. *Discovering Eve*. New York: Oxford University Press, 1988.

Miller, Patrick D., Jr. "The Theological Significance of Biblical Poetry." In *Language, Theology, and the Bible*, edited by Samuel E. Balentine and John Barton, 213–30. Oxford: Clarendon, 1994.

Mitchell, Christopher W. *The Song of Songs*. St. Louis: Concordia, 2003.

Moore, Stephen D. "The Song of Songs in the History of Sexuality." *Church History* 69 (2000) 328–49.

Muilenburg, James. "Form Criticism and Beyond." *JBL* 88 (1969) 1–18.

Munro, Jill. *Spikenard and Saffron: A Study in the Poetic Language of the Song of Songs*. Sheffield: Sheffield Academic Press, 1995.

Muraoka, Takamitsu. *Emphatic Words and Structures in Biblical Hebrew*. Jerusalem: Magnes, 1985.

Murphy, Roland E. "Form-Critical Studies in the Song of Songs." *Int* 27 (1973) 413–22.

―――. *The Song of Songs*. Hermeneia. Minneapolis: Fortress, 1990.

―――. *Wisdom Literature: Job, Proverbs, Ruth, Canticles, Ecclesiastes, and Esther*. The Forms of the Old Testament Literature. Grand Rapids: Eerdmans, 1981.

Neufeld, Jennifer. "A 'Sex'tet on Love: New Visions for Female Subjectivity and Mutuality." MA thesis, Institute for Christian Studies, 2006.

Niccacci, Alviero. "Analyzing Biblical Hebrew Poetry." *JSOT* 74 (1997) 77–93.

Nicole, Roger R. "The Wisdom of Marriage." In *The Way of Wisdom: Essays in Honor of Bruce K. Waltke*, edited by J. I. Packer and Sven K. Soderlund, 106–16. Grand Rapids: Zondervan, 2000.

Noegel, Scott B. Review of *Song of Songs*, by Dianne Bergant. *JHS* 4 (2002–2003). No pages. Online: http://www.arts.ualberta.ca/JHS/reviews/review027.htm.

Norris, Richard A., Jr. *The Song of Songs*. The Church's Bible. Grand Rapids: Eerdmans, 2003.

Oem, Kui Duck. "The Boudoir Lament Poetry of the Six Dynasties." PhD diss., University of Hawaii, 2000.

Ogden, Graham S., and Lynell Zogbo. *A Handbook on Song of Songs.* New York: United Bible Society, 1998.

Osborne, Grant R. *The Hermeneutical Spiral.* Downers Grove: InterVarsity, 1991.

Ostriker, Alicia. "A Holy of Holies: The Song of Songs as Countertext." In *The Song of Songs: A Feminist Companion to the Bible,* edited by Athalya Brenner and Carole R. Fontaine, 36–54. Second Series. Sheffield: Sheffield Academic Press, 2000.

Packer, J. I. "Theology and Bible Reading." In *The Act of Bible Reading,* edited by Elmer Dyck, 65–87. Downers Grove: InterVarsity, 1996.

Parsons, Greg W. "Guidelines for Understanding and Utilizing the Song of Songs." *BSac* 156 (1999) 399–422.

Patmore, Hector. "The Plain and Literal Sense: On Contemporary Assumptions about the Song of Songs. *VT* 56 (2006) 239–50.

Patrick, Dale, and Allen Scult. *Rhetoric and Biblical Interpretation.* Sheffield: Sheffield Academic Press, 1990.

Patterson, Ben. "The Goodness of Sex and the Glory of God." In *Sex and the Supremacy of Christ,* edited by John Piper and Justin Taylor, 47–64. Wheaton: Crossway, 2005.

Paul, Shalom M. "A Lover's Garden of Verse." In *Tehillah le-Moshe: Biblical and Judaic Studies in Honor of Moshe Greenberg,* edited by Mordechai Cogan, Barry L. Eichler and Jeffrey H. Tigay, 99–110. Winona Lake: Eisenbrauns, 1997.

———. "The Shared Legacy of Sexual Metaphors and Euphemisms in Mesopotamian and Biblical Literature." In *Sex and Gender in the Ancient Near East,* edited by Simo Parpola and R. M. Whiting, 2:489–98. Helsinki: Neo-Assyrian Text Corpus Project, 2002.

Pecknold, C. C. "The Readable City and the Rhetoric of Excess: A Reading of the Song of Songs." *Cross Currents* 52 (2003) 516–20.

Penner, Joyce J., and Clifford L. Penner, *Counseling for Sexual Disorders.* Dallas: Word, 1990.

Peterson, David L., and Kent Harold Richards. *Interpreting Hebrew Poetry.* Minneapolis: Fortress, 1992.

Phillips, John. *Exploring the Love Song of Solomon.* Grand Rapids: Kregel, 2003.

Phipps, William E. "The Plight of the Song of Songs." *JAAR* 42 (1974) 82–100.

Pierce, Ronald W. "A Thematic Development of the Haggai/Zechariah/Malachi Corpus." *JETS* 27 (1984) 401–11.

Pope, Marvin H. *Song of Songs.* New York: Doubleday, 1977.

Preuss, Dietrich Horst. *Old Testament Theology.* Louisville: Westminster John Knox, 1996.

Preuss, Julius. *Biblical and Talmudic Medicine.* Translated and edited by Fred Rosner. Lanham: Rowman & Littlefield, 2004.

Provan, Iain W. *Ecclesiastes, Song of Songs.* NIV Application Commentary. Grand Rapids: Zondervan, 2001.

———. "Terrors of the Night: Love, Sex, and Power in Song of Songs." In *The Way of Wisdom: Essays in Honor of Bruce K. Waltke,* edited by J. I. Packer and Sven K. Soderlund, 150–67. Grand Rapids: Zondervan, 2000.

Rabin, Chaim. "The Song of Songs and Tamil Poetry." *SR* 3 (1973–1974) 205–19.

"Rhetorical Patterns." In *Dictionary of Biblical Imagery,* edited by Leland Ryken, James C. Wilhoit and Tremper Longman III, 720–27. Downers Grove: InterVarsity, 1998.

Richardson, John P. "Preaching from the Song of Songs. Allegory Revisited." *ERT* 21 (1997) 250–57.

Bibliography

Roberts, D. Philip. *Let Me See Your Form: Seeking Poetic Structure in the Song of Songs.* Lanham: University Press of America, 2007.
Robinson, Anthony B. "Singing of Sex." *ChrCent* (January 27, 2004) 12.
Rosenau, Douglas E. *A Celebration of Sex.* Nashville: Thomas Nelson, 1994.
Rubio, Gonzalo. "Inanna and Dumuzi: A Sumerian Love Story." *JAOS* 121 (2001).
Ryken, Leland. *Words of Delight.* Grand Rapids: Baker, 1987.
Sasson, Jack M. "Unlocking the Poetry in the Song of Songs." *BRev* 1 (1985) 10–19.
Sasson, Victor. "King Solomon and the Dark Lady in the Song of Songs." *VT* 39 (1989) 407–14.
Schultz, Richard. "Integrating Old Testament Theology and Exegesis: Literary, Thematic and Canonical Issues." In *A Guide to Old Testament Theology and Exegesis,* edited by Willem A. VanGemeren, 182–202. Grand Rapids: Zondervan, 1999.
Schumann, Ruth Antelme, and Stephane Rossini. *Sacred Sexuality in Ancient Egypt: The Erotic Secrets of the Forbidden Papyri.* Rochester: Inner Traditions, 2001.
Schwab, George M. *The Song of Songs' Cautionary Message Concerning Human Love.* New York: Lang, 2002.
Sefati, Yitschak. *Love Songs in Sumerian Literature: Critical Edition of the Dumuzi-Inanna Songs.* Ramat Gan: Bar-Ilan University Press, 1998.
"Sex." In *Dictionary of Biblical Imagery,* edited by Leland Ryken, James C. Wilhoit and Tremper Longman, III, 776–79. Downers Grove: InterVarsity, 1998.
Sigler, Timothy Martin. "Emotional Geography in the Song of Songs: A Literary Study of the Contexts of Love." PhD diss., Trinity International University, May 2008.
Singleton, Laura. "Song Sung Blue?" *Christian Reflection* (2002) 61–65.
Smedes, Lewis B. *Sex for Christians.* Grand Rapids: Eerdmans, 1976.
Smith, Mark S. Review of *Ancient Texts for the Study of the Hebrew Bible: A Guide to the Background Literature,* by Kenton L. Sparks. *JHS* 6 (2006) no pages. Online: http://ejournals.library.ualberta.ca/index.php/jhs/article/view/5715/4768.
Snaith, John G. *Song of Songs.* Grand Rapids: Marshall Pickering, 1993.
"Solomon." In *Dictionary of Biblical Imagery,* edited by Leland Ryken, James C. Wilhoit and Tremper Longman III, 804–5. Downers Grove: InterVarsity, 1998.
"Song of Songs and the Sister-Wife Motif." *Biblaridion* 9 (2007). No pages. Online: http://www.biblaridion-online.net/pdf_archive/2007q1/sister.pdf.
Sorenson, Sharon. "Points of View." No pages. Online: http://herbertholeman.com/writer/povchart.php.
Sousan, Andre. "The Woman in the Garden of Eden: A Rhetorical-Critical Study of Genesis 2:4b–3:24." PhD diss., Vanderbilt University, August 2006.
Sparks, Kenton L. *Ancient Texts for the Study of the Hebrew Bible: A Guide to the Background Literature.* Peabody: Hendrickson, 2005.
Stern, Elsie. "The Song of Songs." In *The Jewish Study Bible,* edited by Adele Berlin and Marc Zvi Brettler, 1564–77. Oxford: Oxford University Press, 2004.
Sternberg, Meir. *The Poetics of Biblical Narrative.* Bloomington: Indiana University Press, 1987.
Stoop-van Paridon, P. W. T. *The Song of Songs: A Philological Analysis of the Hebrew Book.* Louvain: Peeters, 2005.
Strawn, Brent A. "Keep/Observe/Do—Carefully—Today! The Rhetoric of Repetition in Deuteronomy." In *A God so Near: Essays on Old Testament Theology in Honor of Patrick D. Miller,* edited by Brent A. Strawn and Nancy R. Bowen, 215–40. Winona Lake: Eisenbrauns, 2003.
Tanakh: The Holy Scriptures. Philadelphia: Jewish Publication Society, 1985.

Tanner, J. Paul. "The Message of the Song of Songs." *BSac* 154 (1997) 142–61.

———. "The History of Interpretation of the Song of Songs." *BSac* 154 (1997) 23–46.

The Targum of Canticles. Translated by Philip S. Alexander, Collegeville: Liturgical Press, 2003.

Tennant, Agnieszka. "Nice Yet Naughty," No pages. Online: http://www.christianitytoday.com/ct/2003/ 012/35.66.html.

Thompson, Joy. "Talking Heads: A Lesson in Point of View." No pages. Online: http://www.wordweaving.com/articlejan07_00.html.

Travers, Michael E. "The Figures of Speech in the Bible," *BSac* 164 (2007) 277–90.

Treat, Jay Curry. "Lost Keys: Text and Interpretation in Old Greek Song of Songs and Its Earliest Manuscript Witnesses." PhD diss., University of Pennsylvania, 1996.

Trible, Phyllis. "Depatriarchalizing in Biblical Interpretation." *JAAR* 41 (1973) 30–48.

———. *Rhetorical Criticism: Context, Method, and the Book of Jonah*. Minneapolis: Fortress, 1994.

Van der Merwe, Christo H. J., Jackie A. Naude, and Jan H. Kroeze. *A Biblical Hebrew Reference Grammar*. London: Sheffield, 2002.

Vanhoozer, Kevin J. *The Drama of Doctrine: A Canonical-Linguistic Approach to Christian Theology*. Louisville: Westminster John Knox, 2005.

Vargas, Ana R. "Textual Analysis of the "Song of Songs": The Relationship of the Erotic, the Sensual, and the Mystical in Worship." DMin diss., Claremont School of Theology, May 2002.

Viviers, Hendrick. "The Rhetoricity of the Body in the Song of Songs." In *Rhetorical Criticism and the Bible*, edited by Stanley E. Porter and Dennis L. Stamps, 237–54. Sheffield: Sheffield Academic Press, 2002.

von Rad, Gerhard. *Old Testament Theology*. New York: Harper & Row, 1965.

Walsh, Carey Ellen. *Exquisite Desire*. Minneapolis: Fortress, 2000.

———. "A Startling Voice: Woman's Desire in the Song of Songs." *BTB* 28 (1998) 129–34.

Waltke, Bruce K., and M. O'Connor. *An Introduction to Biblical Hebrew Syntax*. Winona Lake: Eisenbrauns, 1990.

Waltke, Bruce K., with Charles Yu. *An Old Testament Theology*. Grand Rapids: Zondervan, 2007.

Walton, Heather. "A Theology of Desire." *T&S* 1 (1994) 31–41.

Walton, Heather, and Elizabeth Stuart. "Editorial." *T&S* 13 (2007) 119–20.

Watson, Wilfred G. E. *Classical Hebrew Poetry: A Guide to its Techniques*. Sheffield: Sheffield Academic Press, 1984; Reprint Sheffield Academic Press, 2001.

———. "Love and Death Once More (Song of Songs VIII 6)." *VT* 48 (1997) 385–87.

Webb, Barry G. *Five Festal Garments: Christian Reflections on the Song of Songs, Lamentations, Ecclesiastes, and Esther*. Downers Grove: InterVarsity, 2000.

Weems, Renita J. "The Song of Songs." In *The New Interpreter's Bible*, 5:361–434. Nashville: Abingdon, 1997.

———. "Song of Songs." In *Women's Bible Commentary*, edited by Carol A. Newsom and Sharon H. Ringe, 164–68. Louisville: Westminster/ John Knox, 1998.

Weiner-Davis, Michele. "When Your Sex Drives Don't Match." *Marriage Partnership* (2003). No pages. Online: http://www.christianitytoday.com/mp/2003 /003/10.52.html.

———. "Sex Starved Marriage." Online: http://www.medicinenet.com/script/main/ art.asp?articlekey=54459.

Weitzman, Steven. *Song & Story in Biblical Narrative*. Bloomington: Indiana University Press, 1997.

Wendland, Ernst R. "The Discourse Analysis of Hebrew Poetry: A Procedural Outline." In *Discourse Perspectives on Hebrew Poetry in the Scriptures*, edited by Ernst R. Wendland, 1–27. New York: United Bible Societies, 1994.

———. "Seeking the Path Through a Forest of Symbols: A Figurative and Structural Survey of the Song of Songs." *JOTT* 7 (1994) 13–59.

Westenholz, J. G. "Love Lyrics from the Ancient Near East." In *Civilizations of the Ancient Near East*, edited by J. M. Sasson, 4:2471–84. New York: Charles Scribner's Sons, 1995.

Wheat, Ed, and Gaye Wheat. *Intended for Pleasure*. Old Tappan: Revell, 1977.

White, John Bradley. *A Study of the Language of Love in the Song of Songs and Ancient Egyptian Poetry*. Missoula: Society of Biblical Literature, 1978.

Williams, Tyler. "The Most Excellent of Songs (The Challenge of Translating Metaphors)." *Codex*. February 14, 2006. Online: http://biblical-studies.ca/blog/wp/category/bible/old-testament/song-of-songs.

Wirt, Sherwood Eliot. "Some New Thoughts about the Song of Solomon." *JETS* 33 (1990) 433–36.

"Women of the Bible." *U. S. News & World Report Special Edition*. 2005.

Wyrtzen, David. *Love Without Shame: Sexuality in Biblical Perspective*. Grand Rapids: Discovery House Publishers, 1991.

Yancey, Philip. "Holy Sex: How It Ravishes Our Souls." *Christianity Today*, October 2003. Online: http://www.christianitytoday.com/ct/2003/october/3.46.html.

Zuck, Roy B. "The Act of Discovery." *HER* 31 (1961) 21–32.

———, ed. *A Biblical Theology of the Old Testament*. Chicago: Moody, 1991.

www.ingramcontent.com/pod-product-compliance
Lightning Source LLC
Chambersburg PA
CBHW051105230426
43667CB00013B/2447